And The Truths That Will Set You Free

MIND LIES

And The Truths That Will Set You Free

© Copyright 2016, Daniel Rechnitzer.

Editorial Team: Sonja Rechnitzer, Jessica Vineyard, Sharron Dorr

Cover Art: Daniel Rechnitzer

ISBN 978-0-9807827-7-6

1st edition, December 1st 2016

Ui Group Pty Ltd
PO Box 511, Noosa Heads, Australia 4567

www.MindLies.com
www.DiscoverUi.com

To Sonja, Oli, and Millie:
Your patience, love, and support during this journey
is what made it possible. We all thank you.

Contents

Introduction 10

"My Beliefs Must Be True" 17

"I Do Not Matter" 18

"I Am Not Respected!" 23

"I Do Not Want To Be Alone; I Want Attention" 28

"I Have To Fight And Compete To Succeed" 35

"People Are Unreliable And Cannot Be Trusted" 41

"I Am Not Wanted" 47

"If I Am Rejected, I Will Be An Outcast" 53

"I Am All On My Own; It Is Every Man For Himself" 58

"The World Is Not Ready For My Ideas" 61

"I Do Not Make The Cut" 65

"Success Takes Such A Long Time" 68

"I Disappoint Everyone Around Me" 72

"I Am Not What People Want" 76

"My Successes Are Mediocre" 77

"I Need To Be Noticed So That I Can Respect Myself" 79

"Who The World Needs Me To Be Is Not Who I Really Am" 85

"I Need To Be A Better Person" 88

"I Am Not Leadership Material" 91

"I Never Grow Quickly Enough;" 93

"I Must Invest Now To Have Happiness In My Future" 98

"Responsibility First, Fun Later" 99

"I Must Maintain Control" 102

"If People Around Me Are Unhappy, I Have Failed" 106

"Everyone Judges Me And Looks Down On Me" 109

"I Do Not Want To Live Being Such A Failure" 112

"I Have Been Way Too Slow To Make Myself A Success" 114

"Success Comes Much Easier To Others" 116

"Other People's Accomplishments Are More Important" 118

"I Cannot Love Myself When I Am Such A Failure" 121

"I Am Not Worthy Of Happiness Or Success" 123

"If Something Is Difficult, It Is More Meaningful" 126

"When I Have Everything I Want, I Will Be Happy" 128

"Stressful Situations Cause Me Stress" 130

"I Need To Contribute To Fit Into Society" 135

"I Do Not Feel Accomplished Or Successful" 137

"I Am Not Perfect, So I Have To Get Everything Right" 139

"There Is Only One Perfect Way, One Right Way" 143

"I Did Not Get Enough God-Given Equipment to Succeed" 144

"I Am The Cause Of My Parents' Hardship And Suffering" 145

"Being An Adult Is Better Than Being A Child" 150

"I Am Not Equipped To Be A Good Parent" 151

"Success Will Not Be Fun Because I Have Children" 155

"I Am Not Smart Enough" 158

"I Always Fail At Being Successful" 161

"If I Do Not Create Something Big, I Will Get Bored" 162

"Everyone Has Their Act Together Except Me" 163

"Time Is Running Out" 166

"My Life Needs To Be Meaningful" 170

"I Do Not Trust Myself, And I Cannot Rely On Myself" 172

"I Disappoint Myself" 174

"I Cannot Help But Disappoint Others" 180

"I Am A Burden To Others" 181

"I Am Stuck With My Mind" 183

"I Am Going To Spend The Rest Of My Life Aging & Dying" ...184

"I Need To Be Liked" 185

"I Need A Naughty And Disobedient Streak" 189

"I Am A Waste Of Time, As Is Everything I Do" 194

"I Cannot Trust Myself To Take The Right Or Easy Path" 196

"The More I Think About Things, The Better My Life" 199

"It Would Be Irresponsible Of Me To Stop Thinking" 202

"Can I Trust My Intuition, This Non-Thought?" 204

"I Am Only As Good As What I Have In My Life" 207

"I Do Not Trust My Life" 209

"What I Want And What Life Wants Are Very Different" 213

"A Simple Life Is A Bad Life" 216

"I Always Come Last, After Everyone Else" 217

"The More Beautiful My Partner Is, The Better I I Feel" 221

"I Need A Way Out, Just In Case" 226

"I Need To Be Distracted; I Need Options" 228

"When I Am With A Sexy Person, I Feel Sexy" 230

"Someone Else Can Validate Me" 232

"I Need To Be Thought Of As Sexy" 233

"What Others Think Of Me Makes Me That" 234

"Everyone Else Knows More Than I Do" 235

"I Do Not Know Enough" 237

"Other People Are More Talented Than I Am"....................239

"I Need What Other People Have To Be Happy" 241

"I Should Be Great At Everything" 241

"I Am A Nobody If I Am Not Really Smart".......................242

"I Am Not Loved, Nor Am I Lovable As I Am"..................244

"The More Things I Have, The More Worthwhile I Become".....250

"I Have To Compete With Others To Improve Myself" 252

"I Am Not Liked As Other People Are"...............................254

"I Am Strange, And Strange Is Unwanted" 255

"Everything Is Always My Fault"..258

"I Need For People To Listen To And Agree With Me" 261

"I Need To Prepare For Failure" 262

"I Do Not Know Who I Am"..264

"I Do Not Deserve To Spend Money On Myself,"................266

"I Need To Be A Somebody" 268

"Clearly I Am Just A Body, Nothing More" 271

"I Need To Make The Most Of My Time"............................273

"I Cannot Trust My Joy To Be For The Greater Good"..............276

"If I Squander What I Have Today…" 279

"If I Am Not Attached, Then Where Is the Fun?" 281

"I Am A Mistake"...284

"I Am A Nobody Without My Parents".................................286

"I Do Not Exist Without My Parents"...................................288

"I Am Wrong To Abandon My Parents" 291

"I Have To Record All Negative Experiences In My Memory" ...293

"I Cannot Grow Faster Than My Partner" 297

"I Must Work To Avoid My Eventual Failure" 301

"I Will Be Sad Without An Identity" 303

"I Am Despised And A Nuisance" 307

"I Have Not Done Enough For The World" 307

"I Am Separate And Disconnected From Life" 310

"I Am Separate And Disconnected From Earth" 313

"I Cannot Tell The Difference Between The Reals & False" 316

Also From Daniel: 320

Who Am I?

Am I the one I say I am?
Am I who I think I am?

Are the ideas in my head the real me?
Am I the one I'm meant to be?

I try to be who you all want me to be,
But in the end I fail dismally.

You may think I am special, but I am not.
You think I can be more, but surely not!

I look in the mirror and I frown,
Because who I see brings me down.

But do I see the truth or something else?
Am I real or just the Mind's self?

Is the truth found out there?
Or is that a path going nowhere?

The more I accomplish, the less I feel.
Have we been misled from what is real?

I see a shadow that pretends it is me;
Is this the truth or the least I can be?

I search for my True Self out in the world,
Where others succeed with gold and pearls.

But what I find is unfulfilling,
Not happiness at all, just more needing.

Will I fail or will I succeed
If my mind is what I believe?

. . . to be continued

Introduction

Beliefs. Everyone has them. We live by them, we defend them, we teach them to our children, we base our sciences and religions on them, we even go to war over them. In fact, our beliefs are at the core of nearly every single decision we make in life. But how many of our beliefs are actually true? We believe they are, but are they?

The interesting thing is that over the years we have come to see just how ridiculous and how untrue so many of our beliefs actually are. Human history is a rich tapestry of beliefs that turned out to be false.

We laugh at the many crazy beliefs of past generations, such as that the Earth is flat, that women should not be allowed to vote, and that smoking is not bad for you. And how about the less familiar beliefs from way back: disease is transmitted by smell; drill a hole in a patient's head to cure a migraine; reading makes women sterile. The list goes on.

We laugh at how anyone could have been so silly. "As if I would believe such nonsense," we say to ourselves. Here is something else to laugh about: your *own* beliefs. Shocked? Do not think for a second that your beliefs today are any less crazy, any less ridiculous, than believing that the Earth is flat. But do not feel too bad; we all carry around crazy, virtually insane beliefs of which we are not aware. This book is full of the beliefs that I have been carrying around my entire life, many of which I guarantee are causing just as much havoc in your life as they have done in mine. These beliefs seem rational, logical, even intelligent. We do not question them because most of the time we are not even aware we have them. And that is exactly why this book was written: to expose the beliefs that have been running—or should I say *ruining*—my entire life, just as they may be ruining yours.

This book is about my journey, it is not directed at you, but do not be discouraged, because it is also ALL about you! "How can this be?" you ask. "A book not written for me but still all about me? That is preposterous!"

Let me explain: As it turns out, you and I are very much alike, far more than either of us may be prepared to admit. On the surface, we appear to be separate—a "you" and an "I"—but the part of "you" that is your mind actually has much in common with "my" mind. Your mind and mine are very similar.

Again you ask, "How can this be? We are born from different families and have completely different upbringings, yet you dare to say that our minds are alike?" I do. It is true.

You see, what our minds consist of—their very matter—is identical. Nearly all our minds—oh, what the heck, I will say it—*everyone's* mind is identical!

"That is a big statement," you think. "An over-exaggeration." I do not think so, because I know minds, and I know what they are made of. And the truth is that your mind and my mind are not at all what we have always believed they are.

For some, the mind is the brain; but in truth, it is not. Others equate the mind with their self-identity: who they really are, the very essence of what makes them a person. Is this how you see the mind? That your mind *is* you?

The truth is that you—or YOU, as in the real, inner You, as opposed to the "you" who identifies with your mind—could not be further from the mind. To believe otherwise is a lie—a *Mind Lie!*

And there you have it, folks; that is what this book is all about.

THE END.

Oh, you want more explanation?

That is the trouble with the mind; it always wants more. Nothing is ever enough; the mind is an insatiable beast! Have you not noticed that about your mind? It has an insatiable appetite, and not just for the obvious things such as stimulation, happiness, love, and affection. It has an insatiable appetite for other things as well—ugly things, such as the need for validation and the need to be right, for example. This is especially true when it comes to how you see your life: no one respects you, people do not listen to you, and others are smarter or more successful than you. And there are other crazy things, such as nothing you do is ever enough, you do not make enough money, and you have not achieved enough. Here is my personal favorite: everyone else knows more than I do.

In its insatiability, the mind is forever desiring something new, something different, something outside of itself, something more than itself. It flips from one need to the next, never content with the present, always living some time in the past or future.

Do you still think this insatiable wanting is who you truly are in your totality? Many do believe this to be true because it is the conclusion they reach in their minds. But the whole point of this book is that the mind is not made up of truth, as many believe it is. The mind is simply *made up*.

The contradiction here is what makes my mind, your mind, and everyone else's minds identical: the mind is fiction, but each day it has us believe that it is truth, that it is what is real. This is where all the problems start, not because the mind rants and raves about who we are and who we are not, or about what would make us truly happy. No, the problems start because we *believe* our minds. We believe our minds so strongly that they become our identities.

Your mind is the snowball effect of one nontruth, one lie, after another, gathering more and more momentum, more and more Mind Lies. It was born not when you were born but as a result of when you decided who you thought you were; and now you have an identity based on one decision after the next about yourself, whether that identity is based in truth or a complete fallacy.

But what about all the good stuff: your smarts, your general knowledge, your skills and expertise? Surely those qualities of yours are all true, right? Let us leave that question for later. For now, know this: even the good qualities you have are not what make you *You*.

Identity is a funny thing. We cling to and defend it because we believe in it. But I have news for you: your sense of identity is not You; it is not who you truly are. The very basis of your identity is fiction—in other words, Mind Lies. But nobody believes or wants to believe that the mind is fiction. They think that would be the death of them, as if clinging to the self-identity of the mind were not bringing death sooner.

Am I just being dramatic? Actually, I am not, as you will discover in this book.

Your mind is the sum total of every belief you have identified with throughout your entire life. It affects everything about your life: your decisions and their outcomes, your health, your finances—*everything!*

In my first book, *The ALL KNOWING Diary*, I devote an entire chapter to how our minds affect our lives and our bodies, even to the point of discussing illnesses and the corresponding beliefs that cause them, so I feel no need to repeat that again here. For a fuller understanding of how beliefs affect your physiology, please read *The ALL KNOWING Diary*.

Suffice it to say that beliefs—or Mind Lies, as I will refer to them from now on—dictate your entire reality and therefore the course of your entire life. Mind Lies determine how creative you are, what income level you achieve, how fast you make money, how well you sleep, how smart you are, how fast you learn, how you react to stress, how prone you are to disease and illness, how fearful you are of confrontation, whether you are likely to quit a challenge, what lengths you will go to in order to avoid failure and risk, how quickly your body heals and recovers, how fast you can run, how healthy

13

your heart is, what your food (and people) intolerances are, whether you get migraines, whether you are a skeptic, how fulfilled you are and will be, whether you stay safe or are likely to place yourself in harm's way, how your kids turn out, what your hot buttons are and when they will get pushed, how intuitive you are, what opportunities come into your life, what types of ideas come through for you, how fast you evolve as a human being, and how long you will live. The list goes on. Your Mind Lies especially dictate how much of this book you are prepared to let in.

Beliefs create your reality by altering your state of being. It is your beingness that dictates your decisions, the quality of your actions, and what you have or do not have in your life. Consider Mind Lies to be the programming language, the coding, behind your entire existence. To use a clichéd food metaphor, your life is a cake and your beliefs are its ingredients. Just as the quality of a cake depends on its ingredients, the quality of your life depends on the quality of your beliefs.

Who you see yourself to be dictates what life you get to live. If you see yourself as a leader, you will create a very different life than if you have been taught to see yourself as a criminal. Basically, your entire reality is driven by what you believe about yourself. Beliefs equal your reality!

What do you do? Seek to upgrade your belief system with more sophisticated or intellectual beliefs? No. You seek truth. Changing your beliefs—your Mind Lies—into truth is the fastest way to transform your life.

Most of us are not used to this way of creating change because we live in a society that is predominantly outward focused, not inward focused. In truth, our outer reality is merely a reflection of our inner reality. The more truth you embrace in your inner reality, the sooner your outer reality becomes what you actually want.

Any belief, whatever it may be, whether you believe it to be positive or not, is a cookie-cutter belief overlaid on an infinite, expansive, limitless reality. The fewer beliefs you have, the more infinite you and your life become.

This is why I wrote this book. It was not to gain more positive belief systems or add to my set of beliefs. Many religions, as well as the media and the "experts," already do enough belief-adding. Rather, I wrote this book to get to the truth of the belief systems running my life, to get to the truth of ME. Perhaps by reading this, you might get to the truth of YOU, too!

Truth is magical; you can feel it in your body giving you tingles, releasing blocks and stagnation. Some feel goosebumps in the presence of truth, others feel relaxed, and still others feel their cells come to life. One thing is certain, though: there is no mistaking it! As far as beliefs go, truth feels like a life-saving drop water on a parched desert, the antidote to the fictitious identities we all carry. There is nothing more potent for getting what you want than embracing truth over Mind Lies.

This brings me to how this book was created. I wrote it by going beyond the mind to a place of stillness, a place of truth. For a long time now I have called this space *Universal Intelligence*, as it is available to all of us and contains all the answers. It is pure consciousness, Intelligence without human beliefs, with only truth.

As you may have read in *The ALL KNOWING Diary*, my life has been about accessing this part of myself, having conversations with it, mastering its wisdom, and incorporating it into my life. This time, when I went to the place beyond the mind, I received the insights and answers I record here in *Mind Lies*.

If these truths bring you even a fraction of the healing, growth, and awakening I have experienced, please share your experience via email at info@MindLies.com. I will thank you now for doing so.

So, are you ready for truth?

Then come along with me on this journey—not into the mind, but beyond it!

Notes to the Reader

The Mind Lies appear in this book in the order they have come up for me to heal. There are no chapters; there are just Mind Lies and the truths as deep as I could allow in at the time. I have inserted the occasional commentary; these are my reflections as I heard the truths being given to me. They are set off as italicized, indented paragraphs.

Throughout this book, a lowercase "y" is used for the made-up "you," the conjured-up version comprising dozens of Mind Lies intricately woven together. A capital "Y" is used to refer to the real "You," that is, who you are in the absence of Mind Lies.

One last point. There is nothing a mind hates more than being exposed. Much of what I say may push your buttons; you may even disagree with some of it, but do not let this stop you. Remember, this book was written for me, it is speaking to me regarding my specific circumstances. But don't be thrown by this, it is at the same time designed to help you too.

The mind hides in obscurity, and when it wants you to avoid learning the truth, it can flare up, find distractions, or even make you sleepy. No matter what reactions you experience, to get the maximum benefit of this book, just keep reading, just keep reading, just keep reading. . . . and then read it again.

The journey begins.

"My Beliefs Must Be True"

This is the first Mind Lie of the day! This Mind Lie is a great place to start, as it keeps most of your other Mind Lies firmly in place, wreaking havoc. Realize that a belief is simply that—something you believe in. It is not a "knowing"; it is just a belief. The problem is, you do not relate to your beliefs as beliefs; you relate to them as truths. Worse, they hide in your subconscious mind, secretly influencing your thoughts, decisions, and view of yourself.

Because they are hidden, they feel far more real and truthful than they really are. That is how they stay so powerful. Like a tick burrowing deep inside, they stay hidden and cause so much damage. This is why it so hard to see something for what it really is. And this is the nature of your beliefs; they were simply ideas you once had about yourself—not terribly accurate ideas but convincing nonetheless.

Think of them as uninvited house guests. These guests were brought over to your house by people you loved and respected. You let them stay, because those who brought them were pretty convinced you would like them; and, admittedly, you seemed to have a lot in common with them at the time. Everyone else at your house confirmed it—"Yes, you are quite alike"—validating that your new house guests should be allowed to stay. So they stayed and stayed. They moved in permanently and have been there ever since. Oh, the mess they have made, the chaos they have created, the havoc they have wreaked! What these house guests have cost you . . . well, you do not even want to know!

You now realize that they were never guests—they were pests all along! They should have been asked to leave right at the beginning. The truth is, you never had anything in common with them at all, so now it is time they leave. After all, these "uninvited house guests" are called be**LIE**fs for a reason.

So be open to letting your beliefs leave and have truths come to stay. They make much better house guests; I hear they even pay their own way!

"I Do Not Matter"

Where did this Mind Lie come from? Where do all Mind Lies come from? Many of them, if not all, have been imprinted upon you since you were very young by those closest and most influential to you. In most cases they come from your parents, siblings, elder relatives, and teachers. What these people have imprinted on you are their stamps, who they believe they are, what they believe they are, and what they believe about the reality surrounding them.

When children are born into this world, they are often led to feel about themselves what their parents feel about themselves. As a child, you felt that you did not matter, but this is not the truth at all. Rather, this is how they felt about themselves.

As you interacted with your parents or those closest to you, their fears and anxieties were activated, causing them to react with yelling, anger, and resentment. Instead of your parents healing themselves of their Mind Lies using the power of truth, they subconsciously chose to express these fears outwardly, projecting their identity onto you.

A parent who is smack-bang in the middle of being confronted has a split second to make one of two decisions: they can either expel the energy they are feeling onto the perceived cause of their reaction, or they can remember that their anger is a reaction from their past, not their present. They must then take responsibility instead of shooting out blame energy.

It is very rare for anyone in the midst of feeling confronted to make the latter choice, and so an exchange occurs. Being a child, new to the world and still discovering who and what you were, you just took on what the adult said—or, more importantly, you took on the beingness the adult projected onto you. In that moment, an intense energy exchange was going on, beyond just the verbal exchange. Looking for an identity of your own as a small child, you took on their energy—their fears—of not mattering. But you were not taking on the "I don't matter" from the adult's perspective; you took on the "I don't matter" from your own perspective. That is how the subconscious mind works; and, without realizing it, you took on the belief that your parents had been led to believe since they themselves were young – I don't matter – thereby creating this as part of your identity, the Mind Lie: 'I don't matter.'

So was it your truth – I don't matter? No, it was just the belief of those who passed it onto you. You activated a memory in them, the "I don't matter" memory. The pain, the confrontation of feeling this way, caused them to lash out at you, causing you to feel this way too. But was it ever your truth? No. Was it ever even their truth? Actually no, it was just one Mind Lie, passed down from generation to generation.

"How Do I Heal This Mind Lie?"

To heal this Mind Lie, you need to learn what the actual truth is. Truth heals Mind Lies. Hearing and integrating the necessary truth changes the chemistry in your brain and body so that a new reality can be experienced. Truth really does set you free!

What is the truth? Do you matter? Brace yourself. The truth is that you don't matter. Let me explain. There is a "you" that you have come to think of as yourself, as true and real. But that "you" is not real, for the "you" to whom this refers is only the total amalgamation of the Mind Lies this book describes.

But fear not, because a real You does exist. The REAL You—the You that exists above and beyond all your experiences, opinions, and Mind Lies—is of sublime significance.

So "you" actually don't matter, but "You" in truth matter greatly.

"What Else Do I Need to Know?"

The Mind Lie of "You don't matter" is a blindfold that hides your actual life purpose from you and keeps you feeling that you don't matter. It weaves its way into the mind, filtering out greatness, hiding the mind-blowing truth: You matter. This truth can be difficult for you to let in, as the Mind Lie that you do not matter has been expressed to you in many different ways and at many different times in your life and came from those who believed the same about themselves.

To break free from this Mind Lie, you must realize that the version of you that is concerned with needing to matter is the very device used to keep you from making a real contribution in this life. In other words, your very identity is a tool that is blinding you from seeing a far deeper, greater, and more significant You. Seek out and live your life as this magnificent version of You. You will see how much you really do matter!

"Who Is the REAL Me?"

It is best you know the ending at the beginning. The real You is LOVE—free from anger, fear, insecurity, and doubt. Letting that in requires either a quick transcendence or a reading of the rest of this wonderful book.

"How Do I Know I Actually Matter?"

Understand this: You chose to be here for a reason. Without this reason, you would not exist. It is your job to discover your life purpose, who you are in relation to it, who you are because of it, and why you have been blinded from it.

Not knowing your life purpose in the here and now does not make you not matter. Not knowing what the switchboard in your home is or what its purpose is does not make it any less important, does it? Of course not. Learning your life purpose can come only from realizing that you matter, not the other way around. If you do not matter, you have little chance to recognize or allow in the full extent of your purpose in this lifetime. Understand that no matter where you are, what you are doing, or what you have done wrong in the past, You matter. The person who did or did not do all those things is not the real You; it was the Mind Lie you.

You are here to bring a gift—your life purpose, unique to you—and in bringing it, you will come to erase or see past all your Mind Lies. Here is an example:

What is your gift, your life purpose? "Being a harbinger of truth."

Who are You because of this? "An embodiment of truth."

Why have you been blinded from it? "Because those who raised me were blinded from the truth."

Who are you now? "The incarnation of truth."

Knowing your gift and life purpose will help ensure that all your decisions are in alignment and facing the real You at all times. When you know your true identity, how important you really are will quickly become apparent.

There are, of course, those who seem to be doing anything but matter. Realize that all people matter, even those who seem to contribute nothing. They are actually contributing the gift of lessons that benefit everyone. All of humanity has a story to tell, a role to play, without which every incarnation of people on Earth would not grow and evolve.

Everyone represents a lesson, a learning, a new understanding, about what works and what does not. Allowing all life experiences to play themselves out is to everyone's greatest good. They are opportunities for all to learn, individually and collectively.

Digging Deeper

No matter how mundane your life may seem, it matters. Although it appears to you that everyone is an individual with individual consciousness, in truth you are all part of human consciousness, with each individual an aspect of human consciousness. All aspects of the human psyche exist as life on the Earth, but many thoughts and concepts no longer serve. It is for this reason that you matter. You are each playing a part in healing and dissolving what does not work and learning to harness that which does.

Think of it like this: Everyone is playing a vital role, cleansing the global human consciousness of impurities; that is, you are learning from your mistakes. As such, you each play a necessary role in a single consciousness that is growing and evolving as it waits on each of its parts to see the bigger picture—to see the light.

The consciousness that runs through you runs through all matter. In truth, it is the *source* of all matter. To say "I don't matter" is actually ridiculous, because you are the essence of matter itself. You are consciousness and consciousness is all matter, so you are the source of all matter. Therefore, to say the source of all matter doesn't matter is clearly untrue, for it is exactly what does matter.

How important you are ultimately depends on how willing and allowing you are to follow through on your life purpose and to be the real You. You all matter, but just how important a role each individual plays changes in every moment.

Ask yourself in each moment, "Will I exist as my Mind Lies, or will I live as truth?" This is a moment-by-moment choice.

"I Am Not Respected!"

There are many times when you feel that those around you do not respect you. It may be someone specific or society in general. Either way, always keep in mind that the complaint you have about others is actually the complaint you have about yourself. If you are presented with people who show no respect, or if this is a general feeling, ask yourself, "Where am I not respecting myself?"

The world is but a stage, and the people you see, the people you notice, are all actors simply acting out your life. People act as mirrors to what is not obvious to your conscious awareness. When you heal the Mind Lie others mirror to you, your new level of self-respect, rather than the old paradigm, will be reflected back to you. The truth is, you do not need others' respect; you just need your own.

You put yourself through the wringer and jump through all kinds of hoops to compensate for the belief that you need other people's respect. You may be compelled to achieve—to in some way summon the respect of others. This may take the form of something drastic or something seemingly courageous and ambitious. You hope that gaining someone's respect will be the missing ingredient you have been searching for. But no matter how this yearning is expressed, it becomes a tool to attract attention and gain respect.

However, the attention you receive, although it may seem to be what you crave, will be a temporary Band-Aid, bringing a short-term sense of achievement and self-worth instead of real and long-term fulfillment, because nothing within you has actually shifted. You may receive increased attention and admiration, but the Mind Lie remains intact. The end result, the respect you longed for, that you got a mere glimpse of, is only skin deep and therefore unable to penetrate past your ultimate belief of "I'm not respected."

The attention you really seek, that will make all the difference, does not come from outside of you. The attention you need is to look upon yourself with fond and proud eyes and realize you are someone worthy of respect. No one "out there" will change this belief for you.

Ultimately, you can have all the respect in the world from others, yet you will never come to experience it until the Mind Lie changes to truth. The irony, of course, is that no hoops need to be jumped through, no drastic action needs to be taken, no conquering of the world needs to happen. It is self-respect you are looking for.

Some of the grandest cathedrals, tallest buildings, and most impressive businesses have been built by people believing "I'm not respected," yet seeking respect. Even these monumental accomplishments did not result in them feeling respected. Outward doing does not heal inward being or feeling.

The parts of you that others don't respect, that get you so worked up and feeling so invalidated, are, of course, the parts of yourself that *you* don't respect. This does not refer to the real You; it just refers to the sum total of the Mind Lies that is present as your identity. In truth, experiencing the need for others to respect the parts of you that you do not respect is a gift. It highlights the parts of yourself that still require healing and dissolving from your identity.

Realize that there is nothing for you to do or achieve to gain respect. To compensate for emptiness with the need to achieve is to attempt to fill a void with the same emptiness that created it. Instead, realize that your greatest achievements will come when you have nothing to prove to others and when you know that your True Self is already great. Respect this as the real You.

Interestingly, because of your Mind Lies, you have reached a point in your society where achieving the respect of others is seen as a worthwhile accomplishment, that it will get you somewhere in life, move you forward. Being respected is seen as a worthwhile feat on its own. Yet, in truth, this respect is meaningless. No one can fill the void within you with respect of any substance or longevity.

This Mind Lie keeps you from learning the truth about how important you really are. The Mind Lies "I am not respected" and "I don't matter" have you continuously looking outside of yourself for validation and a sense of worth.

This is an endless journey, the long route to realizing that the opinions of others are a poor substitute for a high opinion of yourself.

Seeking respect and validation from others also keeps you in the space of comparison, where nothing you do will ever be enough. There will always be someone better than you at something that is not your truth; it is a competition that is impossible to win. In the space of comparison, you will never find your true calling. How can you, when comparison lives externally, with external benchmarks, not internally, where your true calling actually exists?

Life is not a race you win against others. In truth, there are no "others"; there is just one human consciousness, healing itself through multiple bodies with multiple perspectives. The greatest victory is not to race or win against another but to experience moment-to-moment victories through allowing in your true identity in every moment.

A pro golfer or any pro athlete will tell you that you are not playing to beat your opponent; you are playing to master yourself, leaving your old self in the past. Knowing this is what makes them real pros.

Seek not public acceptance nor admiration; seek self-acceptance and self-admiration.

For some, seeking respect is a way to compensate for other Mind Lies buried in their subconscious. For example, the Mind Lies "I am no expert," "I am not a success until I am respected for something," and "If others do not respect me, surely I must not be any good," strengthen the desire for respect from outside yourself.

The truth is, you are great, with or without someone else's respect. Respect is not a prerequisite for great skill or accomplishment. When you sat your driving test, did the instructor ask you to tally up all the respect you had from all the other drivers on the road before they would pass you? No, of course not. Respect is not an indication of skill level or expertise. You are either great at something or you are not. Respect has nothing to do with it.

"If Others Respect Me, Then I Can Respect Myself"

Many people believe this Mind Lie, but respect from others is an illusion. Remember, others are just a mirror for your own feelings and beliefs. Therefore, others are not seeing you when they respect something about you, they are seeing what they respect in themselves. So even when you gain respect, it has nothing to do with you. You do not need other people's respect to get somewhere in life, you just need your own.

As you learn to love yourself, the parts you do not respect will fade away. The only parts of You remaining will be beyond requiring respect.

"I Need Respect from Others to Feel My Decisions Are Worthwhile"

Seeking respect ensures that who you are and the decisions you make are everything but worthwhile. Seeking respect necessitates a degree of conformity, of being in line with or like others. But this world does not need "like"; it needs "different." Different is divine. Different does not come from conforming, it comes from inspiration. Like and conforming come from Mind Lies.

Truth, and then brilliance, come from being just who you really are—from being You. When you are being You, you skip right past getting respect and go into being inspirational. You then see respect as second best. You laugh to yourself and think, "Respect—is that all I get?" and, "Why did I ever crave respect in the first place?"

Respect is what happens when someone sees something in you that they have, or wish they had more of, in themselves. Inspiration, on the other hand, is uplifting, empowering. It reminds people that they, too, are limitless beings with infinite potential.

What would you rather achieve: to be respected or to be an inspiration? There is a key difference. Respect takes a lot of doing for a mediocre result. Being inspirational takes simply being, and with a magnificent result. It comes naturally, takes nothing away from you or anyone else, and is abundant for you and all of humanity.

Being inspirational is an introspective journey of embracing truth. It is not about trying or being concerned with what others think of you; it is only about what you think of yourself. Master this and inspiration will magically happen all around you, effortlessly.

"I Cannot Respect Parts of Myself and Things I Have Done"

To put it simply, the only parts of yourself you do not respect are the parts that are Mind Lies. They are you but not You. They were never You to begin with. They are simply beliefs that you were led to believe about yourself. These very Mind Lies caused you to be and act in certain ways, leading to certain outcomes. But You are not your actions; nor are You defined by your past experiences, who you have been, and what you have thought.

Your beliefs drive the ideas that come into your thoughts. They tell you that these ideas, and your past actions, are your true identity. You are the observer of these experiences and the thoughts that creep into your awareness. You are not defined by your thoughts, actions, and past experiences; they are not what you are made up of, they are not your identity. The real You is none of these things; the real You is without identity. It is pure awareness. You are pure awareness.

Awareness is infinite and indefinable. It is your true nature. That is your True Self. Yes, some of your actions and thoughts were less worthy of respect, but your core self is worthy of more than respect. As awareness, as the real You, you are the entire human consciousness, vastly bigger than the you that feels the need for respect.

You, in truth, are a field of consciousness, an ever-expanding organism healing its way through Mind Lie after Mind Lie. This is both respectable and commendable. No—it's inspirational! This is the real You and describes the journey called life.

"I Do Not Want To Be Alone; I Want Attention"

Being alone in today's society has become one of the worst social faux pas. Why do you resist such a sacred opportunity for reflection and learning? Why has society placed being alone in the "I am a failure" basket? Let us explore.

You do not want to be alone because it feels like rejection from the world. But a deeper truth exists: that being alone represents rejection of yourself. To realize that you have rejected yourself is far too painful, so you seek the company of another to mask the injustice of having rejected yourself.

What is it about yourself that you have rejected? Have you been told that you are boring, annoying, weird, unpleasant, unattractive, or uninteresting? Do you feel unwanted? Whatever the specifics, these are all nontruths; they are just more Mind Lies.

You reject yourself because of these Mind Lies. To be by yourself, on your own, is not boring or a failure or even an act of rejection. In truth, it is where the greatest shifts and breakthroughs can occur. But the feeling of being all alone will persist if you resist this understanding. It is only when you truly embrace your aloneness and harness it for inner connection and realization that the experience will shift forward into something fulfilling. Interestingly, being alone is seen as wrong and undesirable in society for this very reason. While you are controlled and held back by your own Mind Lies, you are envious of anyone who transcends them. You do not want others to break free, to go beyond you, to leave you behind, so the consciousness of Mind Lies has you believe that you must surround yourself with others as often as possible. This keeps you from moving forward and evolving, because keeping yourself surrounded mutes your inner voice, the inner truth that you are so much more than just needing another's attention. When you give yourself loving attention, you will be amazed at how quickly others give it to you tenfold. The secret is to love yourself first, because this is the catalyst for all great experiences.

This sense of being alone stems from considering yourself as not-good-enough company, at least, not enough to fill the void, so you crave others. Yet the void you perceive in yourself is created by undervaluing yourself in the first place. The more you undervalue yourself, the needier you become. You become a slave to your needs.

Do you know why you undervalue yourself? It is because you do not realize the truth. You believe you are the sum total of all the opinions you, and perhaps others, hold about you. These opinions are not based in truth. Believing them makes up your identity, so naturally you undervalue yourself. Simply believing that you are these opinions is the undervaluing.

To understand the truth, recognize that you have these beliefs, but also see that they are not who You are. You currently carry them and experience life as if they were you, but they are not. The attention you crave is to compensate for believing that you are someone You are not. You have been lied to your whole life. Loneliness is a Mind Lie, as is the need for attention.

The next level of truth is to recognize that you are all you need. When you get that, You will find yourself enveloped by love from within yourself and from all around you. You are all you need because You are not the you *you* think you are. You are not you; You are You. If you do not yet understand that, remember that the you that you believe you are is the sum total of all your Mind Lies— which truly is poor company. But when you stop relating to yourself as this poor company and instead see yourself as the extraordinary being that is You, You will realize that You are the best company there is. There will be no need for any other. From that space, any other company you attract into your life will be inspirational and uplifting.

The wisest of self-realized beings know that sitting without distraction brings great fortune. To be in and embrace your own space opens you up, expands you to profound new horizons. You hear the whispers from your True Self in that silence, which catapults your growth to great heights.

As soon as you embrace being alone and wander down the rabbit hole of "Who am I, really?" you will discover an infinite Universe within, one you carry wherever you go. It is a consciousness, a higher aspect of yourself, that always has your back, that is your guardian. You are your best friend, your greatest-ever companion, the best company you will ever keep. You are your True Self. As such, it is impossible to be alone. You are never alone, and you wouldn't be alone even if you were the last human being on Earth. In truth, being alone does not exist in the human experience, or in any experience for that matter. The feeling of being alone comes not from truth but from the related Mind Lie, "I reject myself." That is where aloneness is felt.

When you resist being alone, you surround yourself with distraction after distraction: TV, the Internet, social media, the news, and people who add very little to your life. But you are never alone, because in the stillness of the Mind, when you cease resisting being alone, the unity, the oneness that exists between all living things, becomes apparent.

You can see just how effective this Mind Lie is in keeping you small and stagnant. The resistance and fear of being alone has you avoid the very realization that you are not separate at all. That being alone is bad or in some way detrimental or representative of failure is simply Mind Lie propaganda. Yes, there are times when you may want companionship, when company is what is in your highest good and a catalyst for greater growth. But if that was what you needed most right now, you would not be alone. Being on your own brings space to discover your true nature.

You are more than your mind: you are one with everything. You are a walking, talking Universe, supported in full and loved eternally and unanimously, despite what Mind Lies have to say. Being alone is therefore a physical impossibility and exists only as a state of Mind Lies. The very nature of being is a collective, or universal, experience; it is something the whole Universe is doing each and every moment. To perceive that you are being alone is to engage the Mind Lie and therefore the ultimate self-sabotage, disconnection, and the belief that "I am disconnected." These Mind Lies exist by masking truth with nontruth.

"Why Am I Alone? I Want Company!"

Being alone is not failure, nor is it stagnation, unless you choose to resist it. If you find yourself physically lonely, without friends or loved ones, there is a reason you are alone: it is because to have another around would be a distraction from something that is of greater significance than mere company or companionship.

It is only when you are OK with being alone that your situation will resolve itself to a new level of experience. When you become OK with yourself as alone, this Mind Lie begins to melt away. When you embrace yourself as the only company you ever need, the next level of beingness becomes available: self-love. Self-love opens you up to possibility. It brings you far greater inner strength, which will never have you undervalue yourself, see yourself as alone, or needing attention from outside yourself.

Perhaps without you having ever realized it, self-love is simultaneously all the attention you have ever craved and all the attention you will ever need.

If you had this type of attention when you were young, you would see that you are self-sufficient and full to the brim of what you actually need instead of having this Mind Lie. Beneath these layers of Mind Lies is a well of self-love, never ending or beginning; it just is. Self-love is ever present but is masked by your Mind Lies, so it appears that the only way to feel or perceive it is with the aid of another. This is an act perpetuated by yet another Mind Lie: "I am no good on my own."

When you see the truth, you will realize that this is another Mind Lie that hides your greatness from you, another conspiracy to hide your truth. You fear that who you think you are—the Mind Lies—is the truth. The fear is that without another to comfort you, you will realize that you are not OK as you are, that you are unwanted, wrong, or faulty in some way. To believe this is obviously disturbing and unsettling.

There is no truth to your being unwanted, wrong, or faulty in any way, but hiding from this Mind Lie by seeking company, because you fear it *is* the truth, perpetuates the Mind Lie's longevity. To supplement your need for attention, for company to avoid being alone, pushes in the opposite direction of what will actually cure this need.

Interestingly, to break free from this Mind Lie, you need to see that you are only attracting others who see themselves in the same way as you see yourself. To attract the type of company you actually want to keep, you first need to be OK within yourself.

32

You attract the same frequency at which you vibrate. If you feel you are no good at the core, you attract others who resonate at that level rather than those who have broken free from this Mind Lie. This is not growth, and it is worse than stagnation: it is resignation. Attracting in others who do not feel good about themselves keeps you perpetually feeling low about yourself, never allowing you to come up for air, to see the light, the real truth. Masking your fear with the company of others keeps you stuck in this one repetitive experience of life.

> **Daniel speaking:** *I am reminded of a time when I broke up with a girlfriend after a three-year relationship. I was left feeling very down on myself, undeserving of people's love. Within a few days of the breakup, I met a guy who had just gone through a similar experience. He felt unloved, alone, and unworthy of love from another, just the same as I did. We spent a lot of time together, sharing experiences in great camaraderie; but did it help elevate either one of us beyond this state of despair? No. My need for company attracted in this situation, which did not fill the void but ultimately deepened it further.*

If you are alone because of a Mind Lie, then learning the truth will attract the right company and the right attention.

What attention do you crave? The attention that keeps you stuck but feeling OK and similar to others, or the attention that reflects your greatness rather than your fears? As you radiate self-love, you will draw in a similar resonance from another, the same loving attention you feel and hold for yourself. You are not really OK believing in a Mind Lie, but you are more than OK when truth is present.

Let us go a little deeper. Remember, feeling alone stems from the feelings of being rejected as a child and then continuously as an adult. Yet during this time you made the critical decision that "If others reject me, I must be rejectable," and in that moment the ultimate rejection—self-rejection—occurred: "There must be something wrong with me."

This Mind Lie perpetuated repeat experiences of rejection until it became your truth and a victory for the Mind Lies. But the truth you neglected to see in each and every moment of rejection was this: those who rejected you so that you felt alone and wrong as you were actually felt that *they* were not good enough to be around *you*. They felt not enough, not OK, insufficient to be who you needed them to be. It was literally their problem, not yours!

You need to allow in that it was your greatness that others rejected, not your differences or perceived inadequacies. You were not rejected for who *you* were but for the inadequacies others felt about themselves in your presence. You are therefore the opposite of "not good enough"; you are pure greatness.

Greatness is scary to those who see only weakness within themselves. Greatness is your truth. It is who you really are.

You have been conditioned to fear being alone, as you take it to mean that you have been rejected. But remember, every Mind Lie has a purpose: to hide the ultimate truth from your eyes. Your fears actually go as deep as fearing who you really are. Being alone with yourself is the most significant step you can take toward self-love. When you embrace yourself as the only company you truly need, you are asserting to yourself, "I am lovable. I love my own company." As you do this, you set off a chain reaction where you ascend to new heights in your consciousness—and, frankly, your identity does not want this to happen.

Being alone means loving your thoughts, quieting your busy mind, and being OK with stillness and silence. Why do you fear silence? It is in silence that the answers become clear, that the identity is dissolved, and that the fake self has no presence, no power.

Fear is the working of your mind-made identity, which wants to starve you from the truth because its identity, its very survival, depends on it.

Your Mind-Lie identity wants to live, and it will have you believe all kinds of nonsense to survive.

> **Daniel speaking:** *I am intrigued by how we have been taught to believe in the very Mind Lies that do the most damage to us, that hold us back from learning the real truth about ourselves. It seems to be purposeful sabotage to the human race, disarming us from realizing our true power. It makes me wonder why. For what purpose? How did it all start, and by whom?*

What you truly crave is not what you think you crave; it is far deeper than that. What you really crave is to feel and connect to the nurture that dwells within you. You have just come to accept others' attention as a poor substitute for the infinite well of unconditional love coming from within, which is what is truly life sustaining. Stillness and allowing provide the access to the reservoir of the inner love and true nurture you require to eliminate the false identity.

"I Have To Fight And Compete To Succeed"

For a long time, people all over the world have believed that competition is necessary, that it makes humanity stronger—in the sense of survival of the fittest and so on. Like many other human belief systems, this one has more than reached its expiration date. I know you think that competition is essential in nature, in the animal kingdom, to eliminate the weakest so that only the strong survive. But you are not from primates, nor insects, nor birds. You are part of a unique species, operating from and existing through profound truths.

"What Is The Truth?"

It is not competition that makes humanity stronger; it is a new level of collaboration that very few know about. Many argue that you grow from competing, that it works. But do not become distracted by such mediocre results, which stem from a mediocre approach. There is a better way, and it is raising its hand and saying, "Pick me!"

You observe fight and competition in nature, and you often draw upon the animal kingdom to understand human behavior. Yet, as human beings you have your own laws that nurture you—laws that are not separate from nature but just more evolved than in the animal kingdom. These are your laws of sustainability and evolution. Sustainability does not come from competition. You can evolve because of competition, but evolving this way comes at great cost to sustainability, so much so that the growth gained and the cost suffered cancel each other out. That is what you are facing in the here and now. Let me explain.

To collaborate means working together for a common goal or purpose. This creates more for everyone. To compete comes from the idea that if you do not fight, you will not have enough and will miss out, fail, and perhaps even die. Coming from this place is socially and environmentally eroding. But the true path, the path unencumbered by and no longer generated from Mind Lies, is unlike anything you have seen on Earth. It is not a socialist system, it is not a communist system, and least of all is it a capitalist system, because none of these systems are about bringing people into alignment with their higher purpose; this is why you still feel you need to fight or compete for what is, or should be, yours.

To allow your purpose to be the driver, on an individual level and then naturally on a collective level, means that fulfillment rather than accomplishment becomes the driving energy.

"What is the difference?" you ask. When you base your decisions on attaining fulfillment, you naturally come into flow with the Universe for the simple reason that what brings the greatest fulfillment simultaneously serves the greatest purpose. That is how human nature works, how the Universe works.

Pursuing accomplishment or gains, on the other hand, neglects the attainment of fulfillment, leaving each person empty inside and thereby succumbing to all sorts of Mind Lies to fill that void. You think that you are pursuing fulfillment when you chase money or accomplishment, but you are not. You are chasing what others have misguidedly led you to believe brings fulfillment. In truth, you are coming from "I am unfulfilled." Coming from this place keeps it as the status quo.

A lack of fulfillment perpetuates greed and other self-destructive tendencies, because surely, "If I am discontent, I must need more and more and more." Truly fulfilled people have far fewer needs than those who are unhappy with the life they are living.

Collaboration represents the highest good in all, so much so that it is a by-product of acting in each individual's highest good. In simple terms, collaboration is a naturally occurring phenomenon when all individuals act in their own highest good: from truth, not from their Mind Lies.

The Universe is self-organizing. It does not take your intervention to prosper; it takes only collaboration. The more you fight, the more you become out of alignment with that which generates the greatest success. True collaboration does not need to be initiated; it happens all by itself.

Daniel speaking: I see this kind of collaboration occur quite naturally, without anyone's intention or efforts, in our MIND LIE training courses. Since the beginning of our courses, I have observed individuals being trained in how to come from their highest good. They naturally gravitate toward fulfilling a need humanity has. Groups are formed based on common life purposes without anyone trying to form a group. It happens without effort, without competition, and certainly without a fight.

This evolution of collaboration creates a new middle ground, as you are no longer coming from the position of "I must fight and compete to get what I want," nor are you coming from the position of "I am not worth fighting for or getting what I want." This perfect, divine space is the embracing of the understanding that "I play a perfect role, and the more I nurture this sense, the more I become and the more I get to have and experience." This creates more for everyone, individually and collectively, uplifting human consciousness at the same time.

Fighting is a resistance to what already is. But recognizing your true gift—that you have a gift—and allowing this recognition to steer your path creates what you want much faster. To move away from this recognition will create the need to fight to have what you want. It is like a train that wants to get off its tracks, yet it is the tracks that offer a smooth ride. The minute the train becomes disconnected from its tracks—its path—it will be met with a much more difficult journey.

Creating the smoothest path comes not from forcing change on the outside but from making the change within.

When you find yourself needing to fight and compete, ask yourself, "What within myself am I resisting? Where am I fighting a natural flow that is trying to keep me on my train tracks? What is my truth, and how do I return to it?" You will be amazed at how situations around you shift and change and how people change to support you when you make the shift within yourself first.

Fighting is for those who do not realize that the Universe is behind them all the way. It is for those who fear lack, fear missing out, fear failure. If you trust, you will be in the universal flow, where harmony and abundance exist in the absence of fighting.

To fight to win is like running to stay still. Fight and struggle are acts of aggression toward yourself. The abundance is found in universal flow. To resist flow is where the fight and struggle are found. But what do you really know about flow? Very little, because struggle and fight is all around you.

As children, many of you had to fight, or at least thought you did, for your place in the household—to be able to play, to receive love and attention, to be counted. But another path is available, one that does not come from Mind Lies but from deep truths about your existence here on Earth. Fighting always causes a waste of energy and often resources. It is an inefficient way to get what you want. To flow with the Universe creates abundance for all. The Universe does not have Mind Lies and therefore does not believe in nor needs to create waste, so it has created particular pathways for growth and success. It is your resistance to these pathways that leads to struggle and fight.

"How Do I Know I Don't Have To Fight When That Is What I Have Always Known?"

Fight and struggle are the products of resistance to your True Self. When you are in resistance, you are coming from your Mind Lies. When you are being your truth, there is an absence of resistance. In this space, things happen—opportunities are in abundance, and life works. You know the experience of being in the flow: traffic lights are green, people smile at you, there is no line to wait in at the shops, ideas and solutions come easily to you, and so on.

The fight comes from thinking that you are in control. You are not. The only control you can truly exert on your life is the surrendering of control. You are either in the flow without control or you are out of the flow, believing you are in control but in fact still being out of control. The greater your need for control, the more you inadvertently sabotage your path, making life far, far more difficult than it needs to be. This is the state you find your life in right now. You are stuck in a bog that you cannot seem to get out of.

Control is not needed and is certainly not the answer. In fact, needing control and fearing the loss of it is what got you stuck in this bog to begin with. Control is not needed because it is the Mind Lie—the nontruth version of you—that is seeking control in the first place. This *you* never really existed, and in an absolute sense, it still does not. How can you give control to something that is not even real?

A lot of people confuse surrender with quitting, being lazy, or being apathetic. It is actually quite the opposite. To quit is to abandon hope in yourself and the Universe. To surrender is to abandon the small you, the *you* made of Mind Lies, in order to become the real version of You, which is infinitely grander than the old version.

You are being encouraged to trade in what is not real for what is real. As such, you are trading what is mediocre for what is truly monumentally significant. It is anything but apathy, because apathy is the shadow of surrender. Apathy says, "I have no power, and I don't care what happens to me." Apathy is the denial and dismissal of your True Self, not the embracing of You. It kicks your True Self out of your body instead of welcoming You in with a warm embrace.

"I Have Goals and Ambitions! Surely These Are Worth Fighting For?"

Your ambitions are not necessarily that of your True Self. Your need for admiration and accolades, your need for validation, and your fears are not your truth. The path surrender takes you on may differ significantly from the outcomes or experiences you have planned for yourself. But this is a good thing! The path You lay out for yourself will be infinitely better than the path you planned.

To follow the plans created by Mind Lies may give you the life your head thinks it wants, but it will leave a gaping hole in your heart.

You can test this out and travel the long route to realizing this truth on your own. Alternatively, you can surrender to an Intelligence that already knows: your True Self. Remember, the point is about fulfillment and what will bring in fulfillment in the smoothest, most gentle way. This will not be created in your head filled with Mind Lies!

Start putting the questions out there to the Universe: "What is the perfect flow right now? How can I best surrender? What do I need to let go of? How do I let go? What do I have to look forward to when I do?"

The best possible life for you has already been figured out. It is time to get out of your own way so you can enjoy the ride You had already mapped out before this life even started.

"People Are Unreliable And Cannot Be Trusted"

Many would argue this belief as fact, and there would be plenty of evidence to support it. But how is carrying this belief impacting you? Is believing this Mind Lie helping, or is it hindering you from getting what you want? As with all Mind Lies, this one is a menace to your life.

But this belief stands out from many others. It is different to the Mind Lies discussed so far because it is not about you, it is about others. This gives the belief a unique quality: your resistance to give it up. How ready are you to stop believing it? Mind Lies about others have an addictive nature to them. Notice how quickly you insist on agreeing with this Mind Lie rather than letting go of it.

Could it be that your holding on to this particular nontruth is a way you have of feeling better about yourself? Of feeling greater than you truly believe you are? Does this Mind Lie have you feel you are getting things right, whereas many of the other Mind Lies have you feel like an absolute failure? Yes? Hence the addiction.

Why prioritize the feeling of getting it right over seeing the actual truth? That is the question, because where Mind Lies are concerned, being right never wins over knowing the truth. You live in a society where the pressure to get it right is extreme. Why is this so? Because to get it right means that you have a place in society, a chance for success, and with the added bonus of feeling that you are better than the majority of people. It is a quick and easy source of addictive self-esteem. Yet, in the world of truth, there is no right or wrong.

"How Did Needing to Get It Right Become So Important?"

Centuries ago, when truth was starting to show itself as the way forward, those preoccupied with power were opposed to this concept. They determined to maintain power and control by making truth right and nontruth wrong. It was the dawning of many Western-based religions, which, for some of those in power, were attempts to own and control truth. This approach was taken to such an extreme that truth was soon forgotten about and only "right" and "wrong" remained. Truth ceased to see the light of day, and what began instead were established belief systems based on going to hell and being ostracized, stoned to death, or burned at the stake for getting it wrong. How ironic that those in power punished people and called them sinners, or worse, for living in nontruth.

When you peel back the layers of historic Mind Lies, you can see one absolute truth: truth cannot be owned or controlled; it is more powerful than those "in power." Yet the pressure to stay in favor through getting it right has now become so intense that it is hard to discern whether getting it right is based in truth or in Mind Lies.

This has created the muddle you now have in society. You have ceased believing that you are truth (or that you have it available within you) and have come to believe that others know your truth better than you do. This and many other Mind Lies keep you in the dark, as you have surrendered your true power to those without true power.

But there is a deeper fear inside this Mind Lie, as it is not what it appears to be on the surface. The fear is less about whether or not other people are reliable or trustworthy and more about the questions of "Am I reliable? Can I be trusted?"

When you believe that you are reliable and trustworthy, you stop seeing other people as the problem and yourself as the victim.

Instead, you realize that you are at the center of the experiences you attract and have: "If I am reliable and trustworthy, I will bring reliable and trustworthy people into my life."

The challenge, and the reason that this is such a prevalent belief, is because of its addictive qualities. When you believe that it is all about other people being unreliable and untrustworthy, you are implying that you are reliable and trustworthy, even though secretly you believe the opposite. When you make this judgment, you feel an immediate sense of satisfaction because you are elevating yourself above the masses, which can be very important in certain circles.

Some beliefs make you feel down on yourself and inferior to others. These beliefs have no addictive qualities because of the negative feelings attached to them. Other beliefs intrinsically make you feel superior, which, in comparison, are a refreshing change in your mental state. This is why you want to hold on to them as long as possible. On some level, they make you feel good. They offer a substantial upside, or so you believe.

Because you like this belief, you want to keep it in place to keep you from looking at what you really think about yourself. You engineer circumstances for others to fail so that you can prove your own worthiness and get to shine. Setting these traps keeps you believing this belief and prevents you from ever questioning it or moving away from it. This also explains where you got this belief from: you very likely fell into the same trap set by another believer—a parent, relative, or caregiver—of "I am not reliable and cannot be trusted."

But no matter how many times you succeed at having others fail so that you get to look good, you will still be left feeling dissatisfied and will continue to experience others letting you down. You cannot cure a Mind Lie by attempting to bash it on its head over and over to prove it wrong. This bashing and proving is yet another Mind Lie that goes by the name of "convincing."

Convincing

Convincing either covers up Mind Lies or sweeps them under the rug; it does not remove them. Convincing has you think that the Mind Lies are gone, but they all remain fully functional. Convincing is the shadow of transformation. People use convincing when they do not know how to transform, when they are without the healing power of truth. Transformation is the realization of deeper truths beyond your identity. Convincing attempts to shift your perspective through the grace of the intellect, not truth.

You cannot use one Mind Lie to fix another. All your efforts to thwart your Mind Lies by compensating for them is a form of convincing yourself that they are not the truth. Convincing is an inadequate substitute for truth.

You can see the effects of the "convincing" Mind Lie all over the world as well as in your own life: from convincing yourself to stay in a job or with a partner you do not like to convincing yourself that making money is worth the burnout, the absence from your children, and the demise of the planet; from using fossil fuels and nuclear power for energy to waging war against fellow humans. A lot of convincing occurs among people at all levels of society, including politicians, business leaders, and heads of religions. Society is being dominated by convincing rather than being emancipated through truth.

You as an individual and everyone as a collective need to move beyond accepting and settling for convincing and instead aspire to know the truth in every moment—not just when it suits, but always.

Convincing yourself that you and others can or cannot be trusted is not the answer. As you may now see, as with all Mind Lies, your feelings of having failed and having been unreliable were never yours to begin with. They belonged to the people who used you to validate their own beliefs. It is like spreading a virus: they had it first and spread it all over you. Because you were predisposed to this belief, you caught their virus.

You cannot ever be reliable when you are set up to fail, because the expectations are forever changing. Therefore, being unreliable is not your true identity; you were set up!

Those who set a trap of failure for you—your mother, father, sibling, uncle, aunt, or school teacher—did not know they were doing it; it was one of their Mind Lies. What they subconsciously wanted was to see if you were like them: unreliable and untrustworthy. Being unreliable is not your true identity.

The people who passed this Mind Lie of unreliability onto you actually believed that, sooner or later, you would see just how unreliable and untrustworthy they were, too. They had you take on this identity so that you could not see them in this way, see their ugly truth. You were set up to feel worse than they did, to be less than they were, to be a worse failure than they were, and ultimately, to be even more unreliable and untrustworthy than they were. This immediately caused the problem to be all about you rather than them, which is exactly what Mind Lies do: they have you looking for relief in all the wrong places.

⁂

Digging Deeper

If truth is what works, then a nontruth does not work. This means that when you operate from the space of a Mind Lie, failure is imminent. You will let yourself down, and you will let others down.

Conversely, when you are aligned to truth, you become reliable and trustworthy. The fewer Mind Lies you have, the more trustworthy you are. The more truth is present, and the more victorious you are.

The you who is concerned with being reliable and trustworthy is unreliable and untrustworthy simply because that you is based in nontruth. Stay out of this you and move instead toward *You*, as You will inherently be reliable and trustworthy. Perhaps now another belief will come up for you: "I cannot be trusted to stay out of this Mind Lie identity." This is exactly what it wants you think. These Mind Lies, and your whole identity, live on, based on your belief that these Mind Lies are more in control than you are.

Fortunately, the deeper truth is, it does not matter. It does not matter if you come from Mind Lies or from truth. Making it matter makes staying away from it impossible. Remember, the fear, or getting it right versus getting it wrong, is a devious strategy to have you fail no matter what you do. Life is a series of peaks and troughs, constant oscillations from Mind Lie to truth, Mind Lie to truth. The oscillations become less frequent when you no longer make yourself wrong for stepping in and out of the Mind-Lie space. To make something wrong or bad is what started all these Mind Lies in the first place.

In order to remain in a truthful space more often, you can choose to love both spaces. Love that you have an opposite dwelling within that gives you a stark contrast to truth. Knowing what works and knowing what does not work is how you find your way. It actually keeps you from getting lost. But the reason you have become lost is because you have identified more with the Mind-Lie identity than you have with the truth. That is the definition of being lost.

You have forgotten that truth even exists and that everything became about what is right and wrong, instead of about truth and nontruth, of what works and what does not. Remember not to make that wrong, either. Life is the unfolding of truth, going from one level of truth to an even greater level. Do not make where you are wrong or somewhere else better. Resisting where you are keeps you in Mind-Lie identity, in nontruth.

A core truth has come out of all this: love all your Mind Lies as much as you love your truths. Do not resist or resent this part of you, because it just adds fuel to the fire rather than keeping everything in balance.

The bottom line is this: You will be trustworthy and reliable when you are in truth, but you will be untrustworthy and unreliable when you are in Mind Lies. Your truth is that you will love yourself either way. That is powerful. But wait; there is more.

The whole concept of needing to be reliable and trustworthy is a Mind Lie. It is only your false self, your Mind-Lie identity, that expects this—or anything—from you. Your Mind-Lie identity is a prison where you need to be someone or achieve something. Your True Self, your Higher Self, has no expectations or requirements of you. It is all a joke, really. You are needing to be reliable and trustworthy for that part of yourself that is fictitious. You are trying to please someone who does not exist. You have been bending over backward to chase a ghost. There never was a need to be reliable and trustworthy, and there still is not. It was all an illusion right from the get-go, a Mind Lie created by another Mind Lie.

"I Am Not Wanted"

Feeling as though you are not wanted is nearly as common a human experience as breathing air. This belief was one of the first to be adopted by humanity a very long time ago. Because it is so common and so ancient, it flies under the radar, with very few people ever seeking out the truth. It is part and parcel of the human experience, so why question it, right? You are not meant to question it. In fact, your not questioning it is exactly the effect it is meant to have on you. God forbid that you see the truth about this, because you may find out things about yourself that are even worse than just thinking you are not wanted. What if feeling not wanted is just the tip of the iceberg of deeper painful truths? In this moment, two new Mind Lies raise their ugly heads: Mind Lies are all true, and the truth is likely far worse than what you have come to believe.

But if the other Mind Lies are any indication, you can squash these two pretty quickly. Who you think you are, no matter how bad it is, is never the truth. One of the ways the Mind Lies stay alive in you is through hiding behind the illusion that they are in fact truth. The trick to remember is that any of these feelings you have about yourself—such as "I am not enough," "I am faulty, damaged, unwanted, unloved, unimportant," or even "I am a horrible person"—are not true. This means that you never have anything to be afraid of when exploring the truth about who and what you really are. And you need not take a trip through the painful sludge from your past in order to heal them.

You are a sublime being, period. These thoughts and feelings you have about yourself are not about You, remember. They are about a fictitious being that exists as your mind, that has had painful experiences and may have even caused pain to others. But this is still no reason to intertwine this made-up character with You.

Because you do not fully believe this yet, you are breaking down your identity one Mind Lie at a time. In truth, this is *the* most self-loving act you can perform—to finally allow in the Real You. It is a profound adventure, better than any TV show or movie. With that in mind, what is the truth behind the Mind Lie "I am not wanted"? Prepare to travel down the rabbit hole on this one. And do not be offended by anything I say; just hear me out.

There are several vicious cycles in this Mind Lie, so let us begin the unraveling. As with all Mind Lies, the first truth to realize is that this one is more about how you feel about yourself and less about how others feel about you. Change "I am not wanted" to "I do not want myself," and you will hit the bullseye with what your mind is really thinking.

While it is very likely that you had an experience with someone, or many people, that brought on this Mind Lie, what was most damaging was again the self-rejection. In feeling unwanted by another, you chose to "un-want" yourself. You did this by choosing a part, or all parts, of yourself that you believed were unlikable. Bang! That was the dawning of the Mind Lie identity.

The circumstance could have been not making the group average when you were weighed as a baby. Or perhaps you had a temperature at birth that freaked out the doctors, or your parents were expecting a boy and they got a girl, or vice versa. Whatever the trigger—and it was just a trigger—you believed what those around you believed; not what they believed about you, remember, but what they already had inside them, what they had already decided about themselves.

The truth is that humanity does not know what is normal, what is perfect, what is acceptable. All people have as a reference is themselves and projections from the masses, statistics based on nothing more than Mind Lies.

If you are not the one who conceived of humanity, you do not know how each person, and the species as a whole, is intended to evolve. Not having access to the truth means that the majority of benchmarks on what and how a person should be, whether right, wrong, perfect, or imperfect, are Mind Lies. Your benchmarks for humanity are fictitious and perpetuate the passing of this Mind Lie from parent to child down through the generations. There are countless examples of this throughout history and still in today's society: your perspective on different races, children with autism, children who take longer to learn, and kids who are ignored by conventional teaching methodologies but are in fact truly gifted genii.

You compare yourself to others to figure out what is right, wrong, desirable, and undesirable, which leads you to feeling unwanted. But feeling unwanted has nothing to do with you; it is all about the other person. A person who feels unwanted causes others to feel unwanted. A person who feels wanted has others feeling wanted. It was never about you.

Daniel speaking: My mother was raised to believe that she was unwanted by her parents. Guess how that rubbed off on me. Did my mother compensate by going out of her way to have me feel wanted? No. I have spent my entire life feeling just as unwanted as she did. Why could she not go the other way and have me feel wanted? Because she did not even know she was doing it. This is how easily Mind Lies are transferred from parent to child. To put it simply, your children will believe about themselves what you believe about yourself— until you see the truth. Once you do, space opens for your children to see the truth about themselves. To parents, teachers, uncles and aunts, grandparents, and anyone spending time with children: if you want the future to be incredible for the children—for humanity—then be responsible and practice safe interactions by abandoning the belief systems that no longer serve.

Beliefs can be the most contagious and deadly of "viruses." Be careful what you are spreading around! By reading this book and joining me on this exploration, you are contributing to changing humanity's future.

"What Is the Truth? Am I Wanted? Can I Want Myself?"

Let us begin with the Mind Lie "Am I wanted?" The truth is, you are more than wanted, so much so that the Universe went to great lengths to make you possible, to birth both you as a species and you as seeming individuals.

If you were not wanted, you would not exist.

The second aspect of this may shock you: *you are unwanted.* This aspect refers to the part of you that craves the feeling of being wanted; that part *is* unwanted. It is part of the Mind-Lie identity and is no longer wanted, yet it is present. To resist it is self-defeating, but there is a conflict in your being because of it. It is a nontruth, and it is time to release it from your human experience. Like out-of-date hardware, Mind Lies are unwanted once they have served their purpose. Because your identity is made up of Mind Lies, the you that feels unwanted is right. You do not want that you any longer.

In summary, all that is going on is fictitious, and that self-destructive part of you is unwanted by the part of You that is pure love. Remember, those from your past—and in your present—who actually did not want you were coming from the part of them that was unwanted. In essence, a fictitious part of you is upset that a fictitious part of them did not make that fictitious part of you feel wanted. Do not feel bad about this, because you have believed that the fictitious part of you was real, and that part of you feeling unwanted was painful.

Are you ready for the deeper truth?

The real You is not concerned about being wanted, because the real You knows intrinsically that You are infinitely more than wanted. Being wanted is an infinitesimally small goal to shoot for compared with what is actually the truth.

The truth is that you are way beyond wanted; you are sublimely needed!

You are an integral part of the Universe's structure and functioning. Why aim for merely being wanted when you are fundamentally needed by the entire Universe? That is why you exist. When you truly believe, or even better, when you truly *know* that you are needed, you will be amazed at how many people reflect this knowing back to you and how much you can actually let it in because you now want yourself.

You live in an amazing and generous Universe that is deeply concerned with your—as well as its own—well-being and therefore evolution. The Universe constantly mirrors back to you what you believe is the truth. It does not discriminate and say, "Oh no, that is a Mind Lie, so I will not mirror it back." The Universe mirrors back, no matter what you believe. More specifically, it mirrors back exactly whatever you believe.

Your outer reality is a mirror of every aspect of your inner reality. Thought precedes creation; it always has and always will in this thought-driven Universe. What you believe is what you get to experience. The fastest way to alter and improve your external reality is not through surface-level initiatives but by altering humanity's belief systems at the core. These core belief systems are the root cause of all humanity's experiences, good and bad, light and dark. This is where you need to begin, from kids at school to politicians and world leaders.

This mirroring happens in all aspects of your reality. Your beliefs are reflected outward in your physicality as, for example, your health and your yearning for certain foods and drinks; then in your finances, your relationships, your career, to those around you, to the planet, and so on.

So, are you wanted? You do not need to be wanted, you do not need to be loved, because you cannot need what you intrinsically are.

You are Love.

As Love, You really do matter. You count so profoundly that you cannot comprehend it right now. Best of all, the part of you that is real is needed by the most loving and most real part of your Universe; You have been needed since day one and will be for eternity. Needing to be wanted is a very poor substitute for realizing that "I am love."

"If I Am Rejected, I Will Be An Outcast"

The fear of being rejected is often a subconscious one, yet it is one of the biggest reasons why you do not follow your truth and your dreams. You are terrified of others rejecting you for who you are, your ideas, your bold initiatives, or for simply standing out. But what are you really fearing? What does it mean to be rejected?

If you were to dig just a tiny bit deeper, you would find that to be rejected can result in your feeling alone, or even worse, as an outcast. To no longer belong puts fear into your heart. The feeling is that "If I don't belong, if I don't fit in, then I will be left out of life's riches, its opportunities, and the possibilities of receiving love."

But like all Mind Lies, this is not the truth. To belong does not necessarily mean receiving the spoils, either. Truth be told, it quite often means the opposite. Nevertheless, this fear keeps you vying to belong, no matter the actual cost. So, in many ways this belief creates a race of sameness, of nearly exact clones all over the world, all petrified that if they show their uniqueness and differences, they will be cast out.

While this Mind Lie might be great for businesses around the world, especially those that depend on and thrive because of this need to belong, such as fashion houses, tech companies, car manufacturers, and credit card companies, it is actually quite a suffocating belief to have. In simple terms, holding on to this belief prevents you from ever breathing your unique essence into your life or anyone else's.

This is detrimental to everyone individually and collectively, and to the Earth as well—hence the devastation you are all experiencing now.

You feel that being the same is the only shot you have at validation. This Mind Lie has you believe that if you fit in, you belong. Worst of all, it has you believe that if you belong, you are on the right track. The thought is that "If I do what others do, behave their way, dress their way, work too hard and burn out the way they do, share their goals and ambitions, eat as per the current fad, then I must be OK; I must be on track."

But things could not be further from the truth. Since when does conformity equate to walking your purpose? Conformity does not even mean walking someone else's path. Rather, it means living a life based on what other people or businesses want society to believe is an appropriate way to live. Where do these ideas come from? You guessed it—they come from Mind Lies. These ideas have been passed down from generation to generation, invented by Hollywood, Silicon Valley tech executives, fashion houses, and so on. Somehow, they made it into your mind, passed off as being in alignment with your highest purpose. Remember this Mind Lie: "If I belong, I am on track."

If you are coming from the need for conformity, then you are resonating with ideas coming from Mind Lies. It is an oxymoron to think that you can thrive by fitting in, yet it is a widely held misconception that nearly everyone has fallen victim to at some—or many—stages in their lives.

Funnily enough, those who have ever created meaningful success in their lives did so by being their own unique selves, by not conforming. To fit in is a counter-success strategy. Your Mind Lies will have you believe otherwise; they always do. Interestingly, you can start to see where this Mind Lie gets its strength from: "If I am like someone who is already successful, then I, too, will feel successful."

Conformity equals mediocre life experiences. Divine uniqueness equals divine life experiences.

To step out of the norm, to be bold, to do the work you are passionate about, to live life in the way closest to your heart, is exactly what the world needs. Conformity has gotten you where you are today. Innovation, uniqueness, and a liberated mind will create the tomorrow you so desperately desire. Be bold!

"Where Did This Mind Lie Come From?"

Your desire to fit in came from rejection as a child, from getting it wrong, and from being starved of love and acceptance just when you most needed it. The irony is that those with whom you were trying to fit in were also trying to fit in, even more desperately than you were. You were rejected by those who had rejected themselves far worse than they ever rejected you. The pain of rejection haunts you into believing that you are safer conforming than living at the edge, where differences exist and where a real difference is made.

Fear keeps you from living fully. The fear is that you will slip off into an abyss of unhappiness from rejection and abandonment. You believe that you cannot live until you have achieved the prerequisite of fitting in, belonging with, and being accepted by others. You think that fitting in is living, but life does not really begin until you celebrate your uniqueness. Life happens when you elevate beyond needing anything, beyond there being a prerequisite for life to begin. Needing to conform is not the truth. Waiting until you are successful is not the truth. Waiting until you feel loved by the world is not the truth. Life just is and has always been without requirements; it just is.

The greatest irony in your world is that you are alive right now, yet you are still waiting for something to really begin living.

Let this change right now. All these prerequisites of waiting to live are perpetual. They never end, because in their place will pop up a new version, so the goals are always shifting. You cannot heal a Mind Lie by satisfying it because new and more elaborate Mind Lies are revealed in their place. Realize this: "I do not need to be or do anything."

You worry and fear that you will be rejected if you do not conform in some way. Yet, by believing this, you have rejected your own happiness, putting it off until others believe in and integrate you into their conforming reality. In truth, you had rejected your happiness way before anyone else could ever reject you. You did it first.

Your fear is that the world will reject you if you are everything you truly are. The truth—and it is a big one—is this: You are the world. It exists within you, you do not exist within it. What you therefore see out in the world is what you believe is there in you. To accept and embrace your uniqueness creates a chain reaction whereby those who are out there in the world also lovingly embrace your uniqueness. You dictate what happens; you always have and you always will.

Uniqueness does not exist "out there." It does not exist in how you look, what you say, or what you do. All that is simply an expression of true uniqueness, which is inner and based on how you see yourself and your infinite reality. Strive not to be unique but rather to see uniquely. The more unique your view, the more unique the "You".

Embrace your unique view; never turn away from it because you fear rejection. That would be an even worse rejection.

You live in a world that insists on everyone seeing life through the same eyes. Let it be your gift to see with fresh and enlightened eyes. Let it be your gift to encourage those around you to see with extraordinary, enlightened eyes so that together you can create a unique way of life for everyone.

In truth, this is evolution itself. The Universe you belong to relies on nonconformity for its expansion, and so it is with you. Your expansion, be it emotional, mental, physical, or spiritual, also depends on nonconformity. The Universe says, "If I wanted everyone to be the same, I would not have put billions of people on the Earth." Being different, having a unique edge, is innate, so much so that, like your fingerprints, no two people have the identical DNA.

Let us look at how DNA actually works. DNA is a mind unto itself but not alone or all by itself. It is a current of Intelligence, organizing and harmonizing all living things with one another and with the planets and galaxies as one colossal ecosystem. With that in mind, it is easier to understand why being different is critical: because it is following the path and flow of the DNA mind.

You have a DNA-based blueprint guiding you toward success and expansion in all areas of your life. DNA is comprehensive; it guides both physical development and life expansion. But guess what switches this DNA global positioning satellite off? Conformity, the need to fit in, the craving to belong.

DNA is difficult to describe because there is so much going on in it. For now, understand that within your DNA is a set of immaculate gifts to bestow upon the Earth. These gifts are essential to your success and are needed to transform the consciousness of all humanity. You are a piece of a much larger puzzle. Each of you brings a gift that serves the individual and the greater good. Without having the opportunity to share these gifts, you grow that much more slowly and suffer the consequences of such. To see what these consequences are, simply look around. The lack in shifts of human consciousness are responsible for all the violence, poverty, and environmental damage you are now experiencing on Earth.

It is in everyone's highest good to tap in and see what gifts you have to bring. You want to make a significant contribution, and finding out what gifts you offer is both the best way to make a real difference with your life and the Universe's preferred way you go about it.

You are no different from all other life on this planet. Each species has a role to play, a gift to bring, to create balanced and evolving ecosystems. The difference between humans and other life on Earth is the level of gifts you have to bring. This is truly profound for each and every one of you.

Your skills and gifts from within are deliberately complementary to, not the same as, those that others have. The Universe does not require copies or conformity in any way. The more you live your truth, the more you will naturally express uniqueness. It takes courage and self-belief, but in the end success comes to those who free their uniqueness, who support the growth and expansion of the Universe. You get the reward of even greater growth and expansion in your individual life.

"I Am All On My Own; It Is Every Man For Himself"

Perhaps you are familiar with this belief: "There is no outside help, no one to turn to, nobody and nothing who can or will help me." This Mind Lie is yet another cunning belief that leaves humanity high and dry. It is designed to have you fail, to cut you down from achieving your dreams, to have you feel as though it is all too hard. You begin to think, "Why bother? Someone else will either do it themselves or destroy my chances of doing it."

"What Is The Truth?"

While there is plenty of evidence to justify the belief that you are all on your own, it is nonetheless a Mind Lie. Bear in mind that just because there is evidence for a belief certainly does not mean the belief is true. It only means that particular belief has a lot of followers.

You are never alone and never doing it by yourself. The deeper truth is that no one is doing it all on their own. From the birds in the sky to the bees in their hives, everything is supported and on its purpose. The birds are given the sky in which to fly, the tree trunks in which to make a home, the branches on which to land, and all the bugs in the world to call lunch. You are no different. It is truly amazing just how much support you are given, whether you acknowledge it or not.

Let us look more closely at this so you can clearly see how the Universe supports itself—and you—in every way possible. Have you marveled at the fact that anything you can conceive of as a species can be created? There are enough elements on Earth to make anything and everything you desire—from an iPad, a kitchen sink, a telephone, and an airplane to a skyscraper, a five-star meal, clothes that warm and that stay dry, and every variety of machine that flies! This is just the tip of the iceberg of how supported you really are.

You have everything at your disposal; you are fully supported to achieve your dreams and beyond. And there are even more inner resources than the finite number of external resources. You are equipped with the exact knowledge for how best to flourish, prosper, heal, love, and be loved. You have been designed this way; as above, so below.

As you are supported on the outside, so too are you supported from the inside.

Unfortunately, you do not understand that you are a self-sufficient being; you are fully equipped with all the knowledge and wisdom you will ever need for your entire life. Many refuse to let this in and instead seek answers and direction from anyone and everywhere else, but the truth is that you came here equipped with your own GPS. Now you must learn to hear it above all the Mind Lies that insist that your GPS is faulty—or worse, nonexistent.

A coach exists within everyone. It has to; life could not exist any other way. Let me explain: Life itself is an energy field, but many relate to it as they relate to electricity: power without thought. But that is not how life is; life is *powerful thought*. By the mere virtue of being alive, you have within you all that you will ever need: an advanced medical expert, a career adviser, a best friend, a coach, a mentor, an enlightened guru, and infinitely more. You have felt this being, this presence, in your moments of inspiration and during times of stillness. You have witnessed the genius in the turning points of your life and in those incredible coincidences that come out of nowhere to help guide you. This being within you is the greatest source of help available. However, you have been taught to doubt yourself, and so you doubt that you could ever have all the answers. This creates a predicament.

How on earth can you access this inner wealth of genius if you do not believe it is possible? This is how the illusion of no help being available permeates the entire human species. It has become the case of "If you don't believe it, you won't see it." There is always help available, the best kind of help. But if you doubt it exists, it ceases to exist for you.

Humanity is making an inner shift; people are realizing that everyone is equipped with pure genius. Without this wisdom, the human body could not function. Life exists on the very basis of intelligent, purposeful functioning. This Intelligence lives within, guiding the body's natural functioning, but it is also there to guide the life You live, too. Life force energy does not just power your DNA, it powers the progression of a species from one moment to the next, guiding your life. And it is collaborative, bringing together all the resources life needs to thrive. DNA and life-force are one and the same.

Life on Earth began with all the necessary resources, every amazing, possible support to create and thrive purposefully. It is not every man for himself unless every man denies that life bridges one man to the next, one support system to the next, and one Earth to all of humanity. To deny yourself this reality leads to a dark and lonely tunnel, where there is an absence of support. This is the Mind-Lie identity, and in that mind it really is every man for himself.

The deeper and more practical truth is this: It is not every man for himself, nor every woman for herself. This is just a Mind Lie. The experience is perpetuated not because it is true but because it has a strong following. To allow in support, all people must recognize they are one as humanity. You are one planet. One planet brings all the support you need. Life is collective, not individual, so to thrive in your individual life, let in a life that harmonizes you and supports you by drawing upon the collective. The more you shut this out, the more shut out from this abundance and support you will be.

Support comes in many ways, sometimes unexpected. Be not the judge of what form the support takes, judge not whether you or others are worthy of this support, but realize that in your heart you are the giver and receiver of this support. You are not separate, not more the giver or the receiver. Life works with you, as you, through you. Allow yourself to not scrutinize how support should be given or received; just be open and allow that the support exists in the first place. Do not be the judge and jury of who is capable and who is not. In realizing that you are all you need, you open up to a world of possibilities in which you are mirrored in the arrival of help from others. You are others. Life is one.

"The World Is Not Ready For My Ideas"

Many of you are brimming with new ideas and revolutionary ways of looking at life. You are inventors, pioneers, innovators, engineers, and natural-born leaders with ideas that will change the world. So what stops you? Mind Lies, many of them, once again hold you back. But one Mind Lie stands out as a huge culprit: "The world is not ready for my ideas." By clearing this Mind Lie, you will be nudged that much closer to showering the world with your genius.

When you have an idea, a concept, or new project, your first thoughts are, "Who is ready for this? Who would want this, and who is going to buy it?" The answers to these questions more often than not scare people into holding back their ideas rather than moving forward. The reason is a commonly held view that ideas must be sanctioned by others to support their feasibility and worthiness. This is where the initial resistance comes from. Where there is a nontruth, life cannot flow freely and abundantly.

The belief that you must have paying customers or supporters for your product is actually a Mind Lie. This flies in the face of conventional business or societal thinking, but *from a place of truth, you can see that the world is not your audience; you are.*

You are the customer, and even as a business owner, you will only ever be the customer. How is this? The truth is that the world exists inside you. When you make the shift into realizing and understanding this, then whatever you create, whatever you are ready for, the world around you—and inside you—will be ready, as well.

Human consciousness is a shared mind, a field of knowledge of right and wrong, of known and waiting to be known, of contraction and expansion. It is something that affects and is affected by all of us.

When you resign yourself to waiting for others to become ready, you simply create that experience—people waiting to be ready—as your reality.

Once you realize that "I am the world and I am ready," you manifest a new reality, bringing yourself more in alignment with infinite possibilities, distinct from the reality generated by humanity's Mind Lies.

You are not on the outskirts of human consciousness; you are right in the middle of it, causing ripples throughout. Your every thought creates a chain reaction. Radio frequencies bounce around the Earth carrying signals of information, and so does human thought, coalescing as one enormous bubble of human consciousness. Some frequencies create peaks in consciousness, and others, such as thoughts of hate and anger, bottom it out, lowering the vibrational frequency. The vibrational frequency of truth uplifts everyone and affects the Earth as a whole, unconfined to continents, territories, and governmental jurisdictions, in powerfully positive ways. There is no place that is exempt from the expansive power of truth, so when you yourself realize, the whole world gets to realize.

Conversely, when you have hatred or anger toward a person, race, or country, they are not set free, nor does your attitude make the change you hope it will. Your hatred and anger do not improve their views on life; rather, people are suffocated in that energy of hatred and sent backward even further. When you send hatred at someone or something, they become immersed in hatred. Who is that helping?

Human thought is not confined to you. It is magnetic. It travels to and adds to that which the thought is about, such as a person, place, or topic. Thought behaves in the same way as molecules bonding together. Thought is, in fact, how molecules bond together.

When you set yourself free, when you embody truth instead of hatred, anger, and disapproval, you open up a path to allow others to set themselves free, too. All is one, one is all.

Do not allow the outside world to dictate what thoughts and ideas you have, because if given a choice, the world as a collective prefers sticking with the familiar and not having to change its ways. Comfort is the chief objective rather than truth.

To create and launch what you are ready for invigorates the world, elevating people's creativity, wisdom, and expectations of themselves. Be the one to set new benchmarks, to view things in a way never viewed before. Be the one to bring truth where there has been only nontruth.

Questioning your ability to affect change around the world through thought is what your Mind Lies want you to do. The more doubt you have, the less you affect. The more truth you embody—that is, the fewer Mind Lies you carry—the stronger the ripples you send around the globe that affect change. Remember, hatred will not transform what you do not like into what you want. Pure self-belief and the frequency of love are what create change.

Another Mind Lie that will trip you up in your process of creating is, "If I do all this and the world has not evolved as quickly as I have, I will be rejected." Is this the truth? Of course not. As with previous Mind Lies, rejection does not exist "out there" in the world; rather, it is an internal experience, when you reject yourself. To believe that you need to be validated by the needs and desires of others is just another Mind Lie at play. To believe that profit or people's acceptance is the ultimate judge of your success or failure is yet another Mind Lie. True success is in birthing something new and revolutionary. It is like when a baby is born; friends and family congratulate the parents and bring flowers and gifts. They do not wait until the child has grown up and has made a success of himself or herself. The congratulations and celebration come right after birth. The same needs to apply within you when you birth something great.

To birth the innovative, the compelling, and the revolutionary is what life is all about, not how others receive it or welcome it. Genius just is, with or without validation. Welcome your genius to bubble up, and do not fear how others will respond. No one ever welcomed life-changing ideas with a warm embrace. Every great idea, every revolutionary thought, every concept that caused people to have to rethink their world or themselves was challenged by fervent opposition. Put yourself in the space of welcoming the opposition as a true indication that you have achieved something truly worthwhile and must clearly be on the right path!

Being in a space of truth harmonizes your brain with ideas that need to be birthed on Earth. Ideas that are not ready or that will cause harm or destruction come from a mind full of Mind Lies. The trick is to avoid birthing ideas for others and for their approval, for this is just compensating and leads to the experience of "I have failed." Do it for you and only you, guaranteeing yourself a true winning success every time.

You be ready, so that the world knows what ready looks like.

"I Do Not Make The Cut"

Many like you, may have been raised by parents who were ignorant or unaware of your true purpose, of the gifts you were here to bring to the world. As such, your parents steered you along alternate paths in an attempt to fill their own voids, to elevate their own self-worth by getting you to achieve things so that they could feel accomplished.

The result from such an upbringing is that careers are chosen for you, goals are predetermined, milestones preset. You were born into a pre-organized life of targets toward which to aim and aspire, all because Mom or Dad did not feel they were enough. You can get lost in this artificial dynamic, squeezed into an impossible world, and suffocate under the weight of this burden. Hence this Mind Lie: you ultimately feel that who you are intrinsically does not make the cut, and you are therefore doomed to be a disappointment.

The truth is, it is your parents and those who helped rear you who felt they never made the cut, and still do not, so they look to you to make them proud. But it is not about being proud of their child; it is all about finally being proud of themselves. The result is that you inherit their inadequacies, and they compensate for theirs by hoping you do better than they did. They see your successes as their successes; but because your success is born from a Mind Lie, you suffer through it rather than prosper because of it.

To believe that "I do not make the cut" is clearly not about you, nor are any of the Mind Lies. Who this Mind Lie is really about is humanity and its need to feel on track, to be validated. The problem is that you are searching externally for this validation. The result is that you keep pushing yourself too hard and too far, in too many unhealthy ways—unhealthy for yourself, for others, and for the planet—without ever getting to the real truth about making the cut or not. As always, seeking to heal a Mind Lie by looking externally for solutions only aggravates the Mind Lie.

"What Is The Truth?"

The truth is that there is no cut to make. Because you know this on some level, you made up, manufactured, and invented "cuts to make." Mind Lies will do that! But of course, these cuts are not based in truth; the cuts that exist in society have been created as a solution for those seeking to make the cut. Society creates cuts everywhere: in families, income, success, school accomplishments, business, politics. . . the list goes on. These cuts serve as a means of finding a way to gauge how on track you are. You are literally dying to be on track.

You employ fictitious measures, and it is slowly killing you. It is keeping up with the Joneses on at a whole new level, because there are cuts in every aspect of your life. But remember, these cuts, these benchmarks, are fictitious and have absolutely no relevance in the greater scheme of anything. Making the cut is designed to have you and everyone else feel right on track, but how can there even be a track when the false mind invented it? There is no track, and there is no need to be on it. You are running an invisible race on an invisible track made up by Mind Lies that are not even real.

When you go within, you discover that there is no track, there is only truth and nontruth. The more truth you embody, the better life flows and flourishes. The less truth you embody, the more suffering you experience. The only true indicator of your success is your level of beingness. To focus on being on track is a wonderful yet horrifically conniving way for the human identity to distract from what actually matters and creates success. What creates success is not a goal, not an outcome, not even a track or benchmark. It is your beingness, for your beingness is the only worthwhile thing to focus on. It is the only true measure of success. It is the seed from which abundance, happiness, success, and a healthy body is grown.

It is not about focusing on being on track, but rather about taking the track that focuses on being.

Measuring your life's progress externally is one of the greatest Mind Lies in human history. To hold a space of truth as often as you can is the quickest way to transform any and every situation. Beingness sets the world in action, expands lives, leads to radically new discoveries and new heights of success, and expands your consciousness.

Beingness precedes all creation. To be love creates loving outcomes and experiences. To be greedy creates scarcity and poverty experiences. To be self-loving creates a mirror in the Universe in which others love and respect you back.

Concentrate on your beingness, and great outcomes are inevitable.

The next truth to realize is that, as there is no cut to make, you already inherently make the cut. You are a sublime and divine being: you *are* the cut! You always have been, just by virtue of your true nature. When you understand this, you immediately elevate your beingness, which in turn cements a solid path for your life. When you realize that you *are* the cut, you naturally and inadvertently supersede any cuts and other human-created benchmarks. You effortlessly surpass them without even attempting to do so.

Your greatness from within is far beyond what humanity considers extraordinary or a matter of genius. You in your rawest form already supersede the greatest of all humanity's achievements—or states of being, for that matter. This has always been the case and always will be, because you exist as a shining force of brilliance. Let go of all the running races you are planning to win, all the competitions and the struggles, all the cuts you are trying to make, and you will notice how fictitious they are.

In the absence of trying, what remains is your perfection.

What Mind Lie begins to raise its ugly head now? Perhaps the need to make someone else proud through some accomplishment? Know this: the person you aim to impress must make himself proud first; you cannot do it for him. Furthermore, for this person to expect you to fill his void by doing all the work so that he does not have to do it certainly will not make the cut!

"Success Takes Such A Long Time"

A huge struggle for many people is the perpetual feeling of running on the hamster wheel, wondering when, if ever, success will arrive, as if one knows what it will look like. You wait and wait, hoping one day that when you look out the window, success will be on your doorstep, like a package delivered by the mailman.

This misconception arises because, when you are born, you come into an existing reality. You learn from others, including their definitions of success, which ultimately shapes your expectations and creates preconceptions of what success entails. You watch others as you move through life, learning what success looks like, how you know if you have arrived, and how you will feel when you reach it.

But these measures of success rarely, if ever, disclose the journey and the growth that happens in each moment of that journey, how each experience builds on the last, unlocking new levels of insight and accomplishment. Nearly all depictions and definitions of success are focused on what the outcome is, not on the growth happening within. Thanks to this conditioning, success becomes outcome oriented and therefore appears to take a very long time to arrive. Few people end up assessing where they are on the success meter based on inner realization.

The truth is that success has already arrived; it is always arriving. So much in life is missed; there is so much happening all the time, but it is the measures you employ that create the experience of ongoing waiting.

Daniel speaking: I am reminded of some slow-motion videos I recently watched online. They capture time in such a concentrated way, vastly different from my everyday experience of seeing. When I watched these videos, I observed so much detail—things I had never seen before, another Universe within my everyday Universe. It dawned on me how much we miss, things as simple as a bee landing on a flower, a raindrop sending ripples across a spider's web, a kiss on the cheek by a loved one. People say we sleep 25 percent of our lives, but I ask, How much are we missing out on because we are moving so quickly and we have our attention on everything but that which truly matters? Are we actually asleep more like 75 to 100 percent of the time? If we were all present to the details of each wonderful and wondrous experience, no one would be waiting any longer; everyone would realize that it is all happening right now!

Detail is lost on the outcome-driven mind; depth is gained in the moment-driven mind.

A moment-driven mind is one that is awake for the whole experience: the ebbs, flows, struggles, triumphs, fear, love, and so on. It is the You that rejoices every moment in which truth is revealed. Outcome-driven minds are asleep most of the time, living from one peak outcome to the next, like drug addicts living from one high to the next. For the outcome-driven mind, everything in between is simply waiting—waiting for the next outcome.

"Does Success Really Take So Long To Arrive?"

How many people do you know who are what you call successful but are deaf and blind to it? Success is happening all the time; people just take a long time to notice it. The more conscious you become to different degrees and expressions of success, the less impatient you will be and the less time success will appear to take. Better yet, the sooner you recognize success as a continuum, the more successful you will become. Having realization after realization, celebrating the gaps between each realization, and the realizations themselves are in and of themselves measures of success. When this happens, there is no more waiting!

The more acclimated you become to being the witness of all life experiences, the more you will realize what a hand you play in delaying or accelerating new experiences of success. It is your impatience that robs you of the joys of the journey, the lessons learned, and the growth realized. Your impatience starves you of seeing the inherent success in your life right now.

By focusing on the unimportant things, you starve yourself of realizing the most important things.

Here is another truth: life waits to unveil the next level of success until you are present to the success already created. Just as in a computer game, you cannot celebrate the rewards received from level two until you have reached and earned the rewards at level one. The more fixed you are on your outward goals and the rewards you want, the less able you are to see what bounty already lies in front of you waiting to be recognized and appreciated. You will not move to level two until this occurs.

> **Daniel speaking:** *I remember when I was frustrated about the growth in our business many years ago. When I asked my inner guide, my source of truth, how I could best propel the success of the business, the guidance that came was quite surprising and completely unconventional in terms of business or marketing wisdom; it was out of the box, to say the least. The guidance was not to work harder or spend more money on marketing or practice any of the conventions I had learned about. It was to spend more time with my children, enjoy them, see their magic, and love them fully. Only then would I see them as my successes. I had become so stuck in needing conventional business success and what that meant that I could not see how successful I already was. Needless to say, this guidance was met with much resistance, as it did not appear to give me the answer I needed to achieve business success. After a lot of kicking and screaming, I eventually allowed the guidance in, leading me to the biggest growth we had ever experienced in our business. It was truly mind-blowing!*

There are many revealed fundamental truths from such experience, but the key one is this: every step of the way on your journey is a success waiting to be realized. You need to realize each level of success before moving forward and receiving the next one; there is no skipping ahead. Where would the fun be if you were not able to be present to success until some day in the future?

To hurry success is to miss out on it. You will never see it while you are hurrying to get there. True success is in the realization, not the outcome. True abundance comes from realizing that you *are* a success. From this place you cannot help but be showered in riches from all areas of life.

Success is a state of being; being is free and already present. Being successful does not come from achievement; achievement comes from BEING successful.

"I Disappoint Everyone Around Me"

It is a long-standing belief in psychology circles that children learn their beliefs and ideas about themselves from their parents or those who most closely rear them. This is certainly true to a point, because what most people do not know, and have not even begun to fathom, is that in most cases beliefs are not learned but rather energetically imprinted. It can appear that you believe something about yourself, such as "I disappoint others," because it seems that is exactly what your parents thought about you. But parents, siblings, teachers, and those most influential in your life did more than just teach you a belief; they "gifted" you the energy frequency of "I disappoint others" by the way they were around you.

An energy exchange occurred on such a drastic level that the adults, in their attempt to rid themselves of this affliction, literally extended the energy of that thought, of that belief, to you. Eventually you confused this energy with being your own, and the Mind Lie was successfully created. When this happened, you began to believe that this frequency of thought was somehow self-generated and must therefore belong to you. Yet it was never your real thought to begin with. Instead, you adopted it as your very own, like a stray puppy you found wandering the streets.

Thoughts are like puffs of smoke and can be seen, just as a nonsmoker can see and inhale second-hand smoke from a smoker. People do not realize that "thought energy" travels; whoever believes that the thought energy belongs to them draws it in.

Remember yourself as a child, relentlessly trying to answer the question, "Who am I?" You were so driven to discover who the "I" was that you kept taking onboard thought energy from others until you believed you had found the identity that truly matched. Your body is now full of varying frequencies of other people's thought energies, but just because they now sit in your body does not mean that they belong to you. It is true that you have identified with them, hence why they remain with you. But these thought energies are no more yours than is someone's nicotine smoke you accidently inhaled while walking down the street.

Daniel speaking: I am reminded of times when I was growing up in my parents' house. From around the age of sixteen, I remember a family member being depressed. I remember it brought me down and had me also feeling depressed. I did not need to see them to feel this way, and often I did not see them for a period of time, as they spent a lot of time alone in their bedroom. I did not pay too much attention to this, as I just put it down to them bringing the energy of the house down. It was not until much later that I had a realization.

I had moved out of the house, but this depression was still occurring. One day I would be cheery and joyous, and the next I would feel depressed. As I became more aware of this space, I also became aware that it was how they were feeling rather than how I was feeling within myself. Over time, it became clear to me that they believed if they were unhappy, everyone in the family should be unhappy. This was why I was impacted by their state of mind. Ten years later, I discovered that this connection was because I was storing there energy inside my body.

You might be surprised to learn how many ways you are doing this same thing right now. So ask yourself, "What let this

73

feeling into my body?" For me, I had felt it was my duty to help this person, to be there for them; that was my belief. Why were they embedding their energy into me? It was their way of ensuring that I never left their side.

Ultimately, you cannot be a disappointment because there is no judgment in the Universe; there is just understanding. To be a disappointment is just a label, a judgment, and judgment is ignorance. Wherever you hear judgment, you will find ignorance and a lack of understanding or willingness to understand why someone is the way he or she is. Those who are unwilling to be kind to themselves, to understand why they are the way they are, are the quickest to judge others and are unwilling to understand the cause of another's state of being.

Only the ignorant judge others; the enlightened have compassion, and the greatest compassion comes from understanding. Understanding is one of the greatest paths to enlightenment because it heals all the self-hatred and brings about a new level of self-acceptance. When you have self-acceptance, you have no problem accepting all others for who they are.

When you delve deeper into the phenomenon of disappointment, you will see humanity, not the Divine. If you truly have disappointed others, which is actually more of a reflection on them than yourself, you need to understand that you are on your journey, learning rigorously what works and what does not. The programming you inherited was what was behind your actions, as it was behind the reactions to your actions others experienced. Disappointment does not exist "out there"; it exists within you and in others. It was not your actions that were the disappointment but what they meant to the recipient, who then experienced disappointment. If you look closer, the disappointment they experienced was about them, how they in some way disappointed themselves during their encounter with you. If someone says, "I am disappointed in you," they are really saying, "I would love to blame you for disappointing me, because I cannot bear just how disappointed I am in myself."

What is your truth? Why are you disappointed in yourself? Your disappointment in yourself stems from a lack of understanding about yourself. You have judgments, such as "I could have" or "I should have." But if you were truly capable of doing differently, you would have. Your life has been and will always be a result of you being and then doing the best you can in any moment. Is it the absolute best you can do in the infinite realm of possible outcomes? No, but do not fool yourself. That is not even relevant, despite your mind holding on to such nonsense. You did what you did because that was all that was possible for you in that moment, because of who you believed yourself to be.

There is nothing disappointing about a being of light who is figuring out how best to dissolve old programming and ancient paradigms of human behavior.

You will find an unbelievable truth when you look deeper into this Mind Lie of "I disappoint everyone around me." Exactly who is disappointed? Who is the holder of disappointment? The answer is that it is your mind. "What does my mind have to be disappointed about?" you ask. Everything!

Your mind does not inherently like itself; it is confused. One minute it wants and gets something; the next minute it is unhappy that it ever wanted that something and then got it. It is disappointed in itself, because no matter how hard your mind tries, it cannot escape itself. It is trapped within itself.

But the biggest thing the mind is disappointed by is the fact that it can never be the truth. It can never bring proper happiness; it can only bring quick bouts of it. It can bring nothing truly fulfilling. The mind's absolute essence is that "I am a disappointment"; but the mind does not realize that there is no disappointment unless there is an expectation for more: to be more, to have more, and so on. Realize that being a disappointment is a perfect response, if that is

75

always the expectation. Thinking that it should be more is where the problem lies. Believing that there is more to existence than being a disappointment is where the problem originated, so having a mind that sees itself as disappointing is perfect. However, what makes things truly brilliant is realizing that your mind was never disappointing in the first place.

"I Am Not What People Want; I Can Never Live Up To Other People's Expectations"

The pressure of trying to be what other people want is one that many feel, and it appears as though the problem stems from others as the source of the pressure. Yet where this Mind Lie originates from is in believing that there is an inherent inability or inadequacy deep within you. You feel like this because you believe what others expect of you is just too high. The good news is that it really has nothing to do with what others expect or do not expect; instead, it has everything to do with what you expect of yourself.

This problem was aggravated early on, when you encountered people who set themselves very high benchmarks. These people find it difficult to celebrate others who are not equally hard on themselves. The mirroring occurs when they see how few expectations you placed on yourself as a child. They then immediately recognized all the unnecessary pressure they constantly live with. Instead of dealing with this new awareness, they fought back, condemning you for not being good enough or striving enough. In reality, their complaint was not that at all; their actual complaint was "How dare you think you can live a quality life without enduring the amount of pressure I put on myself!"

In truth, of course, it is not your job to live up to people's expectations. It is your role to discover deeper and deeper truths about yourself and your true nature. In turn, those around you will be blown away by how extraordinarily capable you truly are. To aim to meet or exceed someone's expectations is actually one of the lowest benchmarks you could ever set for yourself. Your skills, knowledge, and abilities vastly surpass what anyone in humanity could ever dream up as an expectation.

You can see now why society rarely excels in any field in terms of what is really possible, because humanity is battling with a collective blockage called Mind Lies. To truly exceed in every area of life, everyone must cease drawing on past experience as their benchmarks and instead reach to the heights that exist within them. Do not confuse what is actually possible with what has already been achieved, for they are light years apart.

Humanity as a whole has no comprehension of what is truly possible. While you exist within the confines of the mind and live according to the lies contained therein, you will never truly know. Even the greatest minds of today and throughout history have barely scratched the surface of what is available to them. Ironically, admiration for what others have already achieved can be the biggest limitation on what you can achieve. You inadvertently cap what is possible for you by admiring the world of others more than yourself. The perfect role model already exists, but guess where— not out in the world, because others are irrelevant to you. The perfect role model lives inside you. Think of your greatest idol, most inspiring leader, and most talented individual; then transfer that admiration, respect, and reverence toward yourself. Now you are ready for greatness!

"My Successes Are Mediocre; Everyone Else Is Doing Better Than I"

There is an illusion perpetuated throughout humanity and history that you are a person, a separate living organism, set up to race against or compete with other separate living organisms. The truth is that you are one organism, perceiving itself uniquely through individuals on Earth and throughout space. You perceive yourself as the identity, and this is what gives the illusion of separation. But remember, this identity is fictitious. You are trusting that reality consists of individuals, yet that which perceives the individuals is made up.

How would you see yourself and others without a mind full of Mind Lies? You would see everyone as being connected, as "one being, being many." As one being, being many, you would see a sublime Intelligence determined that all its parts recognize it within themselves. You would see each person as an extension of yourself, some fully awake and others yet to wake up. You would see people experiencing things you are experiencing and things you are not. But you would not feel as if you were missing out or underprivileged or unfairly better or worse off, because you would recognize that it takes many experiences to take the whole to the next level; it takes many experiences to raise the consciousness of the many.

When you stop focusing on others as different or as more or less accomplished, you will give yourself more power to draw on your own inner resources, to succeed in your own right. It is an injustice to the whole to live in comparison, like a millipede looking at its ninety-ninth leg and becoming jealous that it seems to be moving faster than the others. By looking back at itself, it is likely to stumble and fall, as will you.

Realize that your accomplishments seem big to other people, so they are stuck in the same Mind Lie, too. If you seek comparison, you seek self-doubt. If you seek self-doubt, you will remain stuck. If you seek to acknowledge where you are and where you have been, you seek the fastest growth of all. When you are truly aware, you will be awestruck by the level of success it takes just to be alive in this world. But do you take this for granted?

All successes can be made to look mediocre when you compare yourself to others. But all your successes are superior to where you have once been. If you are going to use comparison, use your own past. If you insist on looking for a bigger fish, there is always one outside yourself.

In truth, there is no one else; there is only the illusion that an "I" exists within you. This "I" looks around and sees others doing and having what it believes it needs to be happy, fulfilled, and recognized. But those to whom your "I" compares itself are busy doing the same thing: comparing, comparing, and comparing. So one "I" is comparing itself to another "I" who appears to have or experience more. Yet both are fictional characters escaping the real truth that they actually have nothing while they believe that all they are is an "I."

Always face forward; never to the side, never behind, because there is no "I" without comparison to others.

It is what You do that matters. Do not pollute it by copying or comparing yourself to others. When you do something, it has your energy in it. It may not look like someone else's or behave like someone else's, or even be up to the standard of someone else's. But it has Your touch on it, Your magic, Your breed of creativity, which is unmistakably Yours. To try to appeal to those who desire other people's creations more than your creations goes against creating in the first place. To love yourself is what creativity is about. To seek recognition is counter-creative. To recognize your genius is true creativity.

To appeal to another's tastes is exhausting. To appeal to your own is a real pleasure.

"I Need To Be Noticed So That I Can Respect Myself"

This is a huge Mind Lie, especially for those who groom, preen, and strut to impress—the bodybuilders, fancy-car drivers, fashion followers, and many others.

Remember that this Mind Lie, and nearly all the others, occurs at a deeply subconscious level. What you are consciously aware of is less the belief itself and more the impact of it. It is your subconscious belief that drives you toward or away from certain outcomes. The belief is that "If others notice me, I will then notice myself. If others notice me, it must be because I am worthwhile and worthy of respect."

If only this were what really occurs. Yes, being noticed has you feel good about yourself, even better than good. It may have you feel on top of the world. But what about the work, the effort, the energy expended to keep up this routine to continue to be noticed? It is exhausting and simply a waste of energy, to say the least. It distracts from what really matters and what sustains you.

Being this way does not come easily, and so it is unhealthy. You will find that so much of these artificial ways of being to get attention take a massive toll on your body and peace of mind. They consume the mind, and if you have the need to placate this Mind Lie, you know how draining the need to be noticed and respected really is. It distracts you from more than the now; it distracts you from being healthy. It is true that this belief can cloak itself to drive you to be in shape and super fit, often under the pretense of it being about health. But it is not what you do that really matters, it is *why you do it*; it is the energy you hold in your space that counts. The energy of the beingness dictates not only the outcome but also the income: your state of mind, health, and well-being. The body can suffer from the healthiest exercise if the motivation is coming from an unhealthy place—a Mind Lie such as "I am not OK as I am, and I need to be better, look better, and look impressive to others so that I get noticed."

In fact, this phenomenon affects people in all areas of life. Skin cancer is a perfect example. On the surface and to the mainstream eye, it appears that the sun causes skin cancer, but it does not. The sun is very nourishing, and your survival depends on it. It is the beingness that has people stay too long in the sun and for the wrong reasons that causes the problem. It is this Mind Lie and others, such as "I am not worthy of looking after and nurturing myself," that cause people to tan and harm their skin, to be careless in the sun. So when the sun reaches and penetrates the skin, it is penetrating into the energy of self-hatred, catalyzing the cancer.

While this Mind Lie might create short-term wins and bouts of success, including the sensation of victory, the overall belief of "I need to be noticed so I can respect myself" has a far greater deteriorating impact on both body and mind. The downside is far worse than the upside of being impressive and being noticed. Where do you think the need for cosmetic surgery comes from? Does the end really justify the means?

"What Is The Remedy?"

The remedy, as with all Mind Lies, is the truth. Realize that others being impressed actually has absolutely nothing to do with you but everything to do with them. They might look at you with awe, but it is not because of who you are; rather, it is because of who or what they believe they should be. Here you are going out of your way to be noticed, but the only people to notice you are those with the exact same belief that you have: that they need to do more or become more to be noticed. When you stand side by side with them they become envious, because in you they see what they think they need in their own lives. All your attempts to be seen and admired backfire dramatically.

No one is noticing you when they see you; they notice only what they want for themselves in you as a mirror.

81

You are going to great lengths and making great sacrifices to be noticed by people who are struggling with the same issue as you are: basically, the need for an identity. If you truly want to be noticed by those who matter, you would go about it in a very different way.

But who are those who matter? They are no one, not even you. Because the you that you think matters is the same you insisting that you need to go to great lengths to be noticed so that the same you can respect itself. Talk about a vicious cycle.

Do you follow? The mind, which is made up, believes it needs to be noticed, so you go to great measures to try and achieve this Mind Lie. You think what the mind needs is real because it certainly feels real. But the mind is actually saying, "If I do not get noticed, I cannot and will not exist." This feels like hell in the body. To remedy it, you feed the mind in the hope that the reward will be real, but you only feed a fake beast something equally fake in the hope that someone fake will give you real fulfillment.

Why are you not noticeable the way you are? The truth is that the way you are is not noticeable, so trying to be content with yourself as you are is virtually impossible until you see through this Mind Lie. This is so because the way You really are is not the way you believe you currently are.

"Hold on; what is this all about?" you say. Essentially, you need to rise above your self-concept for just a minute and assume that your version of reality is skewered, at best, toward a competitive civilization, where one still needs to be the strongest, richest, most glamourous, and most inspiring to be worthy of true love—or even of self-love. You think this only because your Mind Lies tell you to think like this. Once you get caught up in pleasing your Mind Lies, you stay stuck in the loop of discontent until you realize the truth.

"What Is The Truth?"

Self-love and self-respect can come for free—no ambition, plastic surgery, or extreme exercise required. Self-love and self-respect are already present, but they are hiding behind your belief of "I am not good enough or deserving of it just yet." This belief, this Mind Lie, is hiding a truth that you have not wanted to know for a very long time:

"What others think of me is but a very poor substitute for what I think of myself."

But wait; there is more truth to realize. What others think of you will not nourish you as you have thought but will keep you in darkness forever, avoiding a deeper truth. That deeper truth is this: "All others see in me is themselves. All I see in another is myself."

To get to the root of the problem, you need to heal the fear of looking at yourself. You are petrified to look yourself in the eye unless you are pretending that you are more than another person.

"Why Am I Petrified?"

You are petrified because you will see not what you fear or think you fear; you will see something far more terrifying: you will see love. "What? Love is terrifying? How so?" you ask. If you have been trying to be someone else your whole life, it is because you were scared into it, forced into it, but for you to reconcile this information with the fact that you were fine all along makes your upbringing unbearable. How can someone so perfect have been treated so unjustly? To have been told what you were told about yourself, talked to the way you were, and abused the way you were is unjust.

The conflict is this: "If I am and have always been truly perfect, if I am the love you say I am, I would have been treated very differently." The mind fights back on this, lashes out, says, "How dare you say that love is what I will see, when clearly, if I am love, I would certainly not have been treated like I was nothing".

Do not give up on this yet. There's more!

You were treated this way simply because you are perfect, because you are love.

Remember what I said about who others see when they look at you? They see themselves, and in that moment they recognize the discrepancy between how they see themselves and how they wish they could see themselves. In this case, they see the discrepancy between love and how they really see themselves. The bigger the discrepancy, the bigger the reaction in them, and, in most cases, the bigger the resentment.

You cannot look at someone and not see where you are in relation to them. When you look at someone who is pure love, you will either see how far away you are from love—which will make you angry, jealous, and perhaps full of rage—or, if you feel closer to being love yourself, you will feel great affection for this person. When you understand this, you will see that the very reason you feel in need of attention is the same reason why you do not need it and never really have.

Ponder this: If you were actually flawed and an awful creation as a child, those around you would have looked at you and seen themselves. Instead of being angry and wanting to cut you down, they would have felt at peace, validated that they were not the only ones who felt that way. Misery loves company. Because of this, you would not have been made to feel that you needed to be more to get attention or to feel respected. You would now feel fine just the way you are. Yet because you are love—born as pure, perfect, unconditional love—you are already perfect, you are already noticeable and impressive. Others had you feel that there was something "not enough" about you in the first place because it was all about them in relation to you. They were not noticeable and impressive next to you. But you took the hit so they did not have to.

Your truth is this: You are love. You need not be any more than that.

"Who The World Needs Me To Be Is Not Who I Really Am; They Ask Too Much Of Me!"

Very few people on Earth are not brought up with expectations thrust upon them, from the simple "Keep your bedroom clean" to the extreme "Make the Olympic Team and bring home the gold!" Many of these expectations create the Mind Lie of "Who the world needs me to be is not really who I am." But how many of these expectations are based in truth? How many other expectations are you still carrying, even into your adult life, without ever pausing long enough to see the absurdity of them all?

You spend each day slaving on some expectation or another. It could be a social convention, such as phoning a parent once a week because you think you should, attending a family function that you know will end in family World War III as always, or pushing yourself too hard at work because you fear you will miss out on the huge job promotion that means the world to you. All these expectations are based in nontruth.

You have been set up not to fail at life, but to fail yourself. Who you think you need to be for the world, for those around you, for those you imagine judge you, is a recipe for utter failure. This Mind Lie steers you away from being centered and coming from your inner truth. It causes you constantly to question whether you are enough as you are. It steers your decisions, chooses your clothing, buys your cars, and holds on to certain friends and family members. At the end of the day you are run ragged, escaping who you really are by fighting and struggling to become someone you think you need to be.

Is this living, or is it actually dying? If you were to reflect on your life right now from your death bed, would you call spending it this way fulfilling, satisfying, and in honor of your truth, or would you call it insanity?

If you recognize the insanity, congratulate yourself for being in a space of truth. The truth is that you are enough for the world as you are. It is only when you try to be what you think the world needs that you become not enough. That is when you become just like everyone else and join the insanity rat race. Talk about diminishing yourself to be like everyone else!

What the mind believes the world needs is very different from what the world actually needs.

I have already addressed why the world is currently in the state it is: it is a direct result of Mind Lies, and this Mind Lie is a perfect example. The world and its every inhabitant are suffering because you are still pretending you are not enough as you are. You stretch beyond your means to reach some unattainable benchmark, exhausting yourself and the world around you.

The world needs you! Not the you whom you think you ought to be, with all the impressive titles, possessions, and flair. The world needs the real You. It needs the calm, relaxed, centered You to make the right decisions. It needs the content You so you do not exhaust its resources by looking for love and satisfaction in all the wrong places. It needs the soulful you to contribute the amazing gifts that dwell within, that are innate in every cell of your being. The longevity of the world, and your body, depend on this.

The world needs the truthful You. So in a sense, this belief, this Mind Lie, is actually correct. Who you think you need to be for the world is not enough. It is like water thinking that it needs to be gasoline so it can put out fires. *Water is all it takes to put out the fire.* It does not need to be something other than its True Self, as is the case with you. But somewhere down the line, you confused being yourself with not pleasing those around you.

***Daniel speaking:** I am reminded of the time my two-year-old son knocked a glass off our table in a restaurant. Watching it shatter into a hundred pieces caused a surge of anger through my body. Before I yelled at him—and let me tell you, yelling felt like the only way to dissipate this surge of anger in my system—I held it back and placed my awareness on what this anger was truthfully about. It was not about him breaking a glass; it was about me looking like an irresponsible parent in the restaurant, about the fear of others saying, "Look at him! He cannot control his kids!" The anger was about looking irresponsible, as if controlling my kids was what they needed in order to grow up to be great. It was not that my son was not living up to expectations; it was that I was not. But guess who would have worn the brunt of this energy if I had unleashed it? My beautiful, soulful, truthful son!*

Thought energy, then, was sent out to you when you were a child. You embraced it as your own, not knowing that it never belonged to you in the first place. This thought energy got held in your body as if it were truth. It now gets replayed over and over in your mind every time a similar experience comes up. This, ladies and gentlemen, is a reaction—a spark of the past. Every time you experience a reaction, you have an opportunity to see the real truth and heal this thought out of your body once and for all.

"What Is The Truth?"

The world does not need more humans being their human selves. Earth itself wants and needs more people being their enlightened selves. Every time you default to needing to be impressive, respected, admired, or simply validated—needing to be more than your truth—remember that is not what the world needs; that is what got you into the current mess on Earth in the first place. These old ways of being have to come to an end!

"I Need To Be A Better Person"

The Mind Lie of needing to be a better person is where much of the problem stems from, which is having a self in the first place. Stop viewing yourself as even having a self, and while you are at it, stop viewing yourself as a human being; you are not. It is all part of the mind-made illusion. Thinking that you are a person will limit you to what being a person means, especially if it means being like other people. This is not inherently a terrible thing; it is just not what the Earth needs. It does not need people, as people are, for the most part, ruining the Earth. The Earth needs you to be love; not a loving person, just love in a physical body.

Being a physical body does not make you a person. A belief system with a label of "person" makes you a person.

Start to view yourself anew! Begin to see yourself as love, moving through each day on Earth being love, generating love, and doing what love would do.

You are not a person; you are LOVE.

But do not get confused, for I am not talking about love for others, about moving through your day trying to be loving to other people. Instead, I am referring to pure self-love. Love for others can easily be misconstrued, and you can end up sacrificing yourself for others. Love of self does not always flow from love for others, but love for others flows immediately from love of self, so it is the best place to start. To be self-love is a whole new paradigm that barely exists on the Earth plane, so this is why you may have trouble grasping it at first.

To be self-love in its truest essence means to view yourself as an extension of the Earth.

People see themselves as stuck on this blue planet, desperately looking for a way to survive and, ideally, thrive using whatever means they have at their disposal. And you know where that has led you. Burning fossil fuels, polluting your beautiful oceans, fighting over land or even more ridiculous, fighting over beliefs!

When you see your True Self as an extension of the Earth, you will feel abundant, cared for, nurtured, and in the flow. The Earth is enormous and has an abundance of everything you need: enough water, sunlight, animal life, darkness in which to rest, and so on. When you are an extension of this wondrous ecosystem, you will find yourself thriving rather than going without, which is exactly what your Mind Lies say would happen.

In truth, the world does not need more people; the world needs more worlds.

By this I mean that the world needs more people to see themselves as the world. People who see themselves as the Earth recognize that they are intrinsically connected to actions and reactions on the planet and that everyone creates ripples across the Earth's pond and is affected by everyone else's ripples. When you have this level of awareness, you recognize that there is no action without consequence. Unfortunately, this is too much responsibility for some, so they choose to be oblivious, believing their ignorance brings abundance rather than scarcity. How wrong they are.

If you begin with a survival mentality, the human race will create the need to have a survival mentality. If you commence your day knowing that you are supported to be, do, and have what you came here for, then neither you nor the Earth will ever go without.

You can now see how important it is to stop trying to be that someone you have imagined everyone needs you to be. You can begin by being self-aware of what causes you stress and anxiety and what calms and nourishes you. "Trying to be" is stressful; simply "being" is calming. Follow the beingness of the Earth: it just is, without effort or trying. In doing so, a new benchmark will be set for what is aspirational on Earth, and instead of trying to be what you believe the world needs you to be, you will find the whole world growing and evolving to be, just like you.

The truth is that you are the world. You just believed the Mind Lie and stopped seeing yourself this way.

"I Am Not Leadership Material"

The responsibility of being a leader often seems daunting. But it is not actually the responsibility you are afraid of. Many people think the fears, the reservations, the reasons not to pursue a leadership position are, "What if I get it wrong?" or, "What if I lead people up the creek without a paddle?" or, "What if I turn into an egomaniac drunk on power?" In your mind, these are good reasons not to move forward. Believe it or not, this is not what actually stops people; it only appears that way. The real fears are hidden, and one of the major ones is, "My greatest fear is that I will be shown to have flaws and to have them under the microscope for everyone to see and criticize."

You fear that being perfect enough to be a leader is fraught with being seen for all your imperfections. "If I place myself in a leadership position, who am I to have flaws, to have weaknesses? What if I need to indulge in them and turn to a vice to keep me going? Then I will be seen for the fraud that I already worry and fear myself to be."

You are worried about being shown up, seen for all the imperfections you possess. But leadership does not require sainthood; it just requires being unwavering in pursuit of a cause. Being unwavering in pursuit of a cause does not require sainthood. Nothing on Earth does, except sainthood itself; and even sainthood is defined not as having zero imperfections but rather as seeing your flaws as perfect so that you are not trapped into living them over and over again. Buddha did not become enlightened by being born without self-work to do. Buddha became enlightened by recognizing the imperfection as perfection.

And so it is with leadership. It does not work to try to be perfect in spite of your imperfections, for what kind of leader would you be if others felt imperfect because of their imperfections? Rather, it takes the ability to recognize imperfections as opportunities to go deeper into the true You. The more imperfections you have, the more enlightenment you get to share with the world.

Imperfections, or Mind Lies, are not a social status. Having fewer of them does not equate to a superior social standing, as you will see when you clear them. What it does equate to is a superior understanding of what it means to struggle through life. Most leaders, you will find, had the most to push through to get to the other side. That is not to say that your life must be full of suffering prior to becoming a leader, but imperfection exists in everyone. It is only labeled as imperfect through the filter of the mind.

In the light of truth, these imperfections are catalysts for transformation and growth, for the birthing of a new level of awareness. All imperfections, as with all Mind Lies, are catalysts for major growth. The real imperfection is in hiding your imperfect self. By doing so, you cause others to feel their imperfection, showing imperfection as a weakness, as inhuman.

No true leader has been born without blemishes. True leaders have chosen to push through their imperfections by going within to learn the truth rather than remaining in their Mind Lies. Those leaders in the world who have relied on their thinking mind, laying the truth to the side, have only done more damage in the long run. There are countless examples in the political arena, where presidents rely on nontruths, anger, retaliation, and fear to make decisions. Decisions coming from fear lead to outcomes that create more fear. Decisions that come from anger lead to outcomes full of anger.

A true leader uses truth, because truth not only creates the best outcomes but changes the beliefs of those being led. Simply look at the bulk of decisions all world leaders have made throughout history, and you will see example after example of leaders keeping their followers' beliefs intact rather than enlightening them. They do this because they do not want to ruffle the voters' feathers. But this is nontruth, not the trait of a true leader.

Ask yourself how many recent presidents have changed the beliefs of a nation for the better. How many have kept existing beliefs in place? The latter is not the workings of a leader, for it creates followers rather than a new group of leaders.

How many times do you hear world leaders talk about the gloomy economy, the terrible job market, and how the only way forward is to spend more money to keep bolstering the economy? Here is yet another Mind Lie. Spending is not what boosts the economy; the economy is boosted by people growing and evolving. Help your people grow and evolve, help them to see themselves beyond their Mind Lies, and growth will flow more than you have ever seen.

Whoever creates leaders from the truth of their words are themselves leaders.

Whoever stifles the growth of their people because their words have little truth is a ruler, not a leader. Rulers rely on the stagnation of their people. Leaders harness truth, because where there is truth, there is no need for trying or effort. Truth creates growth in people. People who are growing are far easier to lead than those stagnating under fear.

So the truth about whether you are leadership material or not is simply this: you cannot help but be a leader when the focus is on truth. Truth makes the leader, not the mind and not the person. Be truth, and you will find that you are empowering people everywhere around you with no effort whatsoever.

In a world devoid of truth, truth is all it takes. Be truth, and the world will get to see what real leaders look like.

"I Never Grow Quickly Enough; I Am Slow To Recognize My Greatness"

Interestingly, this Mind Lie is actually a factual statement for you and many others, but it is the Mind Lie at work that is causing it to be fact. Being slow to grow and slow to see how much you have grown is a direct product of this Mind Lie. Remember, Mind Lies give you the experience they promise, the one you believe to be true.

The human race is looking for love in all the wrong places.

As humorous as this sounds, it does provide a deep insight as to why and how these Mind Lies wreak such havoc. Your measures for success, failure, and growth are so skewed that most of the time you are looking in the opposite direction from where you will find the success, fulfillment, and abundance you seek.

This keeps holding back your growth, and it keeps you from seeing the growth you have achieved. Your targets are off; you look for growth in things that do not matter, such as gaining material possessions, company acquisitions, and an increasing number of employees or asset base; ticking all the societal boxes—getting married, having kids, and so on; looking at employment numbers and other economic indicators; and seeing how much debt you have. You look everywhere instead of where growth actually exists and can truly be measured.

This Mind Lie keeps it all in place. Instead of measuring your growth by how much happier you are, how much healthier you have become, and how many Mind Lies you have eradicated from your psyche, you look outward to measures deemed by society and by those who came before you for what truly matters.

The truth is that you recognize very little of what really matters on this journey called life. You say you want to be debt free, to own your own home, to be financially independent, to be a CEO, to run your own business, to be a famous musician or film star, to lead a nation; you say this is what matters. Yet when you return home after pursuing these goals, you come back to the same basic questions: "Did they make me happy? Did my health suffer or improve? Am I more fulfilled because of them?" The sad answer is that very few can say that these pursuits are making them happier, healthier, and more fulfilled. When you see it in writing like this, the reason why becomes pretty obvious:. If you want happiness but your focus is elsewhere, how are you ever going to achieve it? "I know," I hear you say, "but those things are meant to make me happy." So, are you pursuing these goals under the illusion that somehow happiness will result from them? Yes.

Who told you that they are the path to your happiness? Whom did you ask whether this was the right path for you? "I just assumed," you say. "I saw it from someone on TV," you mutter under your breath. "Isn't it what makes everyone else happy?" The answer is no, and you are not everyone else! You are not even an "everyone." You are a mind that is chasing its tail, day in and day out, in the hope that someday you will get to experience what you have wanted your whole life. You do not know what will make you happy, so you steal ideas from others, even though you know that they are not really happy, either. But their path looks better than yours, so you blindly pursue it.

The result: a state of being that is unhappy, unhealthy, unfulfilled.

What is the solution? What is your real truth? It is to start again. Hit the refresh button and clear your preconceived ideas about how life works. Start from within, because this is where growth happens. If you are pursuing riches, a new career, or any other life path, that is fine. At the end of the day, it is not what you do but why you do it that is important. Is it coming from truth, or is it coming from Mind Lies?

Coming from a place of Mind Lies will never end in happiness, fulfillment, and abundance. If you are coming from this place, you are basing your life on incorrect physics. Stop doing it.

If you were to come back to your center, from a space of truth, what you would find is love. Being in your center is like a child who plays in the garden because there is nothing more she loves to do. Kids do not play because they are hoping for some outcome in their future; they play because what they do brings happiness and joy in the now. To base your entire life on some future outcome is a fool's way of life. Not only could you be dead before that outcome happens, but the fool's way is a surefire way to accelerate death. What you are saying is, "I am not OK as I am, but doing xyz will lead me to some place in my future where I am content, fulfilled, and happy." No, no, no! This Mind Lie is very bad for your body! Children know better than this. They can see as clear as day that if you put off your happiness for the future, you will never experience happiness in the now.

The truth exists in the here and now, and the truth will set you free. What will bring happiness, fulfillment, and abundance in the here and now? Find out now! Why wait?

A common belief, a part of the Mind Lie illusion, is that "If I am doing what makes me unhappy now, then somehow, miraculously, I will become happy in my future." What?! Slow down! That strategy is not working! When you come from love, you are guided to whatever will be the most fulfilling thing for you right now, for now is all there is. This is true for you as a person whether you are in a job, have a business, or are orchestrating a political campaign. Once you are centered in a space of love, you become one with an energetic current of growth, of flow and expansion. It is like riding on train tracks to a successful existence.

Stop strategizing your life. It is not that complicated. Yes, when you look at others, you see nothing but complication, but you can also see a lack of what they set out to achieve—freedom, peace of mind, health, a sense of self-worth, and self-love. This is what coming from the mind creates: lack.

The writing is on the wall. You are not getting what you want by following your ambitions and goals for the simple reason that those are not your own ambitions and goals, they are someone else's. What are your own ambitions and goals? Truly? They are usually quite simple. Think about how you want to feel at the end of each day. Happy? Fulfilled? At peace? Experiencing growth within? Having a sense of accomplishment? Do you ever hope to feel stressed because you run an exhausting business? Or unhappy because you rushed into marrying the first guy or girl you met? Weighed down by burdens and responsibilities because you were so desperate to lead and manage tens, hundreds, or thousands of staff, thinking this was a worthwhile goal? Why do you make your life so complicated?

The outcomes—running a big business, being a movie star, running a household with five kids—may very well happen, but let them come from truth, from a place of already being happy, rather than of achieving them to become happy. If you are happy first, you can be happy always.

Do not start with ambition; start with happiness. Money will not bring happiness, but happiness can bring big money!

What is the truth about the Mind Lie, "I never grow quickly enough, and I am slow to recognize my greatness"? Growth and greatness come from recognizing the truth where there is nontruth, from seeing yourself as you truly are. How can you do this when you are forever being who you thought you were and chasing what that person thinks he or she needs?

The ultimate growth is in recognizing that you are not that person and those needs are not your real needs. But how are you going to do this when you are still so attached to your Mind Lie-based aspirations, goals, and vision boards? It is simple. Come back to being childlike. A child knows that happiness is not complicated, that it does not require ten steps to get there; it just requires one. A child recognizes that happiness is not someplace in the future. It is now.

A child also sees that to fill your life with things you do not like will never make you happy.

A child knows that happiness does not come from pleasing or impressing or trying to lead others; it comes from giving to oneself. It comes from giving yourself more time to relax, to meditate, to clear Mind Lies; it comes from spending quality time with your kids and your spouse, spending more time in nature, and having fewer tasks to achieve.

Happiness on Earth comes from simplicity, not complexity.

Kids do not need lofty ambitions to be happy, so why do you? Children love the simple things, and so do you.

Be happy in the now, and you will stop screwing up your health and future happiness.

"I Must Invest Now To Have Happiness In My Future"

Investing—meaning taking something you already have and growing it into more of the same—is absolutely viable, such as investing money to make more money. It works the same way with happiness: if you want to create more happiness in your future, you will need to begin with happiness. Zero invested equals zero returned. But when you begin with happiness, you get to invest with happiness, and your return will be an increase in happiness.

Investing never refers to your putting in an absence of something or something different and in return receiving more of the thing you are after.

The Mind Lie that affects this truth is the common human strategy of "If I do something I hate now, it will eventually return happiness later." This is a complete fallacy, because what you are really saying to yourself is, "If I forgo happiness now, then by some miracle I will be able to create happiness later." How can that possibly work? It does not, which explains why so few people, especially in Western culture, are actually happy.

This is a great example of why it is important you make no decisions on the basis of Mind Lies. Do not come from inadequacy, jealousy, lack of happiness, or anger, because these will return only more of what you invested!

Focus on what brings happiness now, and you cannot help but experience happiness in your future.

"Responsibility First, Fun Later"

Many people get stuck in their lives, and they are not doing what they love because of the Mind Lie that "It is irresponsible to give myself what makes me happy in the now. As an adult, I must place responsibility ahead of all else."

Does this Mind Lie pretty much sum up adulthood for you? A child lives in the moment. An adult saves the fun for some day in the future. And you wonder why kids have so much more energy than adults.

This is a quick Mind Lie to deal with, as by now you are 75 percent across the line on this subject. What is missing is the realization that having fun and being playful about your life actually takes care of the responsibilities of being an adult. To be clear, I am not talking about sitting in a bar all day drinking with your buddies or being up all night with friends and then sleeping your whole day away. No, there is a key distinction here, a definable line. For ease of understanding, replace the word *fun* with *truth*. If you are in your truth, coming from truth, you would not drink all day at the bar, nor would you deprive your body of sleep. You just would not do those things that let you down.

"So is living in truth really much fun, then?" you ask. Is making love with the person you love fun? Is spending time loving your children, watching them talk for the first time, and playing crazy games fun? Is learning the secrets of the Universe fun? Is playing a vital role in the saving of the human race fun? Is helping someone survive after a terminal illness perhaps not fun in the conventional sense, but gratifying, even thrilling? Of course, yes! Definitions of fun vary across the planet, but one constant remains: truth leads to fun, whereas Mind Lies lead to pain.

Truth as it has been made out to be is actually the most enjoyable place to come from. Truth takes care of you, provides for you, nourishes you, takes you to fun and safe locations, introduces you to truly fun people, and makes your life thoroughly worth living.

Truth is not what others have dressed it up to be; you are thinking of your parents' version of truth or versions belonging to school teachers and other authority figures who were attempting to be truth but just were not.

Have you not noticed how devoid of fun your life actually is? This is because where there is an absence of fun, there an absence of truth. The more full of truth your life is, the more full of fun your life becomes.

> **Daniel speaking:** *I am reminded of a friend of mine who runs a highly successful vegetarian food company. He tells off his staff for being stressed, working too hard, or rushing around because he knows that there is an absence of truth in where they are coming from. He also knows that a business full of truth is a business that succeeds far beyond a conventional business. Truth is as much a building block of your personal life as it is your business life and your political life.*

Fun can come from living through Mind Lies, too, but it is a different kind of fun, full of short-term thrills and long-term suffering. Examples of fun resulting from Mind Lies include excessive drinking, recreational drug use, dangerous sports, hunting, unsafe sex, bullying—not just kids, but nations bullying other nations—overconsuming, and indulging in retail therapy. These types of fun affect all humanity. Too many have indulged in Mind-Lie fun, and the planet suffers for it.

Truth adds to you and sustains you, whereas Mind Lies deduct from you and ultimately destroy you. Look at the environment as a perfect example. To be in truth is the only way to meld into all the ecosystems to which you belong. Have you ever seen a snake, worm, or caterpillar act outside of their truth? Have you ever seen a snake get up and try to walk on its tail? Have you ever seen a bunch of raccoons try to chop down the tree they live in? Have you ever seen a polar bear try to light a fire on his floating ice sheet? No. And you never will, because animals instinctively know how to live in their truth, and they do so to thrive. The only reason animals on Earth have stopped thriving is not because they are out of their truth but because people are.

You affect not only your ecosystems but everyone and everything else's when you come from Mind Lies. The world as you know it today, with too much pollution, overcrowded cities, engines that pollute the air, not enough trees surrounding people to cleanse their minds, and so on, is a direct result of Mind Lies. There is simply not enough truth in the minds of leaders around the world to have balance in your ecosystem.

When you trust truth to guide your day, you will find that it is infinitely more imaginative than your Mind Lie-filled day. It is infinitely more satisfying than the day you would plan out on your own. It is infinitely safer than the situations in which you would otherwise put yourself, because truth knows what is good for you, what is safe for you, and what will be fun and worthwhile, all at the same time. Truth is You and knows you. Truth is the real You and knows you better than you know yourself. Many accidents, illnesses, disasters, and arguments can be avoided by relying on truth. It is the simple path forward, addressing all your fun needs and taking care of your responsibilities at the same time.

Daniel speaking: The life my Mind Lies had dreamed up for me was running big businesses and being very impressive as a result. As I pursued this path, I was engulfed in stress, anxiety, and a nonstop workload with never a moment for myself. I was completely unhappy—quite the opposite experience to what my mind had promised me. After years of persisting and having arrived at depression and burnout, I finally allowed truth to show me a different path. Surprisingly, after all my kicking and screaming, my life is now infinitely simpler, filled with time to myself to learn and grow. I get to create far more successful outcomes by applying a hundredth of the energy and stress. I get to have fun being more responsible than I could have ever been following the Mind Lie of putting responsibility first and fun last. Life can be so productive and simple with truth as your guide. On the fun meter, I now rate my life twice as high as before. Yes, the fun is different; it is no longer dangerous. The fun now is fulfilling and deep and infinitely satisfying.

Can you let in all this truth yet? Can you trust in truth to be your guiding light? Or do you still need to be in control?

"I Must Maintain Control"

"The more control I have, the more success I will have." What a doozy this Mind Lie is! Notice how the need for control creates the "I" in the sentence—something for you to ponder as you work on this Mind Lie.

Control is an illusion created by the mind. As the mind cannot see the whole Universe, it assumes that it must be in charge—in control—for it to survive. It does not see the interconnection of all matter. It cannot recognize an intelligence outside of itself, and it certainly cannot leave its survival up to anyone or anything else.

Herein lies the root of humanity's greatest problems. To see yourself as needing to be in control blocks you from allowing in that which is actually in control, the Intelligence that devised you: You—your True Self.

Ultimately it is your True Self that is in control, so the minute you rely on your mind's version of control, you become like a trapeze artist without a net, swinging from one life experience to the next, not knowing where you will be taken—to a pit of vipers or to a bed of flowers.

The real You knows the best path for you in every moment; the mind does not. The mind cannot see into the distant future to see how a particular decision will play out. The mind cannot see which airplane will crash into the ground and which will touch down softly. The mind cannot see which thought patterns will create a brain tumor and which will create longevity. The mind only knows what everyone else already knows. It is limited by what humanity knows, which is not much in the greater scheme of things.

Your mind proposes that your future is of top concern, yet its inability to see beyond the already known makes this proposal an impossibility. You see, You are in control from a space of truth, but this type of control is not the control you are used to. Control for a human being means micromanaging every step, taking evasive action when things look hairy, taking what is yours when things look threatening, pulling back on opportunities when they look too good to be true, advancing on something that promises fame and fortune, and holding back when something reminds you of a past bad experience.

You see, control really means doing what you did in the past, or worse, doing what your parents did. For some it means doing what every other human being has done. Control is stifling, stagnating, and in truth, redundant.

Control shuts things down, whereas truth expands and nurtures. Control is the opposite of flow, yet there is a flow in your life called *truth*. To be in truth is to be in a natural rhythm of growing and evolving, and best of all, of receiving the wondrous gifts on offer from life.

But you think, "If I don't control my life, I will end up with nothing!" Au contraire. It is when you try to control life that you are left with nothing. Control harms the body, exhausts the mind; and, ultimately, it starves you of the necessary growth of wisdom for you to see and experience who you really are. Control might make you money, but you will exhaust your life force gaining it and then spend your whole life terrified of losing it. Control might bring you fame, but you will come to resent it, because you will no longer have privacy, or worse, you will come to depend on it for your sanity. Control might even bring you power, but it will not be the power to heal yourself or others; it will only be the power to control or harm.

Control squeezes the life out of the living, like an anaconda squeezing its prey.

To have nothing comes from being without truth. The thought, "Control is the only tool I have to get what I want," is simply a lesson for you. It is showing you that you fear life, losing, being a nobody, missing out, and going without. But why do you have these fears in the first place? Are they actually based in truth, or has it become obvious to you that they are Mind Lies? Having control is a Mind Lie, and so, too, is the need to have control.

You are taught that you must fight for what you want; you must do whatever it takes to succeed, or someone else will take it from you. You are taught that power over others is better than others having power over you, and you have been told how easy it is to lose everything and go back to being a nobody.

What came first, the Mind Lies' need for control or the Mind Lies to do with being on the bottom rung your whole life? The truth is, neither. What came first is the thought that "I am separate and alone." This thought pioneered the need to hustle through life. In this space is an absence of trust; and, of course, if you are separate and alone, what on earth is there to trust in?

With nothing to trust in, you are in danger of your light being extinguished on planet Earth. What eventuates is a race committed to people's own destruction. You can witness that everywhere today, from drugs and alcohol to depression and drowning sorrows in prescription medication. These needs are fed by overusing natural resources and trading the wisdom and knowing of spirituality for science. Science is not a replacement for spirituality; science is spirituality made manifest. If the physical Universe is the body, spirit is the all-knowing intelligence behind the entire Universe.

When you come to realize that the mind is behind your sense of disconnection and aloneness, you will come to recognize a deeper You. This deeper You is the vast and expansive You seeing beyond the here and now. It has been knocking at your door continuously since the beginning of time. You have been knocking since You became a you, attempting to remind you of your true nature as a divine and sublime being, capable of the extraordinary.

Your need for control is irrelevant because only in returning to that which has real control will you be offered the greatest control there is. To insist on control is to insist on chaos. To be without control is to exist with harmony. To fear a loss of control is control itself controlling you. To need control is the fear of loss of control. To live in fear is a life devoid of love, but to act decisively from truth transcends all human concepts of control, because truth knows where control does not.

Allow inspiration to guide you. The more you do, the more it does for you!

Control is an illusion, because thinking that you are in control is the mind thinking that it is in control. Resisting the mind is still control, but nurturing truth returns the control back to its rightful owner.

Believing that you are in control is like a blind person believing they can see. It is both dangerous and untruthful. To know that the absence of control is the best type of control restores sight back to the blind.

"If People Around Me Are Unhappy, I Have Failed"

In your case, much of your upbringing was spent around people bitterly disappointed in themselves. This got projected outward into your space; and you, like many others, felt that you were the cause of those people's unhappiness, thus solidifying the Mind Lie that others are unhappy because of your failure. People blame others for disappointing them or not pleasing them in some way, but it is actually not your job to please or impress others. Their reactions to you have everything to do with their beliefs and very little, if anything, to do with you.

Everyone responds differently to different things because they believe differently about different things. Therefore, you do not generate a positive reaction in someone else; to react is simply to re-enact or re-act out a past experience. Reacting is not a response to a present experience but to a past one. When people are pleased by something you do, it is their vision, their version of reality, that is coming to fruition. It is this that pleases them, not you.

The greatest measure of whether you are doing the right thing is not other people's reactions but your own. How you assess yourself will change over time, but one certainty remains. The more self-loving you are being, the more you are on track. It does not matter what you do; what matters is how you do it. The more self-loving you are being and the more your decisions and actions come from a self-loving space, the happier you will be with yourself and therefore with the outcome.

Life can be made very simple when you understand this: space (i.e. who you are being) equals your outcome.

If people around you are unhappy, it is they who have failed. They have failed to see the greatness in themselves and failed to recognize the greatness that surrounds them. If you are judging yourself for failing because others around you are unhappy, you see them within you. You see parts of yourself that are no longer working for you, such as the need for others to be happy with you, to be pleased or impressed. And what is this really pointing to? The deficit in your ability to love yourself despite how the world sees you. No one really has an opinion about another, so you do not need to take someone's judgment of you personally. You are simply a mirror; their judgment is just a reflection of what they still dislike within themselves. Your need for their judgment of you to be different is a reflection of your judgments of yourself and your need for your own judgments to be different. To judge yourself is to enter the mind. To love yourself is the absence of mind. The love is there, but you will not find it by needing your mind to look for it.

If you are worried or care about what others think of you, it is because you care what you are thinking of yourself. At a deep level, you know your thoughts or actions are harming you.

Being concerned about another's thoughts is a nice reminder to reflect on and correct your own thoughts about yourself.

When you dig deeper into this Mind Lie that "if people around me are unhappy, I have failed," you will find that the part of you that is disappointed in yourself is also the *cause* of the disappointment. The judge and the criminal are one and the same. In other words, the mind is disappointed in itself. Why? Because it knows that it can never be enough, much like Pinocchio wanting to be a real boy even though he can never be. The mind concerns itself with itself; that is how it stays alive. It is like being caught up in a television drama: the longer you watch it, the longer the drama stays alive. You could

107

walk away, but that would kill the drama out of your life. The mind wants to live, so it keeps focusing on itself—not on You, but on itself.

The more you need others to be happy with you, the more your reality will mirror back how unhappy others are with you. You feel like you cannot make anyone happy; this Mind Lie attracts the mirror, and you get to see what you have been fearing.

> **Daniel speaking:** *I saw this Mind Lie with my little boy all the time. I would desperately try to make him happy, to please him with fun adventures, a great house, and a garden. But no matter what I did, I got the same result: a grumpy and unhappy child. Needless to say, this was highly activating! The truth is that I was never happy as a child, and no one could please me, either. The reason for this was the same then as it is today: I hadn't healed the Mind Lie. I felt inherently flawed. No matter what I did, it was never enough, right, or even OK. This anguish played out as needing to have my inner child self-validate its adult self. That was why my son was showing it rather than my daughter. I had to realize that what was inherently flawed when I was being brought up was not me at all; it was the way people acted around me. Their relationships, decisions, family dynamics, religious beliefs, and the life around me were all inherently flawed. In fact, I was not flawed; but to fit in, to try to make sense of the chaos, I effectively became chaos and mirrored the inherently flawed nature of it all to make meaning of my surroundings. This energy had remained in me ever since, and the more perfect my life became, the more the inherently flawed energy showed up in stark contrast; hence the anguish.*

The mind has some very warped ideas about how life should be lived. It is torn between what feels good to you and how others behave around you, which does not feel good. This leaves the mind to be in an almost permanent state of "I am not OK. I am not OK doing what feels right, because that is not how things are done around here. Doing things the way everyone else does them is as OK as it might be in this space, but that does not feel OK. Therefore, I am not OK!" Yet underneath all of this is the realization that others are not OK and that you are perfect!

"Everyone Judges Me And Looks Down On Me"

This Mind Lie is an easy one to clear. By now you know that Mind Lies are less about what others think and all about what you really think of yourself. You feel as though others judge you because you constantly judge and scrutinize yourself.

Scrutiny often begins in a household with very little tolerance of error and comes from people who do not give themselves any margin for error. This scrutiny becomes ingrained in you as a child, and then you become the watcher, the judge, and the critic of your own behavior. You have worked out that if you judge and catch yourself out before anyone else does, then you will not get into as much trouble as before.

There is obviously no freedom in this space and certainly no self-love. What do you need to know to break free from this affliction? You need to know that you judge yourself more harshly than others would judge you, as a form of protection, an insurance policy of sorts. All people judge themselves; you do it because you are afraid to get it wrong around others, as if everyone were watching closely for your flaws and your mistakes.

The truth is, you have been hurt badly and do not want to feel exposed any longer. You do not need to judge yourself; your judgments cause the mishaps you are trying to avoid. Failures, mistakes, and embarrassments all come from not believing in yourself. To judge yourself in attempt to circumvent failures, mistakes, and embarrassments actually guarantees them. To be free flowing with yourself, to allow yourself to unfold naturally, is called living. But how can you do it when you have been so stuck for so long?

There are no benchmarks for life; other people and their progress or lack thereof are not benchmarks. There is no cookie cutter that you must conform to or fit through. The expectations you place on yourself are fictitious and useless. They keep you tied to humanity's norm, to a mediocre version of yourself and life, and purposefully hold you back.

The deeper truth is that you are afraid of not conforming. You are afraid you might—or will—succeed. You are afraid that if others catch on to what you are doing, they will call you crazy, a heretic, a nonconformist, unconventional. This will have you feel that you are unwanted and make costly mistakes. The truth is that people love revolutionaries, unconventional thinkers, and people who behave in a way that demonstrates freedom and self-truth. They are refreshing and invigorating!

Let your hair down and be you! The unafraid You!

You have been led to believe that there is a formula for successful living, an exact recipe. If you fail to follow this recipe, you will be told off and miserable. The irony is that the easy recipe for successful living is an anti-recipe. It is unconventional, unorthodox, out in left field. It is to stray from the recipe and follow your deepest loving truths.

Express your greatest wisdom, unearth your mightiest dance, and draw from a spring of limitless creativity within you, not from anyone or anywhere else. Be free. Be You.

When you find yourself sticking with the conventional formula, change immediately, or you will turn out just like everyone else, miserable and bored. Brighten the world with your individuality, with your difference.

> *Daniel speaking: One of the defining moments that set me up for the Mind Lie of self-judgment was on the day of my bar mitzvah. All those around me made it known that I had better get it right. My parents were there assessing my performance. Their friends, the rabbi, the congregation, and even my school friends were ready to arm themselves with any criticism possible. But at the end of the day, the truth I needed was to realize that just getting there was an amazing feat. We often do not give ourselves credit for arriving at the point before judgment. More often than not, that point is already success. To honor yourself right there and then will free you from any further judgment.*
>
> *The other truth I needed most in that moment was that I will love myself. I will still love myself, no matter the outcome.*

Your greatest fear is not that others will reject you through their judgments but that you will reject yourself. This is more painful than anything else. If you can love yourself unconditionally, no matter the outcome, success or failure, you are truly free!

Celebrate just getting there, and love yourself no matter what.

You are afraid you will do the wrong thing, but what you do not realize is that it is all just the practice of being. The only plausible benchmark to gauge your life against is happiness. You will not find happiness by attempting to conform, be liked, follow a recipe, or live someone else's truth. It all comes back to living your own truth the way it was intended for you. If you can let this in, you will go far. Best of all, you will never be in judgment, because in truth there is no judgment. Truth is like Switzerland: a sanctuary from judgment and right and wrong.

Remember, a fake you is judging itself for not being the real You, whilst hoping this judgement is the fastest path to being the real You. Judgment will not bring you into truth, but disconnection from it.

"I Should Not Stay Alive; I Do Not Want To Live Being Such A Failure"

Feeling trapped in the sense of being a failure often has you also feel that there is no point in living; but you are not actually trapped in feeling this way. This is a Mind Lie.

Loving yourself will end the feeling of failure, but how do you reach this point if you see yourself only as a failure?

Realize that there were never any benchmarks for success—or failure, for that matter—other than the ones you decided to compare yourself to. These benchmarks were put in place long before you were born, and you inherited them as if they were correct and accurate. You were given benchmarks such as "I should be married and settled down by age thirty," "I should own my own business," "As an adult, I should not have breakdowns or cry," "I should drive a new European car so that others know I am successful," "I should always be fit and healthy no matter what," "Bingeing on junk food or alcohol shows I have no moral fiber," "If I put on weight in winter, I have slacked off," and the list goes on and on.

Where did these Mind Lies come from, and how did they enter into your psyche so convincingly? They were all made up and passed down from one generation to the next. But were you given a choice when this Mind Lie was passed on to you? No. You adopted it as quickly as you took your first breath of air. Adopting beliefs and taking in air are quite similar in many ways. You think you cannot live without either one. A breath of air keeps the body alive, and you feel the same way about your beliefs, as though without them you would die. Yes, you need air, but you definitely do not need these antiquated beliefs.

It is time to make a choice, the one you never knew you had. In this moment, a choice presents itself. You can choose to realize that you are not your experiences and therefore you are not your beliefs. It does not make you more evolved to believe that you are your experiences. In fact, it makes you less evolved and more mediocre. This is difficult for you to accept because you cling to your personality and its underpinning beliefs, just as you cling to air. So how do you clear it now?

You are made up of matter known as awareness. This matter permeates the entire Universe. You are aware of your beliefs, but because you have forgotten that you are simply awareness, you believe that you are your beliefs. It is like a fishbowl believing that it is the fish and its experiences. But your mind is limitless until you impose beliefs—Mind Lies—onto it.

Why would you want to die when the real You is the witness, not the experience or even the doer? Imagine you are the doer; do you deserve to die? No, because the doer is the beliefs, not the conscious awareness. Beliefs are the program, and you were born into the program. How can you be guilty of running the program? Life is about running the old program until you realize you are running it. When you finally realize it, freedom beckons. It knocks at your door wanting more, wanting to open you up to something infinitely greater than the Mind Lies. If you are not your experiences or your actions, then what do you really deserve?

You deserve to live out your life in the fullest possible way so that you can realize who you truly are, belief free, in order to pass to new generations who they are and give them a head start in greatness.

It is not You who has failed, it is not You who does not deserve to live. That feeling came from the belief itself, from the energy of the belief, which is not You. It is like walking into a room and feeling a negative energy. Feel it, but do not identify with it.

"I Have Been Way Too Slow To Hit My Stride And Make Myself A Success"

You do not know ahead of time what level you should or should not achieve, what is realistic for you, what will be a stretch, or what will kill you if you try. Yet you assess your level of performance against some self-created benchmark as if it were the God-given truth.

You take your cues from others of similar background, age, and skill. You compare yourself to their accomplishments and think, "I should be able to do that, too!" Yet each of you are running different programs. Different Mind Lies are sending you in different directions, sabotaging your actions in different ways, propelling you forward in different manners. You are not equal, you are different.

What confuses you are two dangerous thoughts: "I know what I should achieve based on what people similar to me have already achieved" and "I know by when I should achieve it based on when similar people achieved it." The problem is that both these statement are erroneous. They are the direct result of this Mind Lie. You do not know what you should achieve, so how can you know by when you should have achieved it?

No two people are created alike for a very good reason. The Universe does not need to have the very same experience over and over again. New experiences are what matter, so to believe that you should enact what someone else has is inherently untrue. It leads to bigger questions, though: "If I am not meant to do or achieve what they did, why am I still suffering and they are not? And what am I meant to achieve?"

Let us explore the first question, "Why am I still suffering and they are not?" You are still suffering because you have more Mind Lies than they do. It is that simple.

Now for the second question, "What am I meant to achieve?" You are meant to achieve exactly what you are currently achieving; there is no way around it. You cannot be anywhere else but where you are right now. This is not to be confused with what becomes possible once you replace more Mind Lies with truths.

This truth goes against your programming. "Surely," you think, "I could have gotten more things right in my life, made better decisions." Yes, better decisions were theoretical options. But this is where things get tricky. If you had been equipped to make those better decisions, you would have done so. But you were not better equipped at that time, so you did not make better decisions, and now you are where you are. By the way, regret is most unhelpful.

Now that you understand this Mind Lie, where do you go from here?

You realize that now is all there is and that the future is created in all the now moments. The way to expand possibilities, to end all suffering, is to heal the lies from within the mind. Remember, that is exactly what you are doing right now. If this is your focus, you are right on track and looking good for making spot-on future decisions.

What matters in the here and now is what you will create when you are free from Mind Lies, now and tomorrow and the next day. The fewer Mind Lies you have, the more time you have. It is the lies in the mind that take up so much time. They seek the longest, most complicated, most exhausting route. A free mind seeks the truth, and the truth is always the best route. What a free mind can accomplish in one year may take a mind full of Mind Lies ten.

You can easily make up for lost time if you stay with your truth and not allow any more Mind Lies to make more decisions on your behalf.

"Success Comes Much Easier To Others Than To Me; I Find It Hard"

You are not wired the same way as everyone else. Your mind is geared toward being highly productive at certain things. Some people have a natural aptitude toward creating music, others to being a steady-handed surgeon. It is not necessary that you all have the same abilities. The trick is not to push in the direction where everything is most difficult for you but to glide your way along your path of truth in the direction that you are best wired to achieve.

Most people do this backward. This Mind Lie steers your career in a direction in which you feel either most accomplished and recognized or the opposite—hidden and unacknowledged. Then, later in life, you realize that you have not been doing what you truly love. The good news is that you are wired to do what you truly love. Your skill set and aptitude will always match what you truly love. But Mind Lies can lead you through quite the labyrinth before you get in touch with what that is.

You convince yourself that you are doing what you love or being with whom you love simply because your Mind Lies are being satisfied—or compensated for. When a Mind Lie rears its ugly head, it can either be addressed and cleared or it can be compensated for, such as being overly ambitious when you believe you are intrinsically a failure. This is the danger of Mind Lies. They can send you well up the proverbial creek without a paddle, and you would not even know it.

Focus on your strengths, and let others step in to support you where their strengths are greater than yours. You can always learn more along the way once your strengths have fired up and you have momentum. You cannot steer a parked car, so it is paramount to get moving.

Those who appear to achieve success more easily than you do are simply those who have learned to use laser focus to pinpoint where they should direct their expertise. They are on their track, and they are showing up for you to see that you, too, need to be on track—not on their track, but yours.

To reiterate, you are as much a part of the laws of nature as any other living creature, yet those beings know their purpose, and they live it. An ant is not trying to be spider, and a bee is not trying to be a butterfly. Bees are best at making honey, so that is what they do. Spiders are masters at spinning webs, not making honey. Yet how often are you being the spider trying to make honey because you have seen the bees do it? How often are you the bee moving away from the honey and attempting the impossible—making a spider web? This is not to say that you are limited in how you can experience life. On the contrary, you only become limited when you pursue pathways that come from Mind Lies rather than from your deep truths.

There is an incredible depth to all your skills and abilities—to who you are—that you can discover. But when you compare yourself with others or write yourself off too quickly because you expected things to be more or different, you do not tap into the full possibility of where your abilities can take you. It is like digging for gold and giving up after digging only one meter down because someone else found gold at that depth. But when you fully trust in your essence and dig deeper, you find real gold—you find an endless reservoir of greatness. So few get to experience themselves as truly great because they stop digging too soon and never get to reap the rewards of these discoveries.

Every skill, every ability, has an endless depth. You have a responsibility to pursue your depth, to explore it and bring it to the surface so that you can be a beacon of light shining to the world what is truly possible. You can then lead by example and allow others to drink from the fountain that has come from perseverance and determination. Be a gift to yourself, and you will bring countless gifts to others.

Explore who you are, trust in yourself, dig deeper, and persevere to move past where you would otherwise quit and just do something mediocre. Be mindful that this advice does not apply to persevering only in a task, job, or business; it is much more than that. Persevere in seeing your real Self and the well of greatness that lies within you. That is where you will find the real pot of gold. That is success in and of itself.

"Other People's Accomplishments Are More Important, More Significant, And More Meaningful Than My Own"

Other people's accomplishments are more important only when you think they are. The Mind Lie of comparison will dull your senses to actual truth. Living in comparison is blinding and torturous. To live in love with yourself is freeing and limitless. At some point you will have to choose. Do you celebrate everything you are while you are on this Earth, or do you stay repressed, green with envy as you acknowledge and watch everyone else's successes?

Those with acclaimed successes did not get there by loving or trusting in others more than they loved and trusted themselves. On the contrary, they took it upon themselves to be the ones to lead, innovate, and create; to make the necessary changes; and to make a better life for themselves and others.

Celebrate yourself, and you will go much further than you will by simply celebrating everyone else.

A pathway to magnificence, to maintaining a worthwhile and meaningful existence while being alive on Earth, is ingrained in your blueprint of life, your DNA life purpose. This blueprint not only addresses your physical characteristics, it also stipulates your plan. But instead you took it upon yourself to make a plan for your life, either when you were a child—when you decided you wanted to be a firefighter, a policeman, or an astronaut—or when you became an adult. But what you have overlooked or forgotten is that a plan already exists. Your mind, the one filled with Mind Lies, contains a pivotal program to sever any memory of a greater consciousness, so you are always starting from scratch each and every lifetime. But your true identity—consciousness—is bored with this scenario. It is time-consuming and repetitive. Consciousness would much rather you carry on from where you left off. "Left off?" you say, "From when I had a previous life? That is crazy!"

Is it? Humanity has been in existence for quite some time, and it would be useful if the wisdom from the ages, from everyone's life experience, were carried forward into every newborn, so that old lessons did not need to keep repeating themselves. But how can this wisdom be carried forward if every child is a new life? The answer is fourfold:

1) If parents can be free of Mind Lies during conception and pregnancy, the number of Mind Lies children inherit would be significantly reduced. In this scenario, people would feed directly into their own blueprints more easily rather than having to go through trial and error before they realize that they had all the answers all along.

2) If the adults in schools nurture the clearing of Mind Lies as much as they do teaching new information, there would be schools full of genii.

3) If society as a whole recognizes that genius comes from within, you would have a society that nurtures inner connection far more than academic or financial accomplishments.

4) If parents and school systems knew how best to put children back in touch with their DNA-based life purpose, the human race would be propelled forward at light speed.

So what is this DNA-based life purpose I am talking about? It is order out of chaos, love out of self-hatred, nurture out of self-torture, harmony out of imbalance. The Universal Intelligence that dwells within you, the Intelligence of your True Self, wants life changed. Chaos is no longer working. Bloodshed has never worked, and self-hatred is leading to all manner of diseases, wars, and other forms of violence. It is time for a change. Your DNA-based life purpose is all about fostering change in humanity. Yours could be about creating breakthroughs in your family line so that Mind Lies are not repeated down through generations. It could be about creating change in business, in education, in politics, or in the environment. It might be creating a new way to reduce dependence on fossil fuels or presenting a workshop that teaches people how to heal their bodies from cancer and other deadly diseases.

All DNA-based life purposes are symbiotic, healing you, others, and the planet while meshing perfectly and supporting this amazing ecosystem that is the Earth and the Universe within.

Do not believe the Mind Lie that acting on your DNA-based life purpose will make you poor; however, not acting might very well make you poor. Your gifts are in perfect balance with what is needed to create the necessary change on Earth. When you support yourself and what is needed, the Earth thanks you tenfold.

You think others contribute more important, more significant, and more meaningful accomplishments than you do? Right now they probably do, but not for long. Seek out your DNA-based life purpose, discover the answers within and the roadmap to living fully, and you will never fall for that Mind Lie again.

"I Cannot Love Myself When I Am Such A Failure"

By now the concept of not being able to love yourself might be getting a little harder to understand. You may not be fully in love with yourself yet, but hearing these truths has no doubt helped you see that the parts you did not love were never the real You to begin with. They were just Mind Lies.

If self-love is still a big issue for you, let us work together to go deep and shed light on how easy it can be to love the real You.

You cannot call yourself a failure; you have acted out of your Mind Lies in the past, and that has brought levels of achievement. At this stage, you might think of them as levels of failure, but this is not you. That would be like getting into a car that has no brakes and condemning yourself for crashing into a tree. Could you have done better or differently in any way?

This is the journey of life: to live as you are with the beliefs you have until you see through this disguise and then see what life can bring.

To love yourself for still being alive despite not realizing the truth about yourself is worthwhile. What an accomplishment that is! Because what it means today is that you have the rest of your life to experience life anew, without the broken brakes.

You get to start afresh, to explore all the different nuances of life, not being who you have always thought you were. You are no longer the old you, which means life cannot be as it always was. It is impossible to repeat the old patterns if you no longer believe the programming that kept them in place.

What stops you from loving yourself now? Is it the anticipation of failure, the likelihood of more suffering, or the impending criticism from others? Or is it that everyone else in the world still sees you as the old version of you? Whatever your reason, it is all Mind Lies.

How do you clear such Mind Lies? As always, with truth. You have chosen to not love yourself in order to protect yourself; there is no other reason than that. You protect yourself from failure, from not living life to the fullest, and from disappointing others. But failing to love yourself is the real guarantee of failure.

Self-love guarantees success in all forms. Self-doubt, or worse, self-hatred, guarantees a most undesirable outcome. You have nothing to gain by refusing to let in self-love. In fact, all you gain is the satisfaction that you were right all along, that life really does suck and is full of struggle and hardship. You can get to the end of your life being right or being happy. Think about that!

Being right is overrated, yet people have continually settled for being right over happiness. It is as if being right brings more than happiness. But if you ask people what they seek, they say happiness, fulfillment, joy, and so on. No one says, "I just want to be right." Yet underneath their own propaganda, few are choosing happiness and joy over being right.

How do you shift this obsession with being right? You guessed it: more truth. You are lovable. That is the truth. You may have committed horrible crimes; let people down left, right, and center; made your family bankrupt; or abused your body. But remember, to say that you are your experiences is a Mind Lie. You were the witness to these experiences, and because you believed you were the Mind Lies that generated them, you also believed that you were the result, the experiences, of the Mind Lies as well.

Life is evolution, and evolution is an unfolding of deeper and more poignant truths. You have watched your life unfold so that more poignant truths could be realized—so that one day, maybe today, you will act from these truths and be a real blessing to yourself and all those around you.

It is not you who is the failure; it is the mind. The mind conjures up ideas and what it is to be a success or a failure without ever factoring in your journey. If you were to look at any successful person's journey prior to being recognized as a conventional success, your mind would label most of it as failure, no question.

A journey can never be a failure. Labeling it as such is the failure.

"I Am Not Worthy Of Happiness Or Success; I Am Not Worthy Of Love From Others, As I Will Only Disappoint Them, Anyway"

This is a very common Mind Lie, one that wreaks havoc throughout society. It is one of the most widespread beliefs and keeps nearly all other Mind Lies in play.

You are deserving of happiness, no matter how you have lived or the choices you have made. Without feeling deserving of happiness, without happiness itself, you are doomed to repeat the same decisions and actions of the past.

This raises some interesting questions about rehabilitation. Is punishment the best way forward when it certifies that what people were already feeling about themselves is actually true? You punish yourself continually, especially under the guise of this belief. You starve yourself of foods you love, of fine clothes or jewelry, of spending time with people you really love, of spending time in nature.

It has always amused me that when people go on holidays, they rarely visit big cities. Most people go to rural areas, tropical beaches, national parks, and places with rivers and mountains. You love the outdoors more than you realize, but how often do you allow it in for more than a few weeks each year? This Mind Lie of not being worthy can be easily cleared when you realize you have been put on this Earth for nice things and to realize you deserve love and happiness.

There is no purpose in creating a life only then to starve it of what it needs most to evolve: love.

Love, rather than money, is what makes the world go 'round. But money has become love's poor substitute. You think, "If I cannot have love, I will get my hands on money; that will fill the void." And there are plenty of people who do not even believe they are worthy of money, either; they think they are worthy only of pain and suffering.

You are here to realize your deservingness, your worthiness. You are here to experience joy and happiness, but it is not without suffering. Like ripping off a Band-Aid, it hurts to tear off who you think you are in order to make space for happiness and joy. It hurts to let go of your identity to make room for something greater. But do not confuse the temporary pain of the process with the outcome itself. Because you have seen this suffering, you have come to think that it is what life is all about. You have confused the middle of the movie with the end. Because of this, few ever reach the end of the movie, the place of joy and happiness. How can you do so, if you truly believe suffering is why you are here?

It is the Mind Lies that are responsible for all the suffering and struggle. Your intrinsic nature, your true identity, is joy and happiness. This vessel of consciousness cannot experience its true nature until the Mind Lies are no longer. Together, you can rip the Band-Aid off so it can end.

You do not know how to be great because greatness is a state of being, not an action. Self-love does not require anything from you, unlike the states of being that come from Mind Lies. All other states necessitate some compensatory behavior, some repairing, proving, or convincing that requires exhaustive effort. Yet self-love requires nothing. It is the full acceptance that who you are right now is perfect.

The mind sorts by reasons and justifications, such as "Am I allowed this? Of course not. I was naughty when I was a child, so that must mean I am undeserving of success and happiness." Yet these reasons are completely out of context, out of date, and were taken too literally in the first place. What is true is that the Universe decides what you are or are not ready for—not in judgment, but as a collaboration.

This is a huge concept to let in, so stay with it as best you can: Your state of being dictates your decisions and actions, so it is ultimately your state of being that sends a signal to the Universe of what you are or are not ready for. The Universe matches this signal by returning to you the same resonant frequency in all areas of life: finance, relationships, type of car, business success—you name it. So you, in collaboration with the Universe around you, are instructing life in what it should bring you for your growth. The process does not stop there, though. As your state of being evolves and you transcend more and more of your mind, the Universe returns the favor by allowing you to realize yourself, your greatness, at a whole new level. The rewards move beyond the physical and into elevated states of awareness. These new states bring gifts of their own: abilities, knowledge, and profound new levels of insight. This means that as soon as you recognize you are deserving of something, the Universe will provide it. The Universe is not some old man sitting up in the clouds with his scales of sin and virtue.

You, as creator, show the Universe what you are ready for.

Even judging this principle is showing the Universe what you are or are not ready for. Allowing it in sends a different message altogether; it shows that you see yourself as great, and now great things can resonate with you.

The only indicators of deserving in your Universe come from you. You are used to the Mind Lie of "deserving" as being a judgment imposed from outside yourself, from teachers, parents, the law,

Santa Claus, and even God. You have been misled to the point of feeling powerless to achieve what you want.

If you feel that you are deserving of happiness, you still believe you are not. If you force success and happiness through your will, you will get a mirror showing you where you are still unhappy and feeling undeserving. But if you trust in happiness and success as a by-product of your state of being, then you are in truth.

A good example of the Mind Lie of deserving is those countless people who finally receive the money they dreamed of and are still unhappy. They are quickly shown that they are without self-love, and so they crave acceptance and respect just as much as they did before receiving the money.

Allow each new gift to flow from each new level of truth at which you arrive.

Being deserving or undeserving is a judgment from the mind. How much you allow in depends on your state of being. In other words, it is physics, not judgments.

Success is imminent when you move beyond being deserving to realizing, "I am greatness personified." You get to see how being deserving was a need created by the mind, a poor label for what you are in truth. The concept of deserving was all made up, so let it go.

"If Something Is Difficult, It Is More Meaningful And Satisfying"

How often do you notice how you and those around you make life so much harder than it needs to be? Whether it is holding a job, rearing a child, making a painting, or embarking on a spiritual journey, the reason you do this is because of this Mind Lie. You try to give meaning to something you believe has no real inherent meaning by making it difficult or making it take a long time or making it hurt you in the process, or worse.

The truth is, if something is difficult, you are not coming from a space of truth. When you connect to truth and your True Self, you find that a path already exists to give the utmost in meaning and satisfaction. But very rarely do you take that path. It could be that your endeavor is not based in truth, that you should not be embarking on it in the first place; or perhaps you are approaching something that is worthwhile, but you are coming from a non-worthwhile space. Either way, this Mind Lie has the power to cause complete and utter havoc.

What is the truth that will set you free? When something must be difficult to have meaning, you are still required to be present to the meaning in the space in and around the activity. This phenomenon does not change. The degree of difficulty is often confused with the level of accomplishment, but this perspective is identity based. It is your identity that wants you to stand out, to be noted and recognized for your efforts; when something is difficult, your ego is given a pat on the back when you achieve it. But the achievement did not need to be hard for you to receive that pat on the back. A pat on the back comes from needing validation and recognition. If you validate yourself and recognize yourself before attempting an endeavor, you will find the activity is that much more satisfying and give yourself the chance at effortlessly achieving.

When you are already significant, a pat on the back pales in comparison to helping others feel significant. You begin to see that the thrill you chase by wanting to be significant actually prevents true significance from being obtained.

Significance is not derived from an activity but from realizing the importance of your place on Earth. This has you stop chasing significance and just be – significant.

The Mind Lie "I need to be significant" perpetuates the need to make life much harder. When you realize that difficulty has no bearing on whether you are significant or not, you can let the Mind Lie go and walk the easy road. Stop making things more difficult than they need to be. It proves nothing other than how adept you are at making things difficult. It is far better for you and far more inspirational to others, to see just how simple you can make your success. Success is simplicity, not complexity.

"When I Have Everything I Want, I Will Be Happy"

You live in a culture obsessed with things to own: cars, houses, TVs, people, and even enlightenment. But what the bulk of humanity has overlooked is it is not things that make you happy; it is you that makes you happy. Each thing you crave has an experiential, vibrational frequency, meaning that it seems to fill a void in you from a childhood experience. Each thing matches a void. For example, if you were denied a BMW for your first car when all of your friends at school got one, then owning a luxury car later in life can be a strong, compelling goal. But these things do not heal the voids, because the voids are Mind Lies. By now you realize that only truth heals Mind Lies.

The constant pursuit of things actually buries you deeper in Mind Lies, making it very difficult to see your way out of the rut you are in. Each thing attempts to hide a Mind Lie from you, acts as another Band-Aid, shields you from the pain and emptiness the void creates. For each thing you buy from this Mind Lie place, you further hide from yourself the need for healing, essentially leaving a bloody wound open to become infected. You never get the full satisfaction of the experience you were hoping for, because you took the thing as a poor substitute for the truth.

Whenever you "must have" the next thing, ask yourself, "From what space is this coming? Why must I have it? What void do I believe this thing will fill?"

These are tough questions to ask yourself, but when you get to the truth, you will either save yourself a great deal of money or buy the thing you want with more satisfaction than you would were you buying it to fill a void. The deeper truth is that it is the space you come from that is fulfilling or not.

Your state of being can be likened to a pilot approaching a runway. If the pilot approaches patiently, gently, and carefully, the plane has the best chance for a smooth landing. If the pilot hurries into the approach, is going too fast, and is anxious about the landing, the landing is unlikely to be smooth. The pilot's approach is another way to explain your state of being.

This awareness creates new rules for humanity: Your state of being creates precise outcomes; focusing on your state of being is the secret to true manifestation; your state of being, not what you do, is what does the creating; your state of being both precedes and supersedes what you do.

What is your every-moment approach? Is it coming from a fear state or a love state?

A true master recognizes that all doing is the by-product of one's state of being. To focus on the doing distracts from what is actually the driver of success. Whether it be seeking love, growing a business, or being a great parent, everything starts with your state of being. Love yourself, and what you do will create results you love. Come from self-hatred—Mind Lies—and you will create the most undesirable results.

What is the ultimate truth? Whenever you feel that you do not have enough of something in your life, know that there is a Mind Lie creating this state of being. To try to fill the void from this space will drag you even further into discontentment and frustration. Where there is lack, there is a Mind Lie, and the fastest way to remedy the Mind Lie is with truth. Truth sets in motion powerful states of being, which in turn attract, expand, and make possible infinitely more than you will ever need to be happy.

129

Remember to focus on your state of being, for that generates abundance.

Do you really need things to make you happy, or is it just the truth you crave? The truth will fill the void.

"Stressful Situations Cause Me Stress"

Everyone experiences degrees of stress at some point, but many people seem to magnetize stress toward their bodies, no matter what the situation is. If this sounds like you, your body will really celebrate this exploration.

Much of the stress you experience is not about what is happening here and now but what happened in the past and how you experienced things then. The stressful events in your life today activate your memories, fears, and anxieties, but they do not have to. You are built to weather stressful situations as if you were standing in a torrential downpour with a sturdy umbrella, staying dry and unaffected.

How do you reach this place of enlightenment? One useful method is to neutralize the most stressful events from your past, but this can be time-consuming and tedious. Another remedy is to breathe truth into the ultimate Mind Lie at play here: "I have to be impacted by my past." This is clearly a nontruth, but it is one that you are heavily invested in.

Why would you want to retain this belief? There are three common reasons: (1) The more you are impacted by your past, the more attention you get from others in the form of sympathy, allowance, and patience. (2) It acts as a "Get out of jail free" card, meaning any disappointments or failures can be attributed to how much you were disadvantaged by your past. It is why you are now OK with failure and disappointment. (3) If you hang on to the lessons of yesterday, you believe you are ensuring that you will never make those same mistakes and never suffer the same way again.

Despite their convincing nature, these reasons are highly counterproductive Mind Lies. Do you really want sympathy and understanding for not having the life you want? Wouldn't you rather get attention, interest, and curiosity because you have everything you have always aspired to? Forgive yourself for needing to hold on to suffering, because it is time to let it go; it is getting in the way of the life you desire. Wouldn't you rather explain to others how you got to be so happy, fulfilled, and enlightened instead of give excuses for why you are still miserable and unfulfilled?

The truth is that you are afraid to move forward. The fear of failure looms over you, yet failure is imminent unless you are prepared to let go of the past. Past failures and sufferings are no indication of future events. You must realize that you are so much wiser today than ever before and attracting failure is not who you are anymore.

What is failure, anyway? It is a judgment you make about yourself and your outcomes. It is a Mind Lie unto itself. To label something as a failure means that you have not been paying close attention to truth. You cannot fail unless you judge yourself unfairly. Outcomes take time, refinement, tweaking, and sometimes abrupt course changes, so where is the failure? Where does it exist? It exists only in the judgment. The surest way to avoid failure is never to judge anything as a failing, because as long as you are alive, you have the time and opportunity to change things.

Failure exists in the mind, not out there in reality. As long as you keep moving forward, failure does not exist; all that exists are lessons, modifications, and new levels of awareness. The true failure is in denying your own greatness, and even that is but a stepping stone to the next level of success.

For example, say you launch a $10 product after investing $1.5 million into it, but only one person buys it. It is human nature and business acumen to label it as a failed product, but in the eyes of truth there has been no failure; there has been only the revelation of truth (or absence of it). A revelation of this kind is anything but failure.

Hanging on to the lessons of yesterday keeps those past experiences alive in your mind and body. Perhaps you will be more deliberate in avoiding those mistakes in the future, but you will deplete yourself of energy, motivation, and enthusiasm for life. The more of this stagnant energy you insist on holding on to, the more depleted you will become. The energy gets trapped inside the tissues of your body, causing decay, illness, and premature death. Why take years off your life as you attempt to prevent further suffering? It makes no sense! Accept that the lessons learned have integrated into your new awareness, but do not drag them around with you.

It can help to journal about what you learned from the past and what the take-home lessons have been, but ignore the drama and self-condemnation. Once the lessons are clearly written out, know that you have gotten what you needed from them. It is time to let go of the experience altogether.

Don't suffer now to avoid suffering later.

The next layer of truth is that once you have had an experience to the point of realizing the deeper truth and lesson, there is nothing left in your field of consciousness to attract that lesson in again. Imagine that the leak has been plugged up by a new awareness. Now you can let go of the Mind Lie of needing the past to continue impacting you.

What is the real truth that will set you free? The past did not happen to you; it happened to the past. The you from the past no longer exists in the here and now; it is like a fading hologram that no longer has significance. All the events of the past happened in and to the past, but the you of today is fresh, invigorated, and exists only in the here and now. Move forward as the new You!

Stress comes from fear, and fear comes from a lack of trust. How do you move into a place of trust when fear has permeated your entire life? Trust comes from realizing that control is not the answer but rather another path back into fear. The more you believe you are in control, the more you fear losing that control. The truth is that you are part of a flow. You are no more in control of your life flow than you are of the Earth orbiting the Sun; it always has orbited and will continue to do so. No matter what control you believe you have, the Earth will circle the Sun 365 days a year, every year.

You have been taught to be in control, to take charge, to own your destiny, but is this the best play? Let us explore. When you understand patterns and systems within an ecosystem, you can plainly see that each element has a function, a reason for being. A spider is a spider and therefore does what a spider does. An ant is an ant and helps the colony function and survive. All insects, plants, and planets form the necessary ecosystems that you exist in as a person. You are as much a part of the ecosystem as the insects, plants, and planets, yet you have taken it upon yourself to make your own rules, to rise beyond the laws of nature and do it your way. The result is the poverty, greed, suffering, and environmental damage you are facing today.

Taking charge does not work. Listening intuitively to the voice within is what works.

When you consider that the flow is designed to harmonize all its aspects to raise all to a higher place of evolution, it is easy to see how much better it is for you to go with this flow rather than rebel against it. The flow is attempting to serve you and improve your life in the most wonderful of ways. Why get in its way?

You fear that to be in such a flow means that you will miss out on what you want. However, you are already missing out on what you want. Do you want stress, fear, anger, illness, suffering, and a lack of answers and understanding of the mysteries of life? Do you want to live with guilt and worry about the impending damage on this planet? This is your life now; it is already what you do not want.

The primary culprit behind all stress is the worry that things will not work out for the best. The worry may take many forms, but in the end you are afraid that you will not get your way—whether or not you know what your way is. The remedy is simply to understand that most of the time you do not know what the right way is; you just know you want it your way. Often a vast chasm exists between what you imagine to be the right way and the actual best way. Surely you have seen this countless times when things did not go your way, but the way things went was significantly better than what you had originally conceived. This is largely because what you conceive for yourself nearly always falls short of the best possible outcome.

In essence, you settle for much less than what is available. Sometimes you grow by force, by life situations that stretch you or are forced upon you, that stretch your perception of yourself and illuminate new levels of truth and new possibilities. In truth, what you imagine for yourself stems from how you imagine yourself. The more you imagine yourself to be, the more you begin to imagine for yourself and thereby become able to create it.

The problem is that you see yourself as separate from the flow. It is like being on an escalator and desperately attempting to move it faster through brute strength and persistence, when you could accept that you are in the flow and surrender to it. You know which perspective brings peace and harmony.

The reason you see yourself as out of the flow or disconnected from it is simply because of ignorance. Were you ever even taught that a flow exists? Mind Lies tell you that to go with the flow leads to mediocrity at best, so those petrified of being average have shunned the flow. Yet it is not *your* flow to which you are surrendering, it is *the* flow. The key distinction is that your flow originates from Mind Lies, while the flow is based in truth. One brings scarcity and failure, the other abundance and success.

What is the flow? Where is it? Who is it? How do you even know it is real? The flow is the superior path masterminded by an

Intelligence vastly greater than your own human mind. It has been placed before you; all you need now is the wisdom to take it. It is the only path you will not regret taking.

"I Need To Contribute To Fit Into Society"

That you need to contribute to fit into society is a common Mind Lie, but why would you want to fit into a society that is running around in circles chasing its tail? Why would you want to be one of "them," when who they are is perpetually not enough? How would joining a group of people who despise themselves teach you to love yourself more?

You are not here to fit into society but rather to help society realize that everyone must evolve to a new awakening—not to belong, but to be different. Feeling the need to belong is another Mind Lie.

Pressure comes in numbers; the more people in a society who blindly follow some invisible system of being, the more that fallacy seems to become the truth. The more truth you think you are following, the more truthful you believe you are; but the fallacy, if it is being followed, is that it is not the truth but a rumor, a self-perpetuating notion hiding the real truth from clear view.

Society is dysfunctional because everyone believes the same thing. It is time to shed beliefs for truth. Truth does not need to be believed to exist; only beliefs do. Without a common buy-in, beliefs dissolve away. Truth is eternal. It has always existed and will always do so, and it is available to all those who aspire to be more.

Once you master your state of being, then growth—the ultimate in productivity—is simply an eventuality, for the Universe does not measure productivity in how much money you have or how many chores you complete but by how much you grow. The magic about using growth as your only measure is that the more you grow, the less you busy yourself with unproductive states of being and therefore unproductive tasks. The more you grow, the more you focus on doing what is fruitful, be that healing the planet, restoring connection and love in your family, or the ultimate in productivity: restoring self-love.

Productivity does not come from useless states of being, such as needing to compensate for inadequacies, fears of rejection, or lack of respect. It is true that empires are built in spite of these states of being, but they are not necessarily productive creations.

Humanity often confuses building something large, such as a factory, city, or company, as being highly productive, but was the thing ever needed in the first place? Often the most productive thing you can do is nothing. Resist creating, resist inventing, and resist that new technology. There are countless examples throughout history of how unproductive moving forward on some ideas turned out to be. The automobile, for example, appeared to be a very productive invention, but the need for oil became one of the greatest causes of war and the depletion of natural resources, and it is one of the biggest contributors to environmental damage. The automobile has taken more than it promised to give.

Without a suitable state of being, innovation and invention only give the appearance of productivity but are inherently unproductive. Here is a simple equation for all of life's endeavors:

$$P^B = O$$

where P = level of productivity, B = state of being, and O = outcome

This means that any state of being will create an outcome. How productive the outcome is depends on the state of being. Master your state of being, and you master your destiny.

Productivity comes from being, not doing. Doing creates, but being manifests.

You do not need to be productive, because productivity inevitably comes naturally from being in truth. Ask yourself, "What is my truth?" in every moment, and you cannot help but be sublimely productive.

"I Do Not Feel Accomplished Or Successful; I Need To Be Productive, I Have To Contribute"

Do you feel discontent unless you have been hugely productive during the day or have contributed to your household?

Remember, Mind Lies exist and survive by distracting you from the real truth and drawing you away from simplicity, grace, and ease. Whenever you find yourself full of hectic energy and unable to breathe, realize that you are at the behest of the Mind Lies.

The busier you are, the less chance you have to see the truth. This is how Mind Lies maintain their control. Everything they do disarms you from gaining power over them, and the Mind Lie that you have to be productive to be content is no exception. In fact, it singlehandedly controls more people than any other Mind Lie does, keeping everyone overly busy for the majority of their lives. It is the slave-driver Mind Lie, promising some form of pleasure the busier and more productive you become. But it is never in the now that the rewards come, which should raise your suspicion. The rewards are always promised at some unknown point in the future, when joy and satisfaction will be experienced. Only when you have done enough, contributed enough, made a real difference in the world will you be counted, worthy, and content.

In truth, you are perfect here and now; just your existence is enough. However, this truth gets buried deeper and deeper the busier you get. You may be productive and achieve great things, but when you rid yourself of the Mind Lies, you will remember that the goal is not doing but centering yourself on the most productive state of being. This requires no movement, no effort, no expenditure of energy or the mind. In this state your greatest service to yourself and others is achieved. So much time and energy can be saved by focusing on your state of being before the doing happens.

Energy in nearly every form is constantly wasted because you have not yet realized that you do not need more; you need less. You cannot see this when you are too busy to stop and realize truth. Just being your natural self, just being You, is a gift to the world. The more presence of mind you can muster, the better for everyone. The more you conserve your energy, the more you conserve energy all over the world.

Digging Deeper

Divine truth explains that productivity comes from realization. Realization comes from stillness. It is only in the quiet of the mind that truth can be revealed in all its glory. It is only in a space of stillness where you can realize who you need to be, and it is not being productive or busy. Both are distractions, diseases that undermine the very fabric of cohesion, logic, and forward thinking.

How can you truly progress as a society when you refuse to slow down enough to see or better put, allow in, what the best path forward is? Inspired thinking is an art form, for true thought occurs without thinking. Thinking is the mind's way of sorting through irrelevant bits of data to come up with something that is in the realm of your identity, of what you consider possible and worthwhile. Then there is pure thought, which goes beyond your mind and originates from far beyond human consciousness. It is this level of thought that changes lives in the fastest way with the least amount of wasted energy and resources.

Pure thought inherently exists; it just is. But you cannot tap into it when the mind is cluttered with beliefs and crazy ideas coming from the human ego.

What is your truth? By being love, you raise the consciousness, the thought potential, of humanity. By being love, you raise your own vibrational frequency, elevating your awareness to pick up on varieties of thought far beyond your own. Thought is everywhere, and it is the defining characteristic of your complete Universe. But as humans, you think you own thought, as though you invented it. In truth, thought invented you, like a cell that divides to create more cells. Thought divides, or thinks of new thoughts. These new thoughts give birth to other new thoughts, just as a dandelion spreads seeds that birth new dandelions with new seeds, and so on.

You are so fixed on the doing side of life that you have missed the important side; the doing is simply a vehicle for honing the state of being.

Being precedes doing, and realizing improves and elevates being. An elevated state of being leads to elevated doing. Doing is not the end game but the inevitable outcome of being in alignment with your truth.

Being productive depends on coming back to love. Let the doing show how aligned to love you are.

The wisest of self-realized beings know that sitting without distraction brings great fortune. To be in and embrace your own space opens you up, expands you to profound new horizons. You hear the whispers from your True Self in that silence, which catapults your growth to great heights.

"I Am Not Perfect, So I Have To Get Everything Right"

When you look at life through human eyes, often what you see is colored by nontruths. In fact, often you see the complete inverse of how things really are. You may have noticed throughout the Mind-Lies journey how what you see is opposite to the truth. This explains why life is so chaotic, destructive, and unsatisfying for humanity. How can it be anything more when you are acting on belief systems that are intrinsically opposite to what is true and real? It is to be expected, really.

The Mind Lie "I need to be perfect; I need to get it right" accurately states the exact opposite of what is true. It is true that perfection exists, it is true that getting it right exists, but what is also true is that you are already both perfect and right just the way you are. Let us explore this so that the resistant mind can allow in the light.

Every human being is made with a mission in mind. Not all follow through or complete their entire mission, but even that is right and perfect. The mission is simply to be and allow your truth to unfold so that you can be an even brighter shining light. That is it. The more love and light there is on Earth, the faster all of humanity evolves. The sooner humanity evolves, the sooner new lessons and new levels of accomplishments can become available.

Humanity is, in large part, the brain, or the mind, of Mother Earth. As a human being, your mind is intended to dissolve into Mother-Earth consciousness, but instead, Mother Earth is suffering from Mind-Lie human consciousness melding with her own. This causes conflict, weighing the energy of the planet down. You need to rise above your individual and collective Mind Lies so that the planet as a whole can rise above its dark history.

Let us look at the perfection that is you. If your purpose is to shed nontruths so that you can elevate the planet, and that is perfect and right, then it can easily be said that you are perfectly on track by virtue of reading this book. That is what you are doing right now. The more nontruths you leave behind, the greater the gift you give to yourself and humanity. You are doing and being perfection personified. Planet Earth thanks you!

You may ask, "I may be perfect, but am I right?" What does it mean to be right? It means to be as your maker intended you to be. You have thoughts and beliefs that are so backward that the word *wrong* could not possibly describe them, but so what? Everyone has such thoughts and beliefs, and that is perfect and right. It is right because this part of your evolution is all part of the plan. It cannot be any other way.

All people need to realize the deepest truths before they can be rock solid in who they are meant to be. Children growing into adulthood depict this process wonderfully. Children eventually learn that throwing tantrums and yelling does not bring happiness to anyone and hopefully stop behaving in this way. Children also learn that weeing in their own beds, while it might be a short-term solution, is not a good long-term strategy. Likewise, children also learn that bullying and being mean to others results in fights or the same behavior being directed back toward them. Children learn what does and does not work, and this shapes them to become the adults they need to be. This is what is happening to humanity. You are still infants learning about tantrums—dropping bombs on each other. You are still learning about weeing in the bed—polluting your environment. And you are still learning about the need for kindness and respect for each other, because in the end how you behave all comes back to you.

You cannot reprimand a child for wetting the bed before he has been toilet trained; in the same way, you cannot reprimand yourself for behaviors bestowed on you in this era of being human. Perfection exists in everyone, as all humans have enlightened within, albeit, hidden under the MIND LIES. One is no more perfect than the other; both have perfection. You cannot say that age six is less perfect than age twenty-five because a twenty-five-year-old knows so much more. In truth, you cannot get to being twenty-five without being six first. So you are already as your maker intended you, except for one small detail, and that is for you to realize this fact.

You need to see, beyond your cultural programming, that the spark of light and life that you truly are is inherently perfect. Getting it right is the trap, the Mind Lie.

The need to get it right is directly proportionate to how right or perfect you believe yourself to be. Those who think less of themselves, who think they have much further to go to be a right human being, deal with the pressure to get their life right more than others. They are trying to correct their inadequacies in terms of what they create and achieve, but change must come the other way. The right creation comes from the mind that sees itself as already perfect. The "wrong" creation comes from a mind that sees itself as wrong, or imperfect

There is no level more perfect than where you already are. All levels are equal. You cannot get to a more perfect level. You seek greater enlightenment because you believe you will be a more perfect human being. Seeking enlightenment for this reason is back to front. Enlightenment comes from, or is, realizing the perfection of what you are, and where you are, not the denial or resistance of it.

There is no such thing as you needing to get it right. There never was, and there never will be. There is only what works and what does not. The need to get things right and perfect dissolves when you see that it once again comes down to something much simpler, much more elegant. When you are being love, when you come from love, what is created makes a loving contribution to life on Earth. Getting it right and perfect is an endless cycle depriving you of fulfillment. Do not chase this Mind Lie; it will always be a step ahead of you. The beingness of "getting it right and avoiding getting it wrong" is a Mind Lie state of being.

The mind is intrinsically flawed, which is why you can never get it right. Trying to get it right, moving away from getting it wrong, is where the problem begins. There are many versions of what is right, and the mind cannot be OK with a concept containing many versions. As is seen in some religions, there is only one way to God and heaven, and it just so happens to be that particular religion's way. Just know that getting it "right" occurs only when you have stopped trying to "get it right". It is the trying that blinds you from your existing perfection.

The mind cannot process many right answers, but the belief that there is a right way, a perfect way, can stop the truth in its tracks. If you inherently believe that there is only one right way, only one perfect solution or outcome, then the Mind Lie "I must get it right and perfect" wreaks havoc.

"There Is Only One Perfect Way, One Right Way, One Best Way, And I Need To Be The Best"

The need to get it right and be the best is actually the need to be counted. But who is counting you? Who is this mysterious group to whom you so desire to belong?

This group is made up; it does not exist in the real world, because trying to get it right to belong to some external group that gets things wrong would have you belonging to more people rather than getting it right. Where is this group you crave? How many people are actually getting it right all the time? If this group exists, it is a very small one. It is certainly not the priests or rabbis, not the politicians or business leaders, not the movie stars or celebrities. So where is this group?

It exists only in your mind. Your mind creates groups for you to belong to. In fact, the whole concept of a group of individuals is a fictitious concept conceivable only by the mind. The truth is that there are lots of minds making things up all the time, but even these coalesce into one human mind that is making stuff up all the time.

The mind says that there must be God's way or the Dalai Lama's way or the good Christian's way. Actually, there is no way; there is only being. That there even is a way is just the mind's way. To have a way is to put the cart before the horse, because only being unfolds itself into a path, not the other way around. Being and the path are one. Way does not exist; only being springs forward direct action and guidance.

Getting it right and following the one right path neglects to address your state of being, yet your state of being is what produces outcomes. Looking for the right way but ignoring your state of being will drive you away from what is actually right for you.

You ask, "How do I know that the result of my state of being will be good enough? What if my state of being does not produce the best result?" This comes back to the Mind Lies of "Who I am is not enough to get the job done" and "I do not trust in myself to get it perfect." Ultimately expressed as "I did not get enough god-given equipment to succeed". Let us explore.

"I Did Not Get Enough God-Given Equipment to Succeed"

This is one of those beliefs that keeps many of the other Mind Lies in place. Letting this one go opens up a whole new world of possibilities, such as allowing you to see the truth about many of the Mind Lies you still battle with. After all, if you believe this Mind Lie, how can you possibly see past the harder ones?

There is a widespread misconception that you need to be great at everything, especially concerning what others similar to you excel at. Yet the world needs different traits and skills, not the old cliché roles of men being carpenters and mechanics and women being housewives. Times have changed, and you need new skills for now and in the new times ahead.

Your skills and abilities are perfect for the role you are here to play. You will find that the things you truly love to do—not the things you should love or want to love but truly do love—are what you are best at. Thinking that you should excel at things you do not enjoy is a Mind Lie that reinforces this Mind Lie and others. We will clear it up for once and for all.

Do what you love, and get others to do what you do not love but still needs doing. If you cannot afford to pay others, either do a work trade so that you both get done what needs doing or focus solely on what you love doing. Given the income from the Universe validating that you are finally playing your role, you will have more than enough to pay others.

Only by focusing on what you love to do will you succeed.

If you look at everyone else's success, your mind will have you believe you need their "right stuff" in order to succeed. In truth, their right stuff would have you fail dismally at what you yourself need to do to be successful.

You only need your right stuff, and of that, you have plenty!

"I Am The Cause Of My Parents' Hardship And Suffering"

You have heard your parents say how much they sacrificed, endured, and suffered as a result of having children. But you may not ever hear how much their suffering way of being affects you. What is even rarer to hear is the actual truth.

It may seem that this Mind Lie of being the cause of your parents' suffering is unrelated to others, but it is related to the clearing of the previous Mind Lie of not being given enough to succeed. Clearing the Mind Lie of "If my right stuff was all I needed, why did my parents complain so much? Why did they have me feel not enough?" helps the last one integrate much more deeply.

You may have been raised to feel like a complete burden to your parents, that you single-handedly ruined their lives, destroyed their marriage, and were the reason for their financial scarcity. Between school fees, your demand for the latest sports shoes, new toys, and so on, you were the ultimate cause of their miserable, unhappy existence; at least, that is how your parents chose to see it.

What is the truth about your being a burden to your parents and causing their misery? It is simple: people blame others—in this case, you—for how they feel about themselves. They feel like the burden, they feel like they are ruining their lives and yours, they feel responsible for all the sacrifices you had to make as a child, and they feel responsible for your unhappiness. They had hoped to be more for you than their parents were for them, but instead, you are the constant reminder of just how much they failed at this. The result is resentful, blaming parents.

Knowing this truth may not immediately take away the feelings you have about yourself, so what will? It is realizing that all those claims about you were false. They were made up to keep you from being the angel you came to your family to be. Consider what would be more confronting to your parents than being responsible for ruining your life. It would be being responsible for your greatness. This is infinitely more terrifying for a parent. When you were born into your family, one of two things can happen. Either you get embraced as the being of light that you are, thus allowing you to help elevate your parents from a low consciousness into a higher consciousness, or you get rejected, accused of doing all kinds of things to your parents' relationship and being the burden that you were told you were. The former requires that your parents were prepared to look at themselves and at truths versus nontruths. The latter took no introspection at all.

If you were raised being taught that you were nothing, a nobody, a waste of space, then you will also have a hard time dealing with a newborn baby. Having a child is scary—not scary in the sense of responsibility, but scary in the sense of enlightenment. You might ask, "Since when does a child have anything to do with enlightenment?" Since always! That is the point.

Children are pure human beings brimming with truth and clarity, innocence and sensitivity. They are truth mirrors. They show up when you are off track, and they teach you patience and love for another. But the scariest, most terrifying thing children do is to show you that you can be loved, that you are worthy of love.

Children love Mom and Dad, no matter what. For many parents, this is too much to bear, because it is the opposite of what their parents taught them. So the children are squashed, criticized, condemned, and blamed so that the parents do not need to see what is staring them in the face every time their children look at them with pure love: that they, Mom and Dad, are needed, worthwhile, lovable: all the things they refuse to believe about themselves. Children are essentially trying to convince their parents—who see themselves as not good enough, who have become invested in this view—that this is not the truth, even though this self-image is all the parents know and cling to. It is just too much; it rocks the very foundation of their existence, because their identities depend on viewing themselves as not good enough. After all, every decision they have ever made was based on this view. Who are these children to question their entire lives?

The truth is, you were resented, blamed, hated, and maybe even abused—not because you ruined your parents' lives, but because you challenged your Mom and Dad's self-loathing opinion of themselves. They dealt with that the only way they knew how: by sending their self-hating energy, thoughts, and intentions right back at you. This happened right until you believed their thoughts were your own, until you felt about yourself what they felt about themselves.

This is tragic in some respects but potent in many others. It is tragic because it was not just one party that was denied self-love but two generations at once. It is potent in the sense that you get to see how terrified you are of being loved and of loving yourself. This is the major truth, and you have done some devious things to avoid it.

As a child, how can you possibly be the cause of your parents' suffering? If they suffered, it is because they caused it. If you were made to feel as though it was your fault, it is because they chose suffering over being like you. They chose to ignore your gifts and resented what you had to bring. They chose to run from you instead of returning to being like you. This is why so many kids feel rejected by their parents; what the parent is rejecting is his or her own inner child, and nothing shows that up better than having a child.

Ultimately, the cause of your parents' hardship was their own resistance to themselves, to being childlike, to allowing in self-love when love was being given to them. In truth, they resented that they were the cause of your hardship, and they blamed you for ever having to feel that resentment. But what did they really resent? That they could not bring themselves to truly love you as you deserved to be loved. You have been believing this Mind Lie, blaming yourself for ruining their lives, feeling their resentment, believing you were insufficient to make them happy, when all along you were exactly what they needed to be happy and more; they just could not bring themselves to allow it in.

The truth is that you were not the cause of your parents' unhappiness but rather the access to endless happiness.

You offered self-realization; self-love; the return to childhood; and the return to playfulness, rest, and fun. It is that which was rejected, not you yourself.

A child is the ultimate blessing, but adults prioritize their careers, their problems, and other people in order to avoid what is on offer through their children: self-realization, self-love, and so much more.

"Being An Adult Is Better Than Being A Child"

The idea of adulthood being better than childhood certainly sounds like truth, and if you ask a child, he or she would more than likely agree. But this type of evidence-gathering is hiding an important truth from you: a child is the cure to being an adult. It is this that parents resist about their children. Believing the Mind Lie that being an adult is better than being a child, many parents get stuck being adults instead of being with their children. Children heal adults. In many respects, being an adult is an illness. You have lost your joy, your moment-to-moment presence, your excitement and anticipation for life, your curiosity and love of life, your adventurous spirit. You have become a slave to money, respect, and completing your work.

Becoming an adult is not what you hoped it would be. And what turned you into an adult? Was it your age or the first time you got drunk or had sex? No, it was when you started believing in all your Mind Lies, especially this one. An adult is essentially a child corrupted by Mind Lies.

It seems that today's version of adulthood has lost its way and its point. You must return to being a responsible, enlightened child. That is the perfect adult. A child is a reminder of what enlightened living truly looks like.

Being child-like does not make you an irresponsible adult, but being adult-like does. An 'adult' is a label just like being a 'human being'. Both are not the truth of You. Unveiling the truth, as you are doing for yourself here, is what releases you back to being child-like. This is the most responsible thing you could ever do.

You are the stuff of happiness. Now you have the opportunity with your own children to let them reveal just how lovable you really are, and who better to share your success with, who better to give it meaning, than with those who love you unconditionally?

Is being an adult better than being a child? It seems being like a child is the best adult you can be.

"I Am Not Equipped To Be A Good Parent, Let Alone A Great One"

This Mind Lie is a burden that you and many others, even those who make parenting look easy, feel. With a plethora of "expert advice" available, it is easy for the mind to have you feel that you are forever getting it wrong with your child.

The first thing to realize is that not all kids need the same thing. Most preconceptions about what is required of you as a parent are false. To fully understand this, you need to have a better grasp of a child's higher purpose and your role in helping him or her fulfill it.

Children come to this Earth with a wide range of paths ahead of them, with differing purposes to fill. This is where the mind likes to play tricks. It begins by having you feel that all children are alike, that they need more or less the same upbringing—the ideal one, at that—and there is nothing you can do to get it right. These are all Mind Lies. What is not mentioned in the traditional view of parenting is that you are as much a part of their purpose as their being here to live it is. Without knowing what their purpose is and what your role is, how can you possibly gauge whether or not you have what your child needs from you? In this case, ignorance is not bliss; ignorance means self-judgment.

The truth is that parents are chosen by their children because those particular parents serve a greater purpose: preparing their children for fulfilling the children's purposes. It is like a running shoe: you choose a shoe that not only fits but is also designed with a specific purpose in mind, such as for tennis, running, or walking. As that parent, you are the running shoe, perfect for your child, so you have to know that you have exactly what it takes to be your child's best parent. If you did not have what it takes for your child, you would be someone else's parent. So breathe a sigh of relief, because everything you are right now is everything they need right now. Case in point: you are reading this book right now; what could be a more perfect thing to do as a parent than that?

The next thing to understand is that children have five basic needs: love, attention, food, water, and shelter. That is it! I point this out because many parents believe that their children need adventure, the latest toys, seeing the biggest blockbuster movies, endless playdates, Star Wars Legos, the latest academic fads, and so. In truth, the less children are given over and above the five key ingredients, the healthier and more evolved they will be.

Let us explore these five ingredients so you can understand what is needed.

Love

To provide your children with love is to show them kindness, respect, and patience, to have them feel that you think the world of them and that they are an important contribution to you and your family. That is it.

This is the single most important thing you can do for your children, and it is free. Having a foundation of love sets them up for a positive experience in all areas of life. It has them feel loved, which has them understand that they are love, and of course they get to believe they are lovable. If your children believe they are lovable, they can love themselves, and loving themselves avoids their having to live lives full of Mind Lies and then needing to look for love in all the wrong places.

What does coming from love look like? Let us consider food and water, as many believe that just giving a child food and water comes before love or even from love. However, many children are given food and water not from a space of love, but from a space of guilt, hate, resentment, and anger. What kind of diet do you think these children receive? A diet that reflects guilt (too many sweets and too much unhealthy food), hatred (not enough fresh and nutritious food), resentment (ill-prepared food and too much fast food), and anger (food that ends up being toxic). Without love, children are not given the right food, the right amount of food, or enough water, and they are not taught the blessing that food and water are in their lives.

Attention

Does giving attention to children mean playing with them all hours of the day? Does it mean your children get their way all the time? Does it mean making sure your children have the childhood other kids have or the childhood you never had? No, no, and no.

Attention simply refers to prioritizing your children, focusing on them, and giving them attention when they fall into nontruth so that Mind Lies do not solidify. It means being in their world enough to make the best decisions for them—not for you or your social standing, their career prospects, or academic achievements, but for them and their DNA-based life purpose. Think of it this way: if society is doing it, do the opposite. Remember, the world does not need more clones, high achievers, or ambitious corporate climbers. It needs people being nurtured into their higher purpose, being their truth.

What better way to help your children achieve a space of truth than for you to be in your truth, living your truth!

Food

Providing good food for your children is easier than you think. Being a great parent involves understanding that how you prepare food and how it is presented to your children is actually more important than the food itself. Loving mealtimes do more for the body than the food itself. If children resent their food or even hate it, then a salad, no matter how nutritious it is, is being digested as resentment and hatred. Food takes on the energy of both the one preparing it and the state of being of the one eating it. Be careful to prepare and serve your food with love, so that it is love your kids eat and drink rather than the energy of Mom and Dad just ticking boxes. Remember, the more in your truth you become, the more truthful foods you and your children will be attracted to buying and eating. Focus on your state of being, and the quality and nutritional value of food will follow.

Water

Water, or lack of it, is a big one for children. But water does not refer just to drinking copious amounts of it; it is also about swimming in it, loving it, and revering it. Water is the most magical substance on this planet, and educating children about its true properties is helpful. For example, as does food, water takes on different energies. Play with your kids when they drink, and get them to use their thoughts and intentions to send different energies into their water: self-love, courage, self-belief, forgiveness, gratitude, kindness, and compassion. Children can even play with the energy of crystals by placing them in bottles or at the bottoms of their glasses. Be sure to choose an appropriate container.

Swimming in nutritious water with minimal chemicals is also important. Ocean, river, and lake swims are very cleansing and healing and teach kids the importance of keeping rubbish out of Earth's waterways. Get kids to fall in love with their friend, water!

Shelter

There is much about building and construction that humanity does not yet understand. Buildings are all about cost, structure and aesthetics, but what about how your shelter feels on the inside? You have had the experience of walking into a house or office and feeling the different energy, but what about getting smart with the energy, beyond anything Feng Shui currently addresses? There are many homes and other buildings that not only allow in negative energies and energetic attacks but actually invite them. These energies come from people and electrical devices. There is a whole science yet to be accessed on optimizing energy for wellbeing and accessing higher states of consciousness, something many office buildings fail dismally at. Another example, hospitals are meant to be places of healing and rest, yet they are devoid of any natural elements, the sources of life on Earth. Where are the plants, the natural materials, the stones? What about including energy-amplifying materials such as crystals and copper? When considering your home for your children, make it an energetic fortress so that all the negative energy is constantly cleaned out and stays out. Then design it in such a way that the good energy inside gets magnified, keeping your kids clean and protected from negative energy. This action certainly ranks high when considering what it takes to be a great parent.

"Success Will Not Be Fun Because I Have Children"

The Mind Lie that children prevent adults from having fun with success leads many adults to choose never to have kids. They may claim all kinds of reasons, such as, "It is just not for me" or "I will ruin their lives," but at the heart of this choice is the fear that kids will ruin *their* lives and subtract from any success they hope to achieve.

You, like many others, believe that kids impair your life experience by limiting your freedom and quality of experiences. In truth, children enhance life experiences far more than they subtract from them. What most parents forget is that there is a time and a place for children. Just as there is not always a time and place to be asleep, there is not always a time and place for kids to be around you. Do not feel guilty about this. Some experiences are not appropriate for them, just as they would feel restricted or limited if you were present for certain things.

Be OK with kids-free time and having experiences away from them. Equally, be open to having only certain experiences with them. These can be the same experiences, such as going to the beach. Sometimes it is fun to have them there to play with, sometimes it is best not to. Be open to a balance of including children in half of your experiences and half the time not. They need independence as much as you do, despite what they say in the moment. Resenting your kids because you choose to lug them around everywhere does not serve either party.

There is another Mind Lie hidden underneath this one, which is almost invisible. It has to do with your notions of success, because when you imagine success, it is rarely if ever imagined with children in mind. You do not see rock stars or movie stars in Hollywood break open the champagne bottle and start partying surrounded by their children. All movies and countless success stories depict success as being free from children. It is this societal perception that causes many people to fear success as a parent. They ask themselves, "What if my kids ruin my success?" or "What if I do not achieve that vision of success I have in mind?"

In truth, having kids is what makes you successful. You have created something that constantly shows you how loved, needed, and important you are.

Not many things in life do that. In fact, many things do just the opposite. So congratulations to you for having children; they are a miracle that brings in enlightenment so much quicker.

The next thing to understand is that success with kids looks very different from success without them. Children are the fast track to healing your past, and it is this that makes parents (and non-parents) shake in their boots. By now you have come to see how quick kids are to push your buttons, and it is unpleasant, frustrating, and downright stressful. But the truth is, they can only push something that no longer serves you. They hold up a mirror to say, "Look Mom and Dad, you still believe these crazy Mind Lies! Is it not time you let them go? They are just holding you back! Imagine what would be possible if you got to see the truth!"

Success with kids is infinitely greater than success without them. You can only get so far without them, but you can go all the way with kids!

You just have to realize the mirror is not the problem; it is your resistance to let go of your past!

Success with kids means being able to break this new generation free from the generational burdens, fears, and limitations that came before them, the ones that came from your generation, your parents' generation, and the ones before that. It is about correcting a mindset and invigorating their thinking with new possibilities—with truth— rather than being slaves to the rat-race mentality.

Set your children free by allowing them and success to coexist. A success mindset changes a generation in a profound way. It does not spoil them; absence and neglect spoil them. Being seen as the center of your success enriches them and enables them to create great things. It is true to say children are the future, so take a stand and decide whether the future is based in truth or on another generation filled with Mind Lies.

Is it true that success will not be fun with children? It will not be success without them.

"I Am Not Smart Enough"

When you relate to yourself as simply human, you default to a comparison state of being, so it is easy to fall into self-doubt and to doubt your own intelligence. Comparison shows up when you believe the Mind Lie that there is always someone somewhere who knows more than you, is more capable than you, learns faster than you, deals with life better than you, and so on. There are always bigger fish than you, thanks to comparison.

But what comparison does not reveal is the connectedness within all of humanity, the oneness to each other, and the oneness to the Intelligence that birthed humanity. It does not show the symbiotic nature of life on Earth and how you are part of a far greater intelligence that underpins all matter and all minds. Comparison fails to put you at the center of this Intelligence; it puts you on the far outer edge and hides a marvelous truth that *behind all Mind Lies, your very nature is Intelligence.*

It is simply a Mind Lie to believe that you are not smart enough. It would be like the sky believing that it is not blue enough or a tree believing that it is not tree enough. Your very nature is sublime intelligence.

How much of this intelligence is needed to fulfill the DNA-based life purpose varies from person to person. You are equipped to draw on what you need—not what someone else needs but exactly what you need. You do not need what others have been given; you just need what you have been given. Believing you need to be like others, is what makes comparison thrive.

Intelligence is innate. It is in every cell, every organ, every muscle. It is even in the air molecules you breathe. The Universe is intelligence.

Mother Nature is an example of this Universal Intelligence (Ui).

To judge yourself as not smart enough without knowing your purpose is the same as a young bee judging itself for not knowing how to make a web. But once that bee realizes that it is here to pollinate flowers and make honey, it recognizes that it has more than ample intelligence to do what it came here to do.

Unfortunately, your world has become such that you think you should be able to do what the smartest person you know can do. You have lost sight of the true purpose of being here. How much of this intelligence you get to funnel down depends on your mind's Mind-Lie filter, which leaves much of the intelligence untapped and unused.

What kind of intelligence matters most? The most pertinent answer is that the most important intelligence is the one inside you. It is an innate gift you have been given, and it feeds you all the necessary answers needed for you to evolve and contribute to the human and Earth ecosystems. It is not an intelligence that requires a book or a college degree; it already knows. It is the one Intelligence that writes the best books and creates incredible learning courses. It is the mind of Intelligence that is never wrong, never fails, and can see well into the future to ensure that you make the necessary course corrections in order to stay on track to being healthy, wealthy, and wise.

What makes you not smart is twofold: (1) the belief that you need to be smart the way other people are smart or the belief that everyone should be smart like you, and (2) the plethora of beliefs that block the sublime Intelligence from coming through you in the same way it does for all living things. Intelligence is not hard-wired, like many would have you believe. Intelligence, sublime intelligence, is an energy—a consciousness that is available to all.

Therefore, it is not about how smart you are—because you are a genius—it is about how diligent you are in accessing this field of inner Intelligence and how committed you are to the process. Do not be easily distracted by what everyone else is doing or believes you should be doing. It is surprising how many things are believed to be more important than accessing this Intelligence by those who do not understand its true power.

The world would look very different if people spent the same time, discipline, and commitment accessing their inner intelligence as they do getting high grades in school. Can you imagine how lives would be transformed all over the globe if seventeen-year-olds and adults said to themselves, "All right, I am going to spend the next three years, minimum five hours a day, learning to access this infinite Intelligence inside me." The economy would go through the roof because it would not be dependent on people getting jobs or spending money to support those without jobs. It would be built upon universal expansion principles of people contributing what they are actually here to contribute.

The "I" that needs to be smarter is in need not because it is not already smart enough, but because it believes it is not enough. Being smart is just another way to deal with this inadequacy. The need to be enough is such a distraction that it prohibits true Intelligence from becoming accessible.

The more you recognize how enough you are and the more aligned with your life purpose you become, the smarter you will become. Intelligence is an energy, and it is attracted to those who need it, not to those who squander it.

You do not need to be smart in the way other people are smart, this would be a waste of you. Be smart in a way that is needed, in a way that no one has ever been smart at before. This is how you make a difference. This is your life purpose. The sooner you see yourself as the knowing Universe, the sooner its knowing becomes your knowing.

Are you smart enough? Not while you believe you are your mind; you are only smart enough when you know you are beyond your mind, natures mind.

"I Always Fail At Being Successful"

First of all, understand that it is a sheer impossibility to fail at being successful; this is yet another Mind Lie. Failure happens either before or after success, but not during it. You are either being a success or you are being a failure; you cannot be both at the same time. Success is to be enjoyed, not failed at, not worried about, not panicked over, and—from a certain perspective—not even have effort spent on it to maintain. It is a place of grace and ease, where building on your successes is light and effortless. Success does not need the same amount of effort it took to obtain it; otherwise, it would not be called success. But do not be fooled; just because many people do put the same amount of effort into both building and maintaining success does not mean that it is required of them— nor will it be required of you.

The true nature of success is that it is virtually self-sustaining, meaning that as long as you remain successful in your beingness, the success will continue to flow.

You live in a society that has giant measures of success, such as buying your first Porsche, becoming a billionaire, or becoming a famous movie star. These are just attempts at quantifying success, but you can achieve these things and still not experience success.

Success is a realization, a level of awareness and consciousness that precedes physical result or outcome. This heightened consciousness nearly always stems from a series of incremental achievements and experiences; basically it is the sum total of many, many life lessons.

Success always happens to those with minds open enough to learn and expand. Success never happens to those with closed minds, because the very definition of success is to grow and expand, to reach new heights, and only an open mind makes this possible.

Why should you have an open mind? Because a closed mind is already a failure; it is a failed mind-space. People say that failure comes from quitting, but failure happens much earlier than that—it comes from being closed. A closed mind is a mind that has quit before a task can even begin. The closed minds of the world are quitters who are too ashamed to admit it. They are dangerous, as they try to bring those with open minds down to their mediocre level. This is not enlightened thinking; it is endarkened.

As long as you believe in yourself, you have already succeeded.

Sometimes the physical world takes a little longer to catch up and reflect what has already happened in your mind. Success in the mind comes before success occurs out in the world.

"If I Do Not Create Something Big, I Will Get Bored"

Why must you create to be content? Since when is contentment about doing and creating? This is a Mind Lie hard at work. Can contentment be like any other state of being, simply a way of being without any necessary prerequisites? Of course it can, because contentment comes from realization, and realization can come from creation. But it does not need to; in fact, realization just is. It exists in the ether, waiting to land on the shoulders of anyone open to seeing the truth. And so it goes with contentment.

To realize that you have arrived brings contentment. To realize that you are loved brings contentment. To realize that you are one brings contentment. Realization, not creation or achievement, is the source of contentment.

Realization does not require creation, achievement, or ambition.

If you do create something without realization, then you will be bored. Without realization, you will believe you need to create and will continue to create to be distracted from the simple yet agonizing Mind Lie of "I am boring."

Could it be that you cannot stand yourself and that, unless you achieve great things, you may never achieve greatness? Are you the source—or the subject—of your boredom? Yes. Your boredom resides in you, as you! So why hang on to it? What is the benefit, the upside? Your mind has you convinced that unless you create something big, others will not find you interesting, respectable, or inspirational. In truth, what others believe or think of you is not the point. Believing this Mind Lie avoids dealing with yet another obvious and undeniable truth:

If you feel bored or that you are boring, it is the mind that bores you. But You are anything but boring.

You are already what you desire to create. You are a work of art, a sheer miracle of nature, inspired, unmatched anywhere in the Universe. You are sublime. Contentment comes from this realization.

You do not need to be more, you do not need to do more. You just need to realize, "I am the Divine!"

"Everyone Has Their Act Together Except Me"

Comparison is the basis of all self-doubt. Without comparison, you would be much quicker to embrace and love yourself. People always show their best side, so to an outsider, peoples' lives look far more on track than they really are. The lesson here is not to take satisfaction from the comparison but to realize that other people's lives are not and cannot be your benchmark. You are sentencing yourself to mediocrity if you continue to use others' achievements as your goal post.

Be present to what you have achieved rather than what you have not. This is not some positive-thinking ploy to make you feel better about your meager accomplishments. It is a ladder to help you climb above the level of situation you find yourself in now, no matter what level of success you have achieved. To doubt yourself by marginalizing or refusing to acknowledge how far you have come creates a holding pattern that continues or worsens your situation.

To succeed beyond where you are requires acknowledging, being present to how far you have come. Only then will the next level become available. It is like a game of pool: despite the rut you were in, once you sink one ball you have the confidence to sink more balls. Sinking a ball is a great affirmation of your success; you can see that you are OK as you are.

One of life's great secrets is that it requires recognition of your accomplishments, so much so that it will not feed you any new opportunities until you understand this. To acknowledge your own greatness, even in small doses, is a direct route to catapulting you higher than ever before.

Part of the need for comparison stems from another Mind Lie: that life is a race—the Human Race. But life is anything but a race. Rather, it an opportunity for you to contribute toward the greater good of humanity, for the Earth.

Another Mind Lie that plays havoc here is the notion that everyone is created equal, when they are not. This concept has been twisted by the mind and used to hold you back rather than propel you forward. What this statement originally meant was that all mankind shared the spark of the Divine within, but by no stretch of the imagination is everyone on equal footing, nor do you need to be; this was never the plan.

You are created with a fundamental purpose and different skills, tools, and circumstances to achieve it. The only true measure of your success is certainly not someone else's success but rather your level of awakening on your journey, how much self-love you are learning to allow in, in each moment. This is not comparing yourself to another but to where you have been. Nor is this measure of success a judgment, because self-love is simply the doorway to greater experiences and higher states of consciousness.

Those who authentically have their act together and are achieving fulfilment and success in a way that you aspire to did not achieve it outside of themselves. They never achieved it by looking at what everyone else was doing. They achieved it the good old-fashioned way: by working on themselves, feeling into their DNA-based life purpose, honoring it, and pursuing it no matter what distractions were thrown at them, irrespective of where anyone else around them was at.

You were born with a GPS guiding you toward success, but you do not listen to it for the simple reason that you are too preoccupied with which way everyone else is going. You cannot hear your own GPS when your head is out the window watching all the other cars go by. By acting this way, you will forever buy into this Mind Lie and feel that everyone has their act together more than you do.

The sooner you stop focusing "out there," the sooner you will be able to realize that you have enough of your act together to be used as a springboard into a greater You, a greater life experience.

It is your inner resources that propel you forward. The reason you are where you are right now is because you have never truly realized this.

When you start going within, you will stop going without.

Time is the trickster. It has become the benchmark against which everything is measured: how long success takes, how much faster everyone achieved success than you, how much younger they were than you when they achieved success, and so on. But what if time were not the measure? What if you were the measure? Consider what happens when you take time out of the equation. What do you have left?

What remains is what you have and what you do not have. If you want to compare, you can look at what others have and do not have. Now remove the comparison. What is left? Simply the possibility to keep creating, keep experiencing; there are no should-haves, no benchmarks, there is just your life. There is nowhere to be, nothing you should have done by now. There is just you.

Remember, you will have your act together only when you stop comparing yourself to others. This in itself is the definition of having your act together.

"Time Is Running Out"

It would be difficult to find any Mind Lie that causes more stress and exerts more pressure than the belief that time is running out. But like all those before it, this Mind Lie is not true. It certainly feels real, but this is one of those forefather Mind Lies that keeps many others in play.

You are convinced that it is true. You think to yourself, "Surely this one has to be the truth. The writing is on the wall and on the clocks, the calendars, your phone—time is ticking away, and worst of all, I am running out of it." But it is not the truth. Something much deeper is occurring. Let us explore.

Time as you know it—the ticking by of minutes and hours—is as real and instrumental in the Universe as the television schedule for cable TV: it is made up, and it has its basis in the past. It has become your enemy rather than your guide. The time that you know, as measured throughout humanity, is fictional; it is just a bunch of highly organized numbers on man-made devices. It is nothing more than a measurement of something over which you have no grasp. But before you begin wondering how your day would function without knowing the time, let us clear this belief before it leads you to your grave sooner than required.

Time is not real but is a fictional notion that you abide by, similar to the mind, really. It is made up! But like all other Mind Lies, it looks real, and you will find plenty of evidence for it because you are the lens from which everything is observed and understood. You are the lens that filters out truth.

When I say time does not actually exist, I mean it. If you were beyond your physical self, you would see time as a choice: there are varying levels of awareness, variations of the past, variations on the now, and many variations of the future. You are aware of time as you understand it not because that is what is real but because *now*—or whatever time you are conscious of—is what you have made up in your mind. You will not find time on other planets, you will not find it in the stars. If you were a star, you would not be aware of time. If you were Mother Earth, you would not be aware of time, other than in the sense of the damage it is doing to the human race. Time is the mind's greatest tool to keep itself alive and thriving.

Time was meant to be a way to harmonize with the planet, not a way to create complete discord, a total lack of harmony with the world and each other as humans. Time exists on Earth as a pressure cooker, rushing people toward certain objectives, outcomes, milestones, and achievements, and ultimately toward death.

Without time, your identity would melt away, because so much of it depends on this external benchmark, which serves as a measure of the level of success you have or have not achieved. But time is in you; it does not exist out there in the Universe. Time is human-based. It lives in you; it always has, and now it will hopefully cease to do so.

How do you see beyond time, if it is such a fundamental way of seeing the world? Let us deconstruct it. Time "out there" is a manifestation of the mind's way of limiting what you see. If humanity could see into the future, it would be powerful enough to change its future. To be blind to such outcomes condemns you to whatever outcomes you are currently on track toward. To be gifted with sight makes you impossible to control, and ultimately, to enslave. But you are a slave right now, a slave to your mind. You are a slave so disempowered that you cannot even see you are one. Time is yet another way of controlling you, moving you away from expansion and into denial of your true reality, of the existence of You, which is inherently timeless and indefinable.

You can always be suspicious of something when it has a label, a definition, a beginning and end point. Can the Universe be labeled—defined and seen as having a beginning and an end point? Nothing that exists as truth can be defined as being just one thing. Labels and time are too definitive for your Universe, so this should again raise your suspicion.

A label is no different from time in that it attempts to manage the unmanageable, define the undefinable. Look at time from this same perspective. You are attempting to live your life within a designated time period as best as you know how, but life is not confined to your lifetime, nor is matter in this Universe. This means you see yourself, your life, as the central theme to life on Earth. You hurry around as if you own the place, but you do not own it. You *are* it. You belong to it, but ownership is another Mind Lie. Wait a few years, and you will see how little you and others own planet Earth. It owns you!

Imagine yourself hovering in the International Space Station orbiting the Earth. Would you perceive time in the same way? Of course not. If you want to believe there is time, then do so. If you want to limit your perspective to one lifetime, that is no problem, either. Alternatively, if you would like to rise above time and just be, you will find that to be much more nourishing for your human body.

Time is your way of setting a parameter around what constitutes your life. But instead of using it to empower you, which is what you believe you are doing, the end result is quite different. To circle time around your life defines you as one short-lived creature, unrelated and disconnected to humanity and the Earth. To define yourself as one lifetime at a time sentences you to the very essence of your identity, of who you believe you are in any moment.

Without time, who are you? Without time, you are not fixed; you just exist as changing matter. Without time, you would not know yourself in the same way you think of yourself now. It is the Mind Lie of time that says, "Right now, and pretty much most of my life, I have been this way. Given the amount of time I have left, it is most likely that I will be this way to the end. It is just the way I am." Wrong!

You are indefinable. You are awareness breathing through a disappearing mask of one belief after another, a mask that is not called your name but is called humanity. When you believe that you are more than time, you see yourself as humanity. The more you transcend the paradigm of time, the less you see yourself as humanity. You see yourself as the life force powering humanity. When you see yourself like this, you come to realize, "How can I ever run out of time?"

You run out of your one body, but who needs to hang on to things once they are broken or damaged?

Time has been seen through your individual lifetime, but when you go beyond this, you realize that energy lasts forever, so what is the hurry? It is not even time that is the problem, though. It is how you relate to it, how you give yourself timeframes for practically everything you engage in—time limits, as if time is limited.

So it is the mind that is running out of time, not You. You are running out of the mind and its grip over your life.

It is your attachment to having everything complete in this lifetime that causes so much anguish. Believing all the Hollywood clichés like, you only live once, you must make the most of life, live on the edge, feel alive—are a death sentence, not a pathway to living a healthy and productive life. These beliefs invariably come from another Mind Lie: "My life needs to be meaningful."

"My Life Needs To Be Meaningful"

It must be said that meaning cannot come from trying to have your life mean something. Meaning is a virtue all on its own; either something has meaning or it does not. You cannot give your life any more meaning than it already has, for that is a Mind Lie and why you try so hard to make meaning out of everything.

Meaning just is or is not. Purpose, on the other hand, is different from meaning. A DNA-based life purpose inherently has meaning. Life has a purpose; therefore, life is inherently meaningful. Can you really add more meaning to something that is already full of meaning? Perhaps you are confusing contribution with meaning: "If I make my life about contribution, surely that gives it more meaning." False. Contribution does not equate to a meaningful life. Contribution is about how meaningful your life is to others, but it has nothing to do with how meaningful your life is to you yourself.

In the moments of reflection on how your life was lived, on how meaningful your life was, you will not be looking at contribution but at sense of presence—at how deeply immersed you were in every moment, for it is your state of being that derives meaning. Your state of being just is. How present were you to your state of being? Or did it escape you while you were too busy creating meaning and trying to make your life more purposeful?

Meaning is in the awareness, akin to depth of observation. Look at each experience you are having now. Are they each meaningful? Do not confuse the doing with the being, though. Doing does not generate meaning; only being generates meaning. This is not *being* in the way I have spoken about it so far. The question is "who you are being about your being?". Is your being deriving meaning? Or is your being overlooking the meaning, too busy focusing on the doing, on the achieving, on making the most out of the short life you have?

Your need to have meaning in your life results in your life not having meaning.-You miss out on seeing life just as it is, as having meaning. It does not need to be added to, because when you add to it to create more meaning, you lose sight of life's inherent meaning.

What drives this need for more and more meaning? The answer is for the mind to have a purpose. If your life has meaning, then who you are is meaningful, and there is nothing your identity wants more than meaning.

Meaning is to your identity like fuel is to a fire. You think meaning is good for you, but meaning is one of the greatest distractions on Earth, spreading itself throughout humanity. If you are preoccupied with your interpretation of meaning and acquiring it in your life, you quickly lose connection with what is actually meaningful. In your pursuit of being meaningful, you cease connecting to your inner knowing of true meaning, your true purpose. You supplement the authentic for half-baked human notions that are not worth anything.

In summary, you cannot add meaning to your life without losing real meaning. You cannot grab meaning outside of yourself, because that is not where it exists. You will never be a meaningful person because you are not a person; you are not any one thing. You cannot add something to something that is everything. Meaning is not found in an activity or in the mind. It is found in the space that is being occupied by activity and the mind. Meaning is not in the content but in the context.

Meaning comes from being love. In this space, love is received and love is given. That is true meaning.

This is why life is inherently meaningful; because love and life are one. How much you choose to access that meaning by being in the space of love determines exactly how much meaning you experience. But can you trust yourself to do this?

"I Do Not Trust Myself, And I Cannot Rely On Myself"

I could go on and on about how trustworthy you are and make you feel warm and fuzzy, but this is about truth, is it not? So, to make this point short and simple, you cannot trust yourself. Your "self" is unreliable and untrustworthy but not unlikable. This is because the minute you dislike this part of yourself is the minute things really start to go bad.

The you that cannot be trusted is only this way because it feels neglected. It is in itself neglect, a big gaping hole in the fabric of time and space, a part of consciousness that has been starved of truth. It is essentially the opposite of truth. While the opposite of truth and its repercussions may be unlikable, to not like this is to dislike opposites in your reality. These opposites are necessary; they are the pairs you see and experience every day: hot and cold, night and day, light and dark, and so on. These pairs are what make you whole.

Pairs are the defining characteristic of your Universe—not separation, just pairs. They may seem disconnected, but they are not. Nothing is separate. To state otherwise would be like saying you want a one-ended stick, so you chop off its opposite end. Not possible, right? The stick will always have two ends; it is a spectrum from one end to the other, as are all pairs.

The opposite pairing of "I distrust myself" is "I am trust."

The energy of realizing that you are pure trust is the next level of your experience to be had. To reach this level, you must recognize that the self that cannot be trusted but deeply desires to be is the self that has no say in the matter, for it is not the real You. Quenching its thirst is futile and impossible.

When you are being your old self, your small self, you are trying to compensate for all those areas in which you still feel small. This creates behaviors and outcomes that you deem as untrustworthy and unreliable. Acting from fear and self-doubt has you be untrustworthy and unreliable, not just to others, but for yourself. Trying to prove you are trustworthy and reliable is of the mind. When you can recognize this, you make the transition to the trustworthy You, and into the awareness that "I am trust."

You can now see that being trust is not a matter of layering false belief and confidence onto yourself but rather of seeing the delineation between your small self and your true You.

To help with this process, realize that there is this persona floating in your field of awareness, like a cloud of belief systems that so desperately wants to be real. It exists around you and has done so for so long that it feels like you; it is how you identify yourself. But it is not You.

It is this self that is untrustworthy, not because it is bad or mean, but because it is inherently incomplete and not whole.

If you feed this aspect, it gets stronger. If you starve it, it gets weaker. But what does feeding it versus starving it even look like? This is where society has it all backward. To feed it means to loathe it, hate it, wish it were not there. It already feels this way about itself, so stop encouraging it! Hating yourself, as you are identifying with it, also feeds it. To starve it means to see it as a natural transition for you, from one end of the stick to the other, from emptiness to fullness, from self-hatred to self-love. To love and embrace its existence is the fastest way to starve it out.

But as part of society, you are taught to hate and reject what is wrong, bad, evil, and dark. How perfect that the mind has been so clever as to keep itself alive in humanity by encouraging you to hate everything it represents.

The good news is that just being in this awareness has moved you light years from where you were fifteen minutes ago. Awareness is power; hiding or running away from this shadow self is "Self"-defeating. It is a catch twenty-two: If you resist the idea that "I cannot trust myself," you fall deeper into it. If you accept it, you immediately rise above it. But there is something else you can do: see the truth in it! The truth is to be one with it, meaning to embrace it as a necessary part of your journey.

Every time you lapse back into your untrustworthy self, you will receive another incentive to put yourself back on track. How could you possibly get more on track without these nudges from your shadow self? Allow it to guide you to seeing deeper into your True Self. Best of all, realize that this is the most trustworthy thing you can do.

"I Disappoint Myself"

Do you expect more from yourself than what you actually get? You must; after all, how can you be truly disappointed in yourself if you didn't have benchmarks? But where are these benchmarks? Can you locate them? Can you define them? Who put them there? How do you even recognize them? Are they fixed or constantly shifting?

In truth, benchmarks are invisible; there are no set benchmarks at all. Benchmarks float, just like the rest of your identity. You do not really know the degree to which you get something wrong, you just know that it is sufficient for you to be disappointed. This is the same as you not knowing the degree to which you yourself are not enough; you only know with absolute certainty that you are not.

In truth, You do not have enough reason to be disappointed in yourself. This is the problem with this Mind Lie. Being a disappointment is imaginary. It is insane, actually. It is not based in actuality. For example - if you achieved 90 percent of your target but fell short on the last 10 percent? Does that make you a disappointment for the 10 percent, or does it make you an absolute master for getting to 90 percent? Despite what your mind tells you about what you have or not have achieved, you can be sure it highlights the missed 10% not the 90% achieved. This is what this Mind Lie does, it has you see past the victories and instead concentrate on what you may believe constitutes a failure. In fact, seeing anything as a failure comes from this branch of Mind Lies.

This is why it is incorrect to say that you are not enough. It is wrong to classify yourself, or what you believe yourself to be, as a disappointment for the simple reason that it fails to take into account the accumulations of all your triumphs, one of which has been staying alive all this time, not to mention being present to this information in this book!

It is easy to overlook that staying alive on Earth is a real accomplishment. No one ever says, "Congratulations on your birthday. You survived another year." They should! Staying alive truly takes mastery, more than you would believe. This is not to say that dying makes you a failure or a disappointment, but it is important to acknowledge the mastery in staying alive.

This is something you can ponder on your own time, because now I have a deeper truth for you to resonate to: the false self exists in and as disappointment, failure, and obscurity. In this small self, there are no concrete benchmarks. If there were, you would struggle much less and be far more congratulatory with yourself than you are. The false self hides all your victories out of view in a shroud of uncertainty because it wants you to focus on the failures, on what you missed, neglected, and got wrong, and keep you in the past. It wants you to focus on mistakes, not the truth. Why do you think you are having such a tough time reading this book? Because it is an exposé on something that has lain hidden for centuries.

How can you feel like anything other than a disappointment when it is your self that is the energy of disappointment? How is water to feel anything other than wet, or fire anything other than hot? You cannot escape your inherent nature while you believe you are that thing. Disappointment is the very substance that you—not You—are made of.

Instead of seeing the truth, you have believed the Mind Lie and been fooled into thinking and believing that you are a shroud of disappointment rather than the awareness that perceives it. It is like walking into a burning house and, instead of reaching for the water to put out the fire, deciding, "I am the fire," which means that you are helpless to save yourself or the house from burning down. You wonder why the house keeps falling down around you. It is because you have not yet realized that You are not the fire.

How do you move your perspective away from being the fire, the disappointment, when you have conditioned every cell of your body to believe this? The answer is, you realize that you began when disappointment began. The first seed of disappointment began a long time ago, further back than you can remember. Disappointment was your first thought about yourself; in the womb, you felt the reluctance of your parents to bring a child into the world, and so the seed of disappointment began to grow. It is not like this for everyone, but it was strong for you.

When you entered the world, this seed met with water from all those around you as they medically judged and assessed you and your well-being. You were weighed, measured, and assessed. You were not the average size, you were not the average temperature, and the energy in the room from everyone's reactions affirmed to you, "I am a disappointment."

Doctors and midwives need to be careful to give only words of love and praise when welcoming a newborn into this world; otherwise, each newborn ends up like you, or worse, believing they are a disappointment their entire lives.

When you dig deeper, you can see that what transpired when you were in the womb was quite remarkable. A baby's awareness is very susceptible to auto-suggestion when it is in the womb. It is desperately seeking affirmation of itself: "What am I? Where am I? Who am I?" Up to this point, the baby is pure awareness.

For some, this sensitivity is strongest in the womb, but some are hit the hardest when they exit the womb. Awareness itself starts having awareness over itself, over its physical form: "I am aware that I am a new being. What kind of new being am I? What am I?"

If your first encounter was in the midst of those who were emanating the frequency of disappointment, then that is what you adopted as your first thought. Babies who are cocooned in love during gestation stand a far better chance at being immune to other energies as they are born. They are therefore more tolerant than those who are shrouded in their parents' doubt, fear, and reluctance while in the womb.

Is the awareness of awareness the genesis of the mind? Yes, although it is more the mind that is aware of itself. You can say awareness is aware of itself, and that creates the mind. But to be more accurate, it is what awareness is aware of that is the genesis of the mind, its contents, and its momentum. So let the mind be aware of something extraordinary when you welcome any living thing into this world.

The first subject a newborn comes into contact with becomes the snowball that gathers momentum, eventuating into either an identity based in self-love or one based in self-doubt.

The bombardment of this frequency continued after you were born, because eight days later, BANG! Circumcision! Nothing could have dried the cement of this Mind Lie faster than the thought that swept over you, the ultimate "I am a disappointment. Why would they feel the need to alter my body unless there is something wrong with me?" This is exactly what you made this 'tradition' mean.

This disappointment had nothing to do with you. Your parents felt disappointed with themselves that they had potentially altered your well-being, making them inadequate parents. The circumcision disappointment was the energy of the procedure itself, the need to please Truth—God—as if I am ever unpleased with my creations as they inherently are. Your life starts out ruined when it begins with you feeling that the Divine, or Mom and Dad, do not see you as perfect.

Shame on anyone who perpetuates such nontruth. It is ironic that there are so many people in the world who have become the source of humanity's problems and at the same time claim that they are the cure.

Interestingly, though, it was not the Mind Lie of "I am a disappointment" that made things so bad for you. It was when you had the thought that to be disappointed in yourself was the most disappointing thing you could do. You made it wrong to feel you were a disappointment, and things began to spiral out of control from there.

How do you recover from that? It is easy, actually. You need to realize that it is only disappointment that is disappointed. There is no you in this equation. Disappointment was not birthed as you, it came after you. It is an energy unto itself. As it is the fire, not you, that is burning things down, so disappointment also is its own energy. Only disappointment can be itself—not you, not the real You. Stop pretending you are it. You are not.

Think of it like toxic gas that you accidentally inhaled. It is toxic; you are not. You just need to stop breathing it in. Stop being it; stop being a disappointment.

This Mind Lie goes back to your first thought of "I am X." If you had not thought you had to be X—a someone or something—you would not need disappointment. Stop needing to solidify your identity into any one thing, because that thing is where you find disappointment. If you move away from the Mind Lie of believing you are a "something"—a disappointment or anything else—and into the true space of "I am; I just am," then you will be able to recognize that you are everything and nothing simultaneously. From this awareness, what is there to be disappointed about? Nothing, of course. It is only in needing to be a something that disappointment exists.

Even to be an "I" is simply not true, for there is no "I" in Me. There is just "Me," the real You—that is all there is. Me, me, me and me. So let go of needing the truth about you, because there is no truth in you.

So, are you disappointed in yourself? Or is it that disappointment is disappointed in itself? Because that is its nature, that is what it is and does. Disappointed is now disappointed, because it believes there should not be any disappointment.

The self is only disappointed in itself, not You.

"I Cannot Help But Disappoint Others"

As you know by now, this Mind Lie has nothing to do with others; it just has to do with you. The truth is that life is not about impressing others or avoiding being a disappointment; it is not about others at all. Yes, there are others on this planet, and yes, you need to be considerate of and helpful to them, but who you are is not in relationship to others; only who you think you are is.

Who you are exists in truth, not in reference to past behaviors or experiences, nor to anyone else. These are indications not of truth but rather of who you thought you were at a particular time. You cannot act outside of this paradigm by trying to. Who you think you are is the governing ruling for all human behavior. You cannot skip over it, and you cannot blame yourself for following its path. Your actions and behaviors are always going to be in direct alignment to or driven by who you think yourself to be, not who you would like yourself to be.

The good news, and the catch, is that who you think you are is a moving target, and it is meant to be. The more close-minded you are, the more rigid you are in your behaviors and ways of being. The clearer you get on what is true and what is fictitious, the sooner you move on to thinking about yourself differently. The more you are prepared to shift your perspective of yourself as an ongoing process, the more success you will create for yourself. Those most stubborn to change will evolve and grow the slowest. That is the very definition of stagnation, which is counter to evolution. You see many people who pride themselves on their intelligence (and skepticism). They are often the most stubborn. It is interesting that people so smart would be foolish enough to be counter-evolutionary.

Why would you refuse to evolve when evolving means growing beyond needing your identity? It is because your identity does not want this. Growing means recognizing that who you think you are today is not who you will think you are tomorrow. It is the realization that disappointment comes from believing you are who you think you are and fear this will never change. Disappointment keeps you from evolving; it is meant to. It is meant to indulge the need for attention from others as a poor substitute for love from yourself. Love for yourself is the fast track to evolving.

Know that who you think you are is always evolving; that is evolution itself. Know that evolving is the opposite of disappointment. You might think that the opposite of the Mind Lie of always being a disappointment is "I always please others," but it is not. The opposite is. In fact, "I fulfill myself by evolving."

If you are having trouble letting go of this Mind Lie, it is because another Mind Lie is at play, one that feels a lot like "I am a disappointment" in your body. That is, you believe "I am a burden to others." Let us explore.

"I Am A Burden To Others"

While feeling as though you are a burden to others feels like the truth and can be hard to shift, the real truth is that the burden is theirs, not yours. People burden themselves with all their self-doubt, self-criticism, and self-judgment and forever feel they are inadequate. All you have done is to mirror it for them to see. But instead of wanting to see the gift you presented, they chose instead for you to feel the burden they feel.

Instead of their having to face you as their mirror, as their pathway out of this feeling, you now, believing you are the burden, mirror back that they are OK and justified as they are. You are still the mirror, but not what you once were. This is what adults do to children. They are saying, "You cannot beat me into seeing my greatness, so I will make you join me in feeling my pain."

Of course, this is not the real truth, either. It goes much deeper. You may feel like a burden to others, but what you really are burdened by is constantly concerning yourself with how others feel about you.

Now you can see where this came from, but to realize it is not the healing you need. Once you realize that others' thoughts are their own, you only need to concern yourself with your own thoughts. Otherwise, the Mind Lie becomes a self-fulfilling prophecy by which the more you concern yourself with what others think of you, the more burdened you become within yourself and the more you perceive yourself to be a burden to others, to the point that they will undoubtedly experience you in this way. But do not concern yourself with this outcome, because that leads you down the road that created it. Rather, remind yourself that your thoughts are your own responsibility, not anyone else's.

There is an even deeper truth. That is, the burden is in believing what the mind presents to you. The mind itself is the burden. It is not the way out of problems, as you may think; rather, it is what creates them in the first place. To think your way out of a problem is like trying to dig your way out of a grave.

Realize that your mind is not your own but merely a record of what others before you and around you have thought, a comprehensive library of what humanity believes but should not. It is a storehouse of what life looks like in the absence of truth.

Believing your mind is your own is certainly a burden. But when you know that it is not yours to carry, another layer of truth reveals itself: you are not stuck with it, because it does not belong to you. As it does not belong to you, it is not who you are, not your whole truth.

Which brings up the next Mind Lie, "I am stuck with my mind."

"I Am Stuck With My Mind"

The Mind Lie of "I am stuck with my mind" is a tricky one, because the more you insist on the truth, the less clear the truth becomes. The mind becomes fixed, solid as a rock, unwavering and unmovable when you resist or reject it. It is like the stranglehold of an anaconda: the more it feels you resist, the tighter it gets.

Hating your mind secures it into place. Embracing it leaves it hanging by a thread. But harnessing it makes it completely irrelevant.

Harnessing your mind does not mean to believe what it says. Do not limit your life by the limited knowledge your mind possesses. Rather, allow your mind freedom to exist and guide you by means of highlighting the opposite of the truth. If it says black, you know to look for white. If it says that you are unwanted, you know that you are deeply loved. If it says keep going, you know to stop hastily in your tracks. Let it become your ally, not your enemy. Flow returns when you see the mind as "Go on red" and "Stop on green."

Your mind is yours forever as long as you identify with it. It will remain deeply entrenched in your life as long as you believe it is safer to have your mind, than to be without it.

But it is no longer yours the instant you see, you are safer without it, that You are bigger than it, that You are awareness itself. For that is what You are, pure awareness that forgot what it was when you came to this Earth. Now you know. It is time to remember!

You are awareness having a human experience. You are not a mind having a spiritual experience. Awareness came first; awareness is your true nature.

"I Am Going To Spend The Rest Of My Life Aging And Dying"

While the thought of spending the rest of your life aging and dying definitely seems true and you can see it in others before you, it is actually not what is happening.

Before I go deeper into this Mind Lie, let us address a Mind Lie blocking your path: "If I prepare for aging, I will be able to cope with it."

This Mind Lie is another commonly held belief, but in reality, you are attempting to have the end justify the means. Preparing for aging is exactly what is aging you more than anything else. Holding this expectation in your body not only ages you, it also binds many other Mind Lies into fulfilling this ultimate prophecy, as if you had requested it to be so.

The truth is that it is not life that ages your body, and it is not even time that ages your body; it only appears this way. It is a nontruth! Believing that you must age, believing what "experts" say about the downward spiral of the body, is a huge factor in the body aging. Think for a minute about how many things experts have said about the breakdown and deterioration of the cells at certain ages, the slowing of restorative processes in the body, and the malfunctioning of cell repair as you get older. Your mind is full of these "realities." It is time to say, "No thank you, you so-called experts. Keep your Mind Lie-based opinions to yourself. You are not helping anyone!"

What these "experts" see in the body is simply a product of what they have been telling everyone about the body.

Following your own truth rather than rumors and observations is what your body craves most. Remember, the body reflects the mind for the duration that you believe you are your mind. The more you populate your mind with nontruths, the faster your body will age.

Your body wants to be embraced and enveloped in high-frequency states of being, such as "I trust myself to know what my body needs" and "I believe in myself."

Believing the mind is what kills you.

You are alive until such time as you believe it is time to die. Some carry that thought from the time they are born, and some never have it until a doctor tells them that it is their time to die.

If you want to live, to really be alive inside your body, fill it with love and truth. Cherish each moment without giving aging or dying a second thought.

Being present to life has you live. Being present to aging and dying begins the aging and dying process. Remember, life transcends all physical bodies, and You can, too!

You are life. Realizing this has your body be stronger and live longer.

"I Need To Be Liked"

You have been conditioned to think that you need to be liked. This Mind Lie is one of the biggest influencers when it comes to human behavior, from influencing your choice of profession, girlfriend, or husband to the clothes you wear, the color of paint on the walls of your house, and which school you send your children to.

The truth to this Mind Lie is rather deep, so follow closely. It comes back to many previous Mind Lies and the questions that arise, such as, "Am I ok?" "Am I faulty?" "Is there something wrong with me?" "Am I lovable or even likable?" But the Mind Lie goes even deeper than that. It comes back to the one Universal Mind Lie underpinning them all: "Are human beings inherently flawed?"

If you believe that you as a species are wrong from the get-go, then knowing that you are part of this species is to know that you, too, are inherently flawed and poorly created. But this is not the truth, as you have no doubt guessed.

There is a pandemic that has been sweeping across the planet for thousands of years. Unless you see through your Mind Lies, it will continue to be present in humanity, creating the flaws in the world that you incorrectly believe exist within you.

It is all about doubt. You believe that to truly know yourself, you must know your opposite self. This is not mandatory, but you believe it to be the case. Creating what you do not want eventually leads to creating what you do want. Evolution of a species often requires it to reach the depths of despair, after which it can create what it truly desires. This process creates resilience in creating only what the species does want.

When you create a happy experience, you keep going, but when you create an unhappy experience, sooner or later you will think twice before repeating that action. Doubt is like an insurance policy for the survival of the human race. It looks like the end of your species right now, but that is because you are in the middle of learning.

Doubt is a mechanism, a warning of what happens when you listen to those outside of yourself.

Your body, your human life, was designed to be self-guiding and self-reliant, and for very good reason. How can human beings be reminded of their life purpose if they get positive reinforcement for following someone else's outer purpose?

Doubt is not a human flaw, but now just another key ingredient to keeping you on purpose. When you come from doubt, you eventually go full circle and learn to trust in yourself.

To doubt yourself can be seen as essential for your growth and for you to be rock solid in your convictions. Doubt eventually leads to trusting in your True Self: You. It leads to mistrust in yourself, which in turn leads to following the advice of others, which then leads to failure, discontent, and ultimately, the awareness that you should have followed your gut the whole time and never doubted yourself in the first place. Having doubt ultimately leads you away from succumbing to it. This conviction that grows in you is essential for your evolution, which is why intuition is becoming a very real and socially acceptable phenomenon. Intuition is the opposite of doubt; it is the self-guiding mechanism at play.

Doubt switches off intuition. Self-belief amplifies it.

What does this have to do with the need to be liked by others? It is simple: the need to be liked is just another expression of doubt playing itself out. Needing to be liked by others is the need for external validation. You believe that if others like you, you will be likable, and then you will be able to like yourself and feel OK about who and what you are.

Alarm bells might be ringing now, as they should, to reveal to you that there are large gaps in your self-conviction and self-reliance. You are still seeking guidance from outside yourself, which is fine because it is part of the learning process. But now that you know the game, be disciplined to catch that doubt and believe in yourself. This is the biggest gift schools and parents should be giving to children. The world would be a remarkable place if every child were raised with self-belief. Schools are meant to prepare children for life, but most schools focus on preparing children for careers. If you are serious about preparing a child, start with the foundation that cements an incredible future.

Self-belief, self-belief, self-belief—sets a child up to live a divinely inspired life.

You ask, "How do I repair this in myself?" Ask yourself this simple question: "If others like me, do I like myself even more or do I like myself even less?" The illusion is the belief that it helps if others like you, so that is the natural answer. But under closer investigation, you can see a different answer.

Think about this: needing others to like you so you can like yourself actually results in liking yourself even less. You may need to reread the paragraph above to get it. Essentially, you are programmed to be ashamed of such a need, which is another mechanism to free you from relying on the mind.

How can you really like yourself if you need for others to like you first? There is nothing likable about that trait, is there? No. What is the remedy? Despite the proliferation of this Mind Lie and the gravity pulling you toward the socially acceptable phenomenon of having people like you being a good and worthwhile goal, what is the remedy to move beyond it? It is to realize that there is nothing likable about you. Truthfully. You are not likable for the simple reason that the you that wants to be liked keeps insisting on others liking you first.

But the real You underneath all this drama is magnificent!

It is like cracking an eggshell, so that a beautiful new chick can emerge. The you that needs to be liked is the plain, boring eggshell with a crack down the center. You, on the other hand, the real You, is this baby bird full of life and divinity, innocent, beautiful, and with the ability to fly.

This is the You that you are getting to as you slowly crack away at the eggshell, one Mind Lie at a time. So, do you really need to be liked? Only by yourSelf!

"I Need A Naughty And Disobedient Streak; I Need To Keep It As An Option In Case I Need It"

This Mind Lie of needing a disobedient streak, of being a formidable adversary, hides in the shadows, often disguised as something useful. It is the foundation for many people's minds, yet it is where all the trouble began. So many lives have been ruined by what looks innocent and harmless.

Melting away this Mind Lie can melt away the some very core Mind Lie foundations, instantly granting you a new source of power within: access to pure light.

This Mind Lie often starts as a survival technique for kids, in order to get away with what they want rather than what Mom and Dad insist on. It is often held on to as you grow into adulthood, as it is perceived as a source of power. The truth is far from it, of course.

Some believe this Mind Lie is what distinguishes them from everyone else. "My naughty streak makes me who I am: different, interesting, and rebellious." Without this belief, people would no longer feel distinguished from the crowd.

This Mind Lie has led you astray time and time again, causing you to rebel, not against the doctrine of others but against the doctrine of yourself. The truth is, having a naughty, rebellious streak is not what defines you but rather what unravels you.

Holding on to this Mind Lie is exactly what starves you of experiencing maximum power in your life. You think that holding on to it gives you extra power, like a secret weapon up your sleeve, so that you can be naughty at the drop of a hat in order to make a quick getaway from unwanted or undesired circumstances. But this is not the case. This Mind Lie actually creates undesirable circumstances.

As a kid, you could depend on it in the event Mom or Dad refused you a treat or a catch-up with a friend. You knew you could always sneak a treat or jump the fence to the neighbor's house in secret. You kept it up your sleeve in the event that defiance was the only way to get what you wanted. But defiance to what? To whom? Defiance to yourself!

You did not know it at the time, but this defiance you carried around in you was self-defeating, not self-rewarding. Truth is a reward unto itself. It brings more rewards than any other state of being known to mankind. Even being clever does not bring anywhere near as much reward as being in truth.

What this belief leads to is quite innocent at the start, but as you got older, the stakes got bigger. Rebelling meant consuming alcohol as a minor, taking recreational drugs, and dating undesirable women; these became your undoing. But even these actions were fairly minor, because what you ultimately rebelled against was life itself and your True Self—You.

What needs to change for you to get this at the deepest level?

Defiance is another word for *ego* or the *mind*. To defy comes from not being of the light. Over time, people began to confuse what defiance offered with true power. Truth was once known as the ultimate source of power, but then came those who saw defiance of truth as power; many still do. How many times did you witness this as a child, watching the naughty kids defy teachers or parents, often feeling envious of the power they seemed to possess. "If only I had the courage to defy," you would think to yourself. Or were you the defiant one at school?

To defy means to go without, to defy, or go without, the flow of what is meant for you. It has been bastardized into being a way out, but a way out of what? A way out of what you know you should want but do not? Why not want something you know is part of your flow toward greatness? Because if you let in greatness, in all forms and all the time, and you actually see yourself as great, something

190

"terrible" will happen: you will be seen as saintly, which has become one of the most undesirable traits a human being can have. Where did this ludicrous notion come from?

There was a time that being saintly was considered dangerously powerful because it was beyond the church, beyond what religious institutions wanted for the people. Those in charge preferred their congregants to be flawed and faulty, because then the people needed salvation. Even more threatening were the true saints, the enlightened beings, who could show up and reveal nontruths where they saw them. When the true saints stood alone, already being what those in charge promised to help others become—of God, of the light—they were ousted.

The same applies today, but not just in religions; the problem is everywhere. If you are being truly great, you are dubbed "holier than thou" or "too big for your boots." To be today what Jesus or any other prophet was two thousand years ago is not socially acceptable. It is tantamount to being a person whom everyone hates.

Thousands of years ago, people had to pretend to the public that they were flawed, no matter what amazing healing gifts and prophetic abilities or inventive skills they had; otherwise, others would not accept them. This pretending became so common that eventually society did not, could not, accept anyone as great unless they were seriously flawed in some way. Being defiant meant still belonging to the Church or holding the common belief system, whatever it was, and thereby sending out the message, "I am not perfect. I still need your help!"

No one was privy to what was really going on: a disease was spreading from one person to the next, a disease that would last millennia, until now. This disease is called "duality."

For someone to be considered a healthy human being, they had to maintain a balance between saint and Satan, otherwise they were not "normal." Psychics were shunned, and you know how witches were treated. Nostradamus had to hide his gifts in stories and quatrains. If

191

people demonstrated true gifts, godly abilities, they were denounced rather than celebrated. In order to be embraced, people had to defy their light and not be too truthful or too great; otherwise they would arouse serious suspicion.

Those who had the gifts, the amazing, extraordinary abilities—heightened intuition, profound wisdom, the ability to heal, telepathy, or some other by-product of being closest to God and the Universe—did not get to belong. Yet the religious leaders, the very people who claimed to be of the light and nearest to God, were the ones who lacked these incredible abilities and condemned them as works of the devil.

Even in this day and age, people still frown at the gifted, whatever those gifts may be; the idea of someone being gifted goes against the concept of the flawed human being. Defiance has come to be considered as being a truly human quality. This is where the problem lies, but more on that later.

Interestingly enough, you can always tell how much truth is in a religion. Does the religion advocate that you are already perfect and lovable as you are? Or does it purport that you are inherently flawed and unlovable? Ultimately, what creates transformation and an enlightened peaceful and harmonious planet—the people who believe in and love themselves, or the people who do not?

Is being defiant your truth? Do you really need to hold on to this naughty streak? The more defiant you become, the less light you have flowing through you. The less light you have, the more you believe you need others to save you. The more you believe this, the less power you exert over your life. The less power you exert, the more you believe in your helpless, false self, the weaker version of you. This self-perpetuating cycle of hating those with real power and real gifts continues. This is why there is an ongoing divide between some scientists and the spiritually aware.

You hang on to being naughty and defiant because it brings you a sense of belonging. But wanting to belong to a collective of people determined to stay flawed and therefore approachable means that you stay in the shadows with no upside at all. To stay in the shadows means that you get to be likable and included in the human population, but at the cost of being liked by those who do not like themselves. This means staying small your entire life, tripping yourself up at every step. You fear your greatness, so you defeat yourself to avoid ever fully getting to it.

The only one you are defying is You.

You—the real you—never gets to be fully present, because the you that thinks defiance works keeps blocking it from happening. You are defying your True Self. Why? Because you are afraid you will let yourself down if you allow yourself to attempt to be great. The Mind Lie has you believe that you will let others down, but it is always you who are let down. The logic goes, "If I let myself down now and stop myself before I reach greatness, then there is no chance that I will let myself down later, when I would be great."

This is a high place to fall from, or so you have been taught. The mind knows that once you know yourself as great, never will you need your mind again. The only way it can remain in power, controlling and manipulating you, is by stopping you on your road to greatness.

And the truth? In greatness, there is nowhere to fall, because this is your True Self—You. You see greatness as being at a great height only because the mind distorts your perception, giving you the feeling that to be great is to be above you, higher than you, not you as you are right now. But to be in greatness is actually your foundation, your natural state. It could also be said that greatness is sky high and you are a cloud that floats until you are weighed down by nontruths. This weight brings you down to ground level, making where you belong seem too high, somewhere you could fall from. But a cloud does not fear heights, nor does it fear falling; it naturally floats sky high.

People think that being naughty and rebellious defies societal norms, but it actually *is* the societal norm. Rebelliousness is the mind rebelling against the light, desperately trying to stay alive. To indulge in rebelliousness is to engage the mind to steer the ship, which takes you further and further away from what you desire.

To be in your truth is the ultimate rebellion to society. If you truly want to defy and rebel, then move toward the light, toward your truth, to where the extraordinary exists. Any other way is mediocre at best and keeps you in the norm you are trying to get away from.

You do not need a naughty streak to get what you want. A naughty streak only gets you what you do not want. What you really need is a truth streak!

"I Am A Waste Of Time, As Is Everything I Do"

It is now important to stop looking to the past for who you are in the present. Looking to the past fuels your identity and is what your identity wants. But you have massive evidence to support the Mind Lie, "I am a waste of time, as is everything I do," so what is the real truth?

The truth is that you are not living in time, so you cannot be a waste of time. Remember, time is a Mind Lie unto itself. Time is a measurement, not an actual thing. You cannot be a waste of a measurement, and what you are doing cannot be a waste of a measurement. The measurement of time is the measurement of the experience of life itself—a measurement of existence—which is ludicrous. If existence is infinite and time is simply a measurement of one expression of existence to the next, how can you possible waste it? Existence is inexhaustible, unable to be wasted.

What this Mind Lie does is trick you into thinking that you have a finite amount of something that is actually abundant; it has you think that no matter what you do with it, you are wasting it. It is like saying that all the water you have drunk your whole life was a waste of water. How could it be, when water is in abundance and gets recycled from you back to the Earth? It goes through you, just as time does.

Life is happening, and it has been happening long before time was ever a concept. Life is not dependent on time, but time is dependent on human life, or the human mind, to be exact. Animals and children do not experience time the same way as human adults do.

How can it be true, then, that you have been so wasteful with time? Is it because you believe you have finite time left to experience and achieve all you desire? This is what the mind says. Or is it that you believe you will never experience and achieve what you desire?

You see, you convince yourself that time exists. But time exists only by virtue of your need to achieve. In other words, time exists because of your need to perpetuate your identity. So time is identity based, not physics based. You do measure time with clocks, but that does not make it who you are.

Could it be that your fear of running out of time is actually your fear of death, and you fear death because you feel unaccomplished, unfulfilled, or worse, unrecognized?

Time is nonexistent and therefore cannot be wasted.

You see time as linear, but the Universe sees it as all events coalescing into multiple probabilities that offer varying levels of experiences. You have the perception of linear time-flow for two reasons: you have the concept of achievement, and you have the concept of lack of achievement. If these concepts were not among your Mind Lies, you would immediately see time very differently. The need to achieve and the need to avoid not achieving—in other words, to avoid living fully—perpetuates the human experience of time.

Imagine that you have done everything you always wanted to do: saved the planet from corporate negligence, fed all the starving children, lived your every fantasy, traveled everywhere you desired, and became an enlightened master. How would you feel about time? You would see an absence of time, because there would be nothing to do and nothing to fear not getting done. There would only be existence, and that would be it. Time is directly proportional to the contents of the mind.

What about death? The body seems to die at a certain point in time—or does it? Could it be that the body changes form from one to the next to the next in a continuous cycle of life and death, giving the Self a never-ending experience of living, rather than dying in time at all?

Is this where the fear comes into play? The belief that "I die with my body" gives you the perception of limited time. But remember, there is no "you." More importantly, there is no limit of bodies, so why the limit of time? The mind has limited time before your awakening happens, but You exist forever.

There is only existence. You are existence.

"I Cannot Trust Myself To Take The Right Or Easy Path"

You have made your life so difficult that it is nearly impossible to conceive of a future filled with grace and ease. But as with all Mind Lies that engineered the past to be what it was, this one can be changed so that you can emerge into a new future, one that will feel so comfortable once you take a deeper look at what is real.

Remember that the more truth you let in, the faster your future will change. You cannot repeat the past if you no longer carry the same beliefs. Beliefs generate your decisions and behaviors and therefore the types of experiences you create. To change a belief, to eliminate a Mind Lie, is to change your entire reality. Understanding this truth is enough to ensure that your future will not be a repeat of your past.

Your future is a by-product of all your beliefs and truths. If you want to believe that your future will not be a repeat of the past, consider how many nontruths have been healed up to this point, thanks to this book. Dozens! You can no longer make the mistakes of the past because you have eradicated the very source code that created them.

It may still be difficult to trust that life can go smoothly from this point on. Realize that difficulty comes from appeasing Mind Lies, appeasing the false you, and ignoring truth. The more you dissolve the you that created difficulty, the less difficulty you will experience. The more you dissolve the need for things to be difficult, the less need you will have to make life difficult.

One of the key obstacles to making life simple is the fear of what you will do if you are not dealing with something. How will you feel accomplished or productive? Without drama and huge challenges, what will you occupy your time with? How will you feel that you are not wasting your time on Earth?

The identity thrives on problem-solving; on the need to fix, remedy, and conquer things; and on the never-ending need to preoccupy itself with something. It thrives on problem-solving because it hides in and among it. You would gradually see the falseness of your identity if your awareness were not constantly consumed by nontruth-based busyness.

Letting go of the need for distraction is one of the fastest ways to cease creating chaos. Simply realize that chaos is not actually feeding you but punishing you. Despite how productive you feel being busy is, busyness occurs as chaos inside the body. Chaos is not the source of growth and enlightenment as you might think; it is quite the opposite. Chaos creates a holding pattern, delaying growth and enlightenment, which does not serve you in the fullest way. Enlightenment comes from being aware of your nontruths and bringing truth where there is none. How can you do this when you are constantly wrestling with problems you have created to avoid looking at truth in the first place?

It is true that you learn from struggle and hardship, but do not fool yourself into thinking that these are the only ways to grow and learn. This is the mind's best trick; it convinces you that hardship leads to growth. This Mind Lie condemns millions to living a life of nontruth, as they are too distracted and too busy to look where truth actually exists, where growth and learning come easily.

To let go of distraction is to realize that it does not bring you what you truly want; it gives you only glimpses of it. It is like craving the rich, milky flavor of an ice cream, ordering one, and then eating it as you watch television. You get a hint of the ice cream, but the experience is muted because your awareness is elsewhere. Simplicity is the key. The best way to eat ice cream is to focus on it without distraction—savoring it and absorbing its full flavor.

Fully absorb life's flavor, enjoy it to the fullest, and stop creating distractions from it! This is a motto for life.

You have come to think that distractions are life; but life exists without them, so how can they *be* life? There is life and there is nontruth, or distractions. Which one do you think makes you fulfilled?

The need to create distractions stems from the need to make life full and rich, but it is the opposite way to achieving what you desire for yourself. Richness does not come from a full life of activity; it comes from being still enough to savor each moment as it comes.

How can you savor something when you are too busy to focus on it? The reason you do not trust yourself is because you are in need of a new outlook. The strategy that you have been employing is inherently flawed, and you feel this on a subconscious level. In fact, nearly all human strategies are inherently flawed. Nearly all human strategies are outcome focused, not moment focused. You need to imagine the moment you desire, not the outcome. You imagine that life will be fulfilling the busier you become, because you know that rich people are busy. But what you neglect to see is that what makes you happy is not the busyness but the moment-to-moment awareness—savoring the ice cream. Busyness for busyness's sake achieves chaos. The next time someone asks you, "How are things going? Are you busy?" try answering, "No, I am aiming for less busyness and more savoring. Thank you for asking," instead of replying, "Oh, yeah, flat out busy, thank you!"

The sooner you change this game plan, the sooner your future will change from chaos and hardship to grace and ease. Constantly thinking about how to be more productive and how to make life more satisfying is not the solution but the problem. What do you do? Stop thinking!

"The More I Think About Things, The Better My Life Will Become"

To reiterate that last point: STOP THINKING! Thinking does not equal peace and fulfillment. This Mind Lie will do nothing but hold you back from bliss and enlightenment.

You cannot think your way into blissful, enlightened states because bliss and enlightenment are the absence of the thinking mind.

Contrary to human belief, your brain was not designed to think your way through life. Thinking is what you do when you cannot access truth. Truth and inspiration are one.

Allow inspiration to bubble up and be the guiding force in your life. Get out of needing to be in the driver's seat, because the you that insists on driving does not have a driver's license. How can you? You are made up, which means that your license is also made up.

The thinking mind is not what you believe it to be. Yes, it can be smart, and yes, it can retain mountains of information. But it is the false you, and it is making decisions based on your limited knowledge about the Universe and how things work, viewed through a filter of fears and belief systems. The thinking mind is the snowball of one Mind Lie after the next. The mind has awareness, and it is this awareness that thinks it is the real you. All thoughts have awareness; self-aware ideas are the true nature of the entire Universe.

To rely on the thinking mind is to kowtow to every belief you have, and this is a certain way to end up in chaos. Wondering what to do with your time, wondering how to stay busy, and the persistent conversation of "What should I do now?" engages the mind. Here you are, attempting to think your way through life. How absurd. Does a bee think its way through life, or a dolphin or a tiger? Nothing else thinks its way through life. They do what they feel to do.

"But hang on," you say, "they are not sentient beings like us, with family responsibilities and bills to pay. The defining characteristic of a human being is the thinking mind, something that animals do not have."

What is sentient about human beings who are so disconnected from nature that they are destroying themselves and all of nature? Perhaps honoring the thinking mind is exactly what has gotten you into this mess on Earth. Ask yourself who is sentient: those who destroy their habitat and everyone else's, threatening their very species, or those who keep the balance on Earth to ensure their long-term survival? It is not the thinking mind that makes you a sentient being; it is your ability to see the mind as nontruth, to see yourself as awareness itself, as the creator of the Earth and all that dwell upon it.

It is clearly time for a strategy change. You have used thinking to get you where you are today, so perhaps now you need to use your brain the way it was intended. The human brain was entrusted to run the functions of the body, to support and guide immunity to diseases, and to keep the body alive. It has the capability to process information, but it functions better as a storage device that as a decision maker. The real thinker is the Intelligence behind the brain; that which designed the brain.

To better understand the brain, imagine it as like a modem or an antenna. Intelligence just is; it is everywhere and everything. Why create a lesser version of what already exists to ruin everything that has been created? You would not.

You are the very same Intelligence that designed you, so you can draw upon it. You were designed this way to keep evolution flourishing and the human species moving forward. This is what is available now: a mind beyond your own and an Intelligence superior to any human intellect. This Intelligence is inspiration; it is sometimes felt or perceived as subtle messages, pictures, and feelings, but it is subtle only because you have become accustomed to the clanking of the loud and boisterous human mind.

This Intelligence, existence itself, is a field of knowing that supports all life to prosper and harmonize. Allow this current of knowing and inspiration to propel you from one moment to the next. This is what a sentient being does, and if you think for a second that this inspiration will neglect your needs, then STOP thinking!

"It Would Be Irresponsible Of Me To Stop Thinking"

This might be hard to read and accept, but just because you can think does not mean you should. You ask, "How can I possibly give up the one thing that keeps me from financial ruin, that keeps me off the streets?"

Do you really want someone who is fictitious doing all the thinking in your life?

"But," the mind argues, "how can I ever give up the biggest thing that makes me human?" What is so desirable about being human? Letting go of being a conventional human is exactly what this book is about. It is time to elevate beyond what is conventional and into what works. This is what makes letting go of doing all the thinking yourself so easy. Take the burden off your shoulders; it is not your job, anyway. Allow me to explain. The Mind Lies in your mind really *are* your mind. You have been taught that having a mind is pivotal to what makes you human, and never have truer words been spoken. It is exactly what makes you human but not extraordinary. When you examine what being human stands for, you understand that the mind and being human are one.

In truth, the mind invented the concept of a human being. That an energy as limitless as You are could ever have a suitable label is a mind-made concept. The more you insist on believing what others say about you and being human, the more your mind develops. A developed mind is not a gift but a severe hindrance, because the more developed it becomes, the more sure of itself it is, the more it filters out the light and showers you with opposites. That becomes its only purpose.

Even now, as you are reading this, buttons are being pushed because your mind is desperate to exist and desperate to persevere with having you do the thinking. The mind has you get upset in order to live, so you will reject the very premise of what I am presenting here. But consider that it is not your mind that makes you great; it is not your mind that is the best part of you. What makes you great is something else, something you are getting closer to with every truth you integrate.

The mind is like a slot machine: it gives you some wins, enough for you to think it serves your greater good, but it also gives you more losses so that you never evolve beyond it. Have you noticed this before? You have "perceived wins." These are victories only because they are a version of what other people are achieving. In relation to other minds, you feel successful.

It is funny when you reflect on what you used to count as victories. Go back to when you were a child, and let us recount some of these victories for your awareness. Your earliest victories involved getting attention from your parents. Then you moved on to getting attention from the naughty kids at school. Then your victories returned to getting attention from your parents by earning good enough grades to get into a university, and then again for getting a good graduate job; this also got you attention from friends. From that point, you sought attention from men or women whom you thought society deemed important or attractive, but who would otherwise serve your heart on a platter. Soon after that, you believed your biggest victory was getting attention from complete strangers for appearing successful and driving a flashy car.

These are the victories your mind delivered to you; yet all that time, during all those pretend victories, the mind never took away your anxiety, fears of rejection, fears of being a disappointment, or your self-doubt. It only added to these feelings by piling up more and more pressures and stress. The wins of the mind are short-lived and illusory, taking away more than they give. Underneath all of this is You, a still, quiet voice holding you together so that you do not snap under the weight of the pressures of the mind. Over all these years, the real victory has been allowing You into your life enough so that

You could play that steadying role. *You* are the victory, not the mind.

Listening to your mind will be your undoing, because there is something else available to you, something vastly more useful and truthful. It is You, which goes by other descriptions and labels, some of which have been touched on throughout this book: the Superconscious, Universal Intelligence, Enlightenment, and the True Self. You are not the thinker; You have knowing. You are this knowing, so there is no need to "think."

The mind acts as a barrier to You, a barrier to infinite Intelligence, filtering You out like clouds filter rays of sunlight. The more you listen and act on what your mind says, the more spot fires you will need to put out. You believe that it is irresponsible to stop thinking, but when you look at what your mind has done thus far, you will find it irresponsible to trust your thinking at all.

Knowing, on the other hand, is powerful. Thinking is a form of uncertainty, whereas knowing is certainty. You are that knowing. The Universe is a perpetual state of knowing. This is where the concept of the Divine as being omniscient and omnipresent is derived from. In a sense, the Universe is a mind—the greatest mind, a brain unto itself. Within this mind there are many varieties of thought; some are thoughts of not knowing, and this is your mind: simply a thought within a brain, an idea about itself.

What is the responsible action? How will you ensure that your finances grow in abundance and ensure that your appreciation for yourself and others continues to grow? These are achieved by retiring the mind, by retiring from thinking altogether.

Thinking is not a prerequisite to being.

"Can I Trust My Intuition, This Non-Thought?"

You were not taught that learning comes from within, so you came to trust information coming from outside sources more than that coming from your inner source—from You—and from the Universe. Herein lies society's problem: the Mind Lie that you cannot trust your intuition. Nearly all knowledge on Earth has come not from stilling the mind and meditating to get answers, not from the very Intelligence that founded life on Earth, but from the process of trial and error. This is how you learned everything you know about life; you took the long way around and were often sadly mistaken.

You and all of humanity have been avoiding going to the real source, the source of it all, to get your answers, and instead have settled for the hard road, the less exact path. This is like wanting to ask a girl on a date, but instead of asking her directly, you talked to everyone but her. The result was a bunch of opinions, not the actual truth. Hearsay rather than truth has governed your life to this point and still does.

Everything that can be known is already known. This is why I refer to the Universe as a "knowing Universe." Not knowing exists in the human mind; it is a mind-made paradigm. To be in truth, simply swap learning from outside yourself with learning from within, which is where the great library exists.

You have been taught to rely on scientific study rather than your inner wisdom, your intuition, for exact truths. But scientific study is filtered through the mind; inner wisdom can come through only in the absence of the mind. Who better to ask about anything on Earth than the very Intelligence that thought it up? A gap exists in your total knowing, not because you are not smart enough but because you insist on consulting the mind for answers instead of your all-knowing, Universal Mind.

Spirituality is the true mind, the Intelligence behind the Universe. The best news is that you are an extension of this Intelligence, so the answers that come from within, like the truths you are now reading, are from the very same Universal Mind that designed and pioneered life on Earth. And not just life on Earth, by the way; the Universal Mind designed all life—and this life, too, is an extension of you. The view that you are alone in the Universe and that life does not exist anywhere else comes from the Mind Lie, "I am alone, separate and disconnected."

Your mind is the filter. You cannot see what you refuse to believe or what you are not ready to believe. Belief is the key that either gives you unlimited access and borrowing privileges to the great library or limits you to borrowing only the books you have already read a thousand times.

It does not matter how smart you are; you cannot think beyond the filter of your mind. To think is to be in the mind and constrained by the filter of the mind. You have a mind limited by your identity; you cannot see anything bigger than you see yourself to be. This is the identity-driven intelligence, not truth-driven Intelligence. One is limited, the other is infinite.

Without spiritual awareness, you will struggle. As long as you still believe your mind is the superior intelligence on Earth, your growth will be stunted. This is a tough Mind Lie to give up, because the fear of being without your mind is the fear of being without an identity, which you believe to be tantamount to death.

The mind has been so powerful that it has convinced you that if it is not the one making decisions or thinking—if thinking were handed over to your intuition or inner wisdom—the result would not be the truth. You have been led to believe that somehow intuition is not scientific because it is not the convention, even though the convention has left you high and dry.

It is time to wake up now. Intuition is not scientific because the meaning of *scientific* is limited to "our understanding to date," whereas the meaning of *intuition* refers to something, or better stated, a 'knowing' being "beyond our understanding."

The mind says that you cannot trust information coming from outside it, when in truth you cannot trust what is coming from your mind. So keep reading, keep clearing your Mind Lies, and, once you are done, pass this book out to the world so that thought leaders, doctors, CEOs, politicians, scientists, academics, military personnel, music teachers, school teachers, and moms and dads can be the change the world seeks now.

Remember, thinking is a poor substitute for knowing. In fact, thinking prevents a still enough mind to even perceive your inner knowing. Do not settle for thinking, know that knowing is available instead.

"I Am Only As Good As What I Have In My Life"

You feel assessed by what you have in your life; you always have. This Mind Lie has you believe that the car you drive, what your partner looks like, what type of house you own, how much money you make, whether you own the latest iPhone, and so on determines how good you are. This Mind Lie plagues people on a daily basis.

In this new spiritual age, there are many new assessments and spiritual accomplishments you must pass to be socially and societally embraced and accepted. Some of these include how long you meditate for, how strict a vegan you are (it is no longer OK to just be a vegetarian), how often and for how long you practice yoga, and the list goes on.

None of these are the truth, however; none of these benchmarks are the path to happiness. Assessing others and yourself in this way comes not from truth but from insecurity. Instead, there is a new way to look at life, a new way to look at yourself.

How can you be assessed for what you have? It is not what you have that is important but who you are, because who you are is the sole determinant of what you can give.

Think about it like this: you assess others to evaluate what kind of relationship you will have with them: friend, employee, husband or wife, business partner, accountant, or doctor. But what each of you can give is the real determinant of the quality of life between you. People who come into your life may have all the money in the world and never give you a dime. They may drive the fanciest sports car but never lend it to you. They may have amassed an abundant property portfolio, but you will never learn their secrets. She may look like a supermodel but be a completely wrong match for you and your evolution. But if people are loving, you will receive love. If they are respectful, you are likely to receive respect. If they are enlightened, you will receive enlightenment. So why do you assess others? It is because you assess yourself this way continuously. Is this all starting to feel like déjà vu?

It is hard not to feel that you are only as good as what you have, because your belongings and your life situation are seen as a reflection of how good you have been in your life: how smart, how strategic, how patient, how impulsive. But is it not more accurate to say that your belongings and life situation are reflections of how many Mind Lies you have, or rather, how much truth is present in your life?

Decisions, strategy, and patience are derivatives of your belief systems or lack thereof. You are quick to judge others because you judge yourself, but you deserve more understanding and compassion than that. You cannot act outside of your belief systems. When you understand that you could not have done your past—your life—in any other way simply because you were programmed that way, you will start to see others in the same light: with compassion.

Your life is not a reflection of how good you are but of how good you believe yourself to be. You now know where this is coming from: not from the truth, but from the mind.

You cannot comprehend right now how good You really are. Learning to comprehend it is exactly what this book is about. But there is an even deeper truth to be understood. Release the need to see yourself as good in the first place. This need is a Mind Lie that locks you back into a personality, a definite perimeter. It stems from the Mind Lie, "I need to be good." It keeps you in a spin! With the need to be good comes the need to look good, to have good things, to act good . . . and so the cycle goes on.

In truth, good does not come close to describing what you are in the absence of Mind Lies. Why aim for good when you can aim for truth? You will end up with infinitely more, you will be infinitely better off, than the result you gain from attempting to be good.

"I Do Not Trust My Life"

You are not alone in experiencing the fear of getting out of bed in the morning. Your heart pounds at the mere thought of what the day has in store, what life will throw at you today—or worse, what is in store for the rest of your life. This fear, this Mind Lie, has become more prevalent as you have gotten older, a symptom not of something true but of something that was handed down to you, forcing you into a victim state.

At what point did you forget that you play a pivotal role in what life throws at you? When did it change from life being your ally to life being your adversary? Perhaps a better question might be, when did you forget that you *are* life?

What you receive or do not receive, what you experience or do not experience, is not subject to the whim of the Universe, as you may believe. Life is far more directly related to you than you give it—and yourself—credit for. This is a touchy subject, especially when looking at the horrible experiences you have endured.

No matter what your experience has been, you are not separate from life, not simply a bystander. You are innocent perhaps, but by no means simply a victim, unless that is what you choose.

You interact with the ebbs and flows of the Universe and are either flowing or resisting on a daily basis. This is the driving force behind not only how you experience life but also what challenges, opportunities, and gifts come into your life.

Your mind is central to your Universe; after all, the Universe is one giant mind. But how fast your experience expands beyond poverty, suffering, violence, arguments, and struggles depends on how fast you are prepared to move beyond these concepts within yourself. The longer you hold on to them, the longer they remain the pervasive experience, individually and globally; hence the need for this book. The faster you transcend your Mind Lies and thereby the need for these lower-level, low-vibration experiences, the sooner you will be rid of them on Earth. That is the point to all this; that is the game in which humanity is currently involved.

You attract and allow in what you think, but what you think is rarely what you would consciously choose for yourself. Your Mind-Lie mind does not choose experiences to punish you, even though it seems this way at times. But that is just your manifestation. The upside is that this process is a healing one, healing you back to truth, back to the real You.

Just as you cannot see more than you believe for yourself, you cannot allow in experiences that are beyond you. Unveiling truth in your life and for others is the single most important activity in which you can engage. This is your life purpose: to give to others in this way.

Truth is what drives growth and expansion in your Universe and therefore in your life. Any and all struggles that come up for you are simply truth trying to be restored. Look at any battle you have ever experienced, and you will find that there was more than one nontruth present. Likewise, look at every war that has ever happened on Earth, and you will again see how nontruths play out. These nontruths will play out again and again until humanity realizes the truth.

Humanity believes that remembering wars and past tragedies is what prevents them from happening again, but this is not true. What prevents them is learning the truth and restoring it to human consciousness.

Children at school should not be studying wars and battles but the truth that was learned from them. How have you evolved? If the truth is not written in the textbooks, let this be the assignment for students: What was the truth? After all, history's biggest battles were global manifestations of humanity's battle with nontruth.

There are many other influences occurring all around you, but what you experience and how you experience it comes down to you. But remember, there is the you who plays a part, and then there is the real You. Your not getting what you really want is the result of an age-old tug-of-war between you and You. Guess who is going to win every time? The one who has the power; which is not you, by the way. The more you struggle against the real You, the less power you have. The source of all great power is truth. The more aligned to truth you are, the greater your power.

People often blame outside forces for many of the things that happen to them, whether tragic, empowering, or magnificent. Many of you realize that there is some type of power or force behind life that both gives and takes. But what if this external power, which is clearly at play, was always in your corner, working for you rather than against you? What if you could see yourself as this external power? Be the power. Harness it to nourish and support you. Be You!

You have lost loved ones and undergone horrific experiences, but is this because of an external power or the absence of it? you are quick to blame God, the Universe, karma, or whatever you believe in, but have you ever stopped to realize that tragedy occurs not because of this power but because you get in the way of it, you ignore it when it doesn't suit, stubbornly choosing your own path, still insisting on this illusionary "free will"?

By now you know the importance of remaining unattached to things, whatever they may be: possessions, professions, goals, outcomes, and relationships. This is because the more you attach, the less life can give you of what you truly want. Attachments block you from receiving the things and experiences that are even greater than what you are attached to. You just fear you will get less.

Attachments come from insisting on how life should look but then blaming someone or something else for life not being everything it can be.

Life's tragedies can be easily avoided when you listen to You, your True Self, and when you release attachments in your life. The more you do this, the more you become the power of life, able to direct life toward the highest good rather than being kicked around by it.

It is like playing in the ocean waves. You can stand in their path, stubbornly asserting your free will to stand wherever you like, and get pummeled. Or you can become one with the waves as surfers do, riding them all day long until your heart is content. Choose either to be part of the wave or to be in its path.

The question now changes. Is it life you do not trust, or is it yourself? Could it be that you do not trust yourself to get out of the way of the oncoming waves? What if you are not listening to the messages of life? What if you get stuck in your identity, miss the timing of the wave crashing, and get thrown head first into the sand? What if you are lazy and cannot get motivated to do the right thing in the right moment? These are just your Mind Lies talking.

Being on the path of life takes no more effort; actually, it takes less. Life the way you have lived it to date is where great effort has been required, because you have been doing it all your way, the alone way. If you stop insisting on being the one to set the navigation, you will be surprised at how fast that wave comes to swoop you up to the highest point on its crest, carrying you forward on a wild and beautiful ride to your destination.

Be prepared for some life lessons along the way. Wherever you are still stubbornly holding on to nontruths, life will teach you the way. Life likes to shake you around a bit to pry your fingers off what is not working for you. But remember, the tighter your grip, the harder the lesson.

It is not you that you need to trust, it is life. Once you allow life to work its magic, there will not be a "you" left to stop it.

Trust life!

"What I Want And What Life Wants For Me Are Very Different; I Will Never Get What I Want"

This Mind Lie is actually factual because most of your wants are in response to your other Mind Lies. Many of your ambitions and goals are compensations for how you feel about yourself on the most subconscious level. What life wants for you and what you want for yourself differ, but this does not mean that what life wants for you will make you unhappy—quite the opposite.

Consider what happens when you get what you want based on your Mind Lies. You get the world as it stands today: oil spills, trees being chopped down by the millions, drug overdoses, nervous breakdowns, corrupt politicians, plastic bags . . . the list goes on. All these and more are the result of getting what you want as a race of mind-driven people coming from a space of appeasing your Mind Lies.

Consider the belief, "I do not get enough attention, so I want a V8 sports car or a Harley Davidson so that people will notice me."

Ponder for a moment what goes into making these things possible. These noisy, attention-seeking machines require gasoline, mined metals, plastics created at great expense to the environment, roads for them to ride on, and so on. The point is, your needs are not congruent with your wants. What you think you need, that is, what you want, does not give you what you actually need, such as clean air, zero landfill, peace instead of wars over oil, and so on. You say that life is not giving you what you want, yet every day the planet suffers because you are getting exactly what you want; it is just not what you need.

The more in alignment you become with the energy of life, with your truth, the less you will want things that destroy you and the Earth, and you will start having exactly what fulfills you.

You see this already starting to happen in your own life: the more nontruths you shift, the more you gravitate toward what serves you and move away from all those things that have harmed you.

The more connected you become to You, your True Self, the less you crave what harms you, and interestingly, what harms the Earth. You become one with life. Soon there will be a time when the very thought of war will be unconscionable, abhorrent to even the most corrupt of human minds. A time is coming when self-destructive thoughts will hurt the human body so much that people will have no choice but to move toward self-love and love of others.

The secret to happiness is liking yourself. The secret to peace is liking what you do with yourself. The secret to loving your life is loving yourself.

Do you want life to give you what you want at the expense of life on Earth, or would you rather life show you an even better way? You may still want the fast cars, big house, flights overseas, and so forth. When you are living in truth, experiencing these things will actually be in your highest good; that is what life wants for you. But be prepared that the closer you get to the true You, the less you will desire what is no longer sustainable.

By now, you may be feeling like a spoiled child, throwing a tantrum and demanding that you get what you want. Consider that feeding or compensating a Mind Lie does not actually bring the level of satisfaction and fulfillment you are expecting or hoping. How many times have you finally reached your goals, anticipating a colossal life change, only to end up feeling indifferent or unsatisfied? The big purchases, the accumulation of more and more stuff, does not make you feel more accomplished but burdened and cumbersome. Satisfying Mind Lies is the fastest way to being unhappy, which is quite the opposite of how it is all perceived.

> *Daniel speaking: I wanted a jet ski my whole life. When I finally got one, I could not stand the feeling of being weighed down by this gas-guzzling machine. It did not add to me in the way I had hoped, but it did add to me in terms of feeling burdened. What I was really after was to be close to the water, to connect with the ocean, to be in it. Notice how I say "be in the ocean." Following my Mind Lies, I ended up on the ocean with an expensive machine that took me not closer, but away from, what I wanted. All I really had to do was swim more often. Simple.*
>
> *Conversely, I never wanted a wife or children, because my mind convinced me that they would take away from me. Needless to say, my life is fulfilled now that I have allowed both these precious gifts into my life, despite the stringent objections from my mind.*

Your needs are simple and non-disruptive. Keep them simple and light, always.

Can life get what it wants and you get the same? Yes! Consider that you do not really know what to want. The clearer and more aware your mind becomes of your Mind Lies, the clearer you become of what will bring happiness and contentment. It is similar to standing in the center of a labyrinth trying unsuccessfully to peer over the three-meter-high walls to the outside: all you can see is what the mind wants, what it tells you to want, what it tells you that you need. But it is not you that needs these things, it is the mind. Once you get them, you wonder why you are not any happier.

Seek the path outside of the wants, and you will be surprised and amazed at how life knows exactly what you really want—things you would never dare to desire for yourself so generously.

How quickly can you have what you desire? As quickly as you remove all the Mind Lies that say you cannot have them. Life wants to give you more than you have ever allowed yourself to dream of. Life wants to show you how. Life just wants you to listen.

"A Simple Life Is A Bad Life"

Then there is the Mind Lie that a simple life is bad. You have become suspicious of life being simple. Simple has come to mean stupid, lazy, corrupt, criminal, deceitful, or worse. For some reason, a simple mind is considered to be a bad thing. You have made having a simple and free-flowing life mean something negative.

You strive for a busy life, as if being busy equates to more happiness. Does it? Does filling your life with complexity and activity—which are actually barriers and opposition to enjoyment— ensure that you have more enjoyment? Obviously not.

A simple life is an enlightened life.

The beliefs of "Life is not meant to be easy" and "Success takes a lot of hard work" forget to mention that the work is not out there in the world but inside of you. The work of clearing the Mind Lies and seeing the truth not only cuts down on the outer work but has what is left be simple and enjoyable. Remember, success takes 10 percent

216

perspiration and 90 percent inspiration. Have you forgotten this age-old truth?

You go to great lengths to enjoy life, yet it takes very little effort to enjoy something so simple and beautiful.

"I Always Come Last, After Everyone Else's Needs Have Been Met"

Let me be straight: you come where you put yourself. That is it. So why put yourself last? Are you being generous, altruistic perhaps? Or are you just being self-defeating?

The truth is that putting yourself last serves no one, as you have no doubt come to see. It is not enlightened to put yourself last, nor is it chivalrous—or any other admirable trait you are using—to hide the real truth from yourself. Your mind would have you think that the hallmark of a selfless human being is to put yourself last, but your mind is incorrect.

To put yourself last does not come from self-love but from lack of self-love. You create further suffering for yourself whenever you forget to practice self-love. What is worse, those whom you believe you are helping miss out. They miss out on the awareness and experience of equality, because sooner or later, those whom you were seeking to help become those whom you can no longer tolerate.

A shift is needed from your coming last to coming first, and "coming first" is not what its reputation would have you believe. It is not selfish but rather without self. If you deduct the mind-self from the equation, then what is left is equality: all beings giving and receiving what they need to prosper.

The challenge is that you have convinced yourself that coming last and neglecting yourself is in some way nurturing or character building, but it really comes down to feeling a lack of worth. You feel a subconscious anxiety that you are undeserving, you do not have what it takes to be counted, you are not special enough to be recognized and tended to.

The thought simply is: the benefit of coming last outweighs the cost, at least in your mind. You allow yourself to come last because you believe that this offers you something greater in return. Do you know what it is? Can you feel it rising up into your awareness? The *perceived* benefit is that you get to stay a victim. "How is that a benefit?" you ask. Being a victim offers a whole suite of subconscious wins. Let us explore them so that you can let go of them one by one.

- A victim receives sympathy. Sympathy is an attractive form of attention, and sometimes any attention will do, especially if you were starved of it growing up or if it was the only form of attention you received. The problem with this type of attention is that you need to keep failing, hurting yourself, or creating chaos to keep receiving it. So as nice as the attention might appear, the life you need to live this way is not worth it. This is not a life you want; it is painful, unfulfilling, and downright boring—and it is because it is so boring that you crave the extra attention. How else are you going to feel that your life is worth living?

  Stop failing. Stop hurting yourself, and the attention you will get will be much more fulfilling, because you will receive it by virtue of how wonderful you are rather than how much suffering you endure. When you receive attention, when you are not failing and not suffering, you will see attention for what it truly is: a reflection of your self-worth, not your self-doubt. This is the fuel required to spur you on to keep creating amazingness in your life. Sustaining a space of self-doubt is deadly.

Daniel speaking: *I am reminded of what I often tell my seven-year-old son. He starts arguments just to get his mother's attention, and I remind him that yes, he is getting attention. But he is getting angry attention when he is seeking loving attention. I remind him to be loving in order to receive loving attention.*

- A victim does not have to try. "If I never get to try, I cannot fail" is the motto of the victim mind. It is the get-out-of-jail-free card, the note from your mom for permission to skip gym class. The failure is not in the trying and not succeeding, it is in holding yourself back from even attempting a better life. Not trying, not believing in yourself, is the failure. Even worse is believing the thought in your head, the Mind Lie that says success is beyond you, unreachable. But moving forward toward a better or clearer life amounts to success whether you reach your mind-made goals or not. Success is in seeing yourself as more than your mind says you are.

- A victim has a fear of being abandoned. Someone needs to give you sympathy and attention, and being a victim gives people around you a role in your life, keeping them close by. You have people around you now because they pity you. But wouldn't you prefer that people want to be around you because you are a source of wisdom and inspiration? Why sentence yourself to a mediocre life, attracting people through being mediocre instead of by shining your true light? The truth is, you are worried that people would be scared of your light, that you would actually turn them away. You learned this as a child; there were those around you that didn't want to see your brilliance, and they certainly did not want to give you attention for it. They much rather wanted to support you when you were in despair. But the truth is that those who now stay because of your suffering are suffering, too. It is far better for both of you to wake up, for you to be light rather than darkness.

- A victim gets to make people feel useful. Your mind tells you that being a victim gives others a role in your life; they get to help and comfort you. And you like making people feel useful. The truth is, it is not at all about them but rather that you like to feel useful by giving people a use. They might feel useful or even special, but what a waste of time for them and for you, because being a victim stops you both from actually being useful. You create this useless way at being useful. It is far more useful for you to be useful than it is for you to be a victim.

- A victim gets concessions. There is a spectrum of concessions, like having people understand when you are unable to do something with your life. When you are a victim and need sympathy, people are more understanding, more compassionate, and they do not put the same amount of expectation and judgment—and therefore pressure—on you. Why would you want this? Because it removes the pressure you feel from society to be something you are not or do not believe you can be. But stifling your own growth is not a remedy to relinquishing pressure; it just adds to it. The way to rid yourself of the perceived pressures of needing to be something, to achieve or obtain something, is to realize the truth. You are already those things! You are the energy of all things, so there is no need to feel pressure to be or achieve something that you already are. It is like water feeling pressured and overwhelmed at the thought of becoming wet.

Being a victim or putting yourself last is a no-win situation. You do not win, the people around you do not win, and, by holding yourself back, you hold back the very evolution of the Earth. By putting yourself last, you suffocate mind and body from growth. You suffocate those around you from growing, because all they see in front of them is someone who depends on them for mediocrity, not success. That is unfulfilling for everyone.

Realize that your path is not to dwell, or to have others dwell, in mediocrity; rather, it is a path to greatness and awareness. Putting yourself last cancels out awareness in the same way as a blanket smothers fire. It blocks you from receiving the necessary oxygen for your health to thrive, the mind to triumph, and the soul to fulfill its higher purpose.

Putting yourself first is so important that it is singularly the most enlightened thing you can do. It allows your purpose to be in play for this world. You have a purpose; no one gets to know about it, least of all you, if you keep putting yourself last. Lead by example, because it gives others the permission to do exactly the same, and you will all thrive in unison as one living organism. Teach everyone around you: your children, your family, your colleagues, and your friends.

The importance of living your life purpose is that it is one for all and all for one.

"The More Beautiful Or Handsome My Partner Is, The More Accomplished I Feel"

This Mind Lie speaks to the need and desire for a trophy wife or successful husband and the need to keep looking to see who else is out there.

You live in a society that portrays glamorous, sexy woman as targets, as something to aim for, and rich, successful men as something to catch. But the damage this causes to both men and woman is astounding. Very few men are being fully present to their truly beautiful wives when a beautiful or stunning or sexy woman walks past. Many men become like putty, drifting off into fantasyland. It

221

might be days before they come back to seeing their wives or girlfriends for what they are: the best thing that ever happened to them. And women, on the other hand, behave the same way when they become interested in and drawn to men other than their partners or try to catch a "sugar daddy."

The allure of a beautiful woman or handsome man can be very strong; it can be as strong as a drug high. But what many people do not realize is that this high, just as with drugs, has catastrophic side effects. And just as with drugs, this allure comes from Mind Lies, not from truth. The mind has you convinced that your attraction to someone is the real, meaningful, heartfelt truth. But most of the time, the attraction is only masquerading as truth, and this is what gives it so much power over you. Misunderstanding attraction for the truth is so dangerous to indulge in that it can easily lead to divorce, energetically or in actuality.

Divorce for the wrong reasons can be one of your biggest regrets. Let me explain. When a spouse is energetically seduced, his or her energy is distracted away from the loved one, causing a disconnect in their relationship. Fights begin, dissatisfaction is experienced on both sides, and the one being seduced often begins to feel a desire to move on, feeling that what the partners once had is over and that this new interest shows more promise.

These thoughts can lead to having an affair or secretly fantasizing about being with such a person and what it would be like. This is devastating to the energetic connection within a couple. Having such fantasies may cause you to feel, in the moment, like a success and truly alive, but repeatedly breaking the connection with your partner is actually the fastest way to end up feeling anything but alive and successful.

Sexual allure may well be one of the most addictive sensations, yet it is also the biggest obstacle standing in the way of true success. Certainly cavorting with glamorous women has been continually portrayed as being manly and successful, especially by Hollywood.

But if the need for this stimulation comes from feeling unmanly and having the need to validate and prove yourself, you will end up validating these Mind Lies, not changing them. Women experience the same Mind Lie by falling for the myth that catching a wealthy, successful, or famous man validates them as sexy, desirable women.

A marriage is a union of souls to support one another, to bring in wealth, abundance, and fulfillment, so the cost of losing sight of your partner because of the allure of a pretty woman or handsome man is devastating to your success, abundance, fulfillment, and especially your finances.

The cost of ruining a wonderful relationship is infinitely worse than the benefit your Mind Lie portrays. Remember, as the mind is made up, so too are its promises. If it promises adventure and a sense of being alive, know that it will deliver a lonely life and the feeling of being half dead. Why jeopardize perfection with energetic flings? But all this knowing does not stop the surge of energy when a good-looking man or stunning woman appears. In this moment, do not fool yourself; the sense of attraction and rush of excitement in your body is a reaction, just like all other reactions you feel when your Mind Lies are at play. The difference is that you believe it to be a good reaction because it feels good, but all reactions point to nontruths—and you know where making decisions based on nontruths lead!

Let us explore in finer detail what this reaction is really about: The energy you feel coming up when you react this way is twofold. The first part of this sensation feels like all your inadequacies will be healed in one fell swoop by attaining the goal of attracting a beautiful woman or handsome man. This is a very addictive sensation. The second part is letting the other person's perceived sexual energy into your body. This perceived energy is like a pheromone but infinitely more powerful, as it can reach you across great distances—through a TV screen, for example—or merely by the thought of being with such a person.

Basic physics about thought energy shows that thinking of someone creates an energetic gateway, a bridge to connecting with that other person. When you are connected, that person's perceived sexual energy dislocates you from your partner. The void that is left and felt by both of you, even subtly, is the cause of many fights and separations.

For the partner on the receiving end, the effects are quite devastating. She or he is left with the perpetual experience of feeling inadequate, not enough for you, always needing to stay young and thin or muscular and fit and not being able to meet your impossibly high standards. Your wife or girlfriend can never measure up to all the different types of women you are attracted to, as she cannot be all those different shapes and colors. She can only be her beautiful self. Your husband or boyfriend, likewise, cannot hope to meet the standards of wealthy, handsome, fit, successful men who are held up as what all men should strive to be.

You can guess how this scenario diminishes your partner's health and sense of well-being—your partner responds to your ego mind instead of your heart. The perpetual feeling of "I am not good enough" is a common cause of aging, moodiness during menopause, and long-term disconnection from one another, which is why you see so many older couples completely disconnected at the breakfast table, as though they are living separate lives.

Women are often more ready for a long-term connection than men are. They recognize the partnership and the importance of it. But it has become such a part of society for men to "gawk at women" that men have not stopped to understand that this behavior will ruin their lives. But many men feel as though they do not stand much of a chance to do otherwise, as images of women are plastered everywhere out there in the world: calendars, TV shows, big screen movies, magazine covers, even just walking down the beach.

It is obviously not true that women need to or should cover up, but men need to be hyper-aware that sexual attraction is like a drug, addictive and toxic. Sexual imagery is everywhere and will be for some time. The effect is that many people have a desire to be with—or be—a sexually desirable person. The movie gets its audience, the ad gets its viewers, and the magazines keep getting bought. Sexual imagery is a legal drug and is not healthy.

This is not about being prudish or conservative or taking your fun away. Despite what the mind thinks, the truth is that you are not actually having fun entertaining such thoughts and desires. What you think is fun is in reality a symptom of the most powerful drug on Earth: sexual energy. From the mind's perspective, this energy is a cure-all for all your belief systems, but from the perspective of truth, sexual energy, when focused on one person—the one you are meant to be with—is a very different experience. It is so powerful that it brings life into this world. If people could focus all their sexual energy on their one true love, the little souls that come in to be their children would come in as infinitely powerful beings, pure and protected from other people's energies. This phenomenon will become a big part of pregnancy and birth in the future, a science unto itself.

The Mind Lie-based sexual energy is very seductive and overpowering and feels like the solution you have been searching for. It knocks you off your center and sends you up the garden path. On the other hand, the sexual energy found within a soulful connection is not destructive, as it propels you forward together.

If you want to feel accomplished as a man or woman, focus your energy inward toward yourself, your partner, and your family. Destroying your marriage and your children's future just because a pretty girl or sexy man walks past is hardly anyone's definition of success.

Do not let yourself get seduced by the sexual energy of other people; it is not meant for you. It is meant to help them flourish and move to the next level of their development and evolution. Just as you have your gifts to get you where you need to go, they use what they have available to them. Stop making it personal, even if they are personally interested in you. Being seduced will not eradicate your problems, it will just magnify them. It will not eradicate your Mind Lies, it will only cover them up until you realize that the basis of the attraction is purely because of Mind Lies, which leads to chaos and destruction.

This is not to say that you cannot leave your wife or husband if you are energetically incompatible; in fact, please do, and make it quick. But do not get fooled into leaving, on either the actual or the energetic level, just because you are enveloped by another person's sexual energy.

Realize that these other people are not the ticket to healing your Mind Lies but will lead you to perpetuate them. You will notice a trend within yourself that you only look at other women or men when your Mind Lies come up for healing. The biggest realization is that "I think this is what I need to be happy, but in truth, it is my needing that is making me unhappy."

"I Need A Way Out, Just In Case"

Another reason men and women hold on to the experience of looking outside their relationships is because of the belief that they need a way out, a back door, a back-up plan in case they become unhappy. This can become a self-fulfilling prophecy in the sense of "what you fear, you create."

You will not become unhappy while you are focused inward in your relationship; you will only become unhappy when your mind takes you into the world of comparison and ogling at other women or having affairs with other men. This is, in fact, one of the biggest reasons people become dissatisfied in their relationships. It is not because you change over time and your compatibility changes; it is because you sever your compatibility every time you look and fantasize elsewhere. Of course, this behavior is going to lead to dissatisfaction. It is like buying the brand new car you have always wanted, but instead of enjoying, it you keep looking at your neighbor's new sports car. It does not matter what you yourself have because you never notice it.

Having a back door creates the need for a back door. Rather, maximize the present moment by being present, and let the future evolve. After all, what better way to ensure a brighter future than to feed and nourish the present?

This brings up another Mind Lie, one that is addressed to men only: the more successful a man becomes, the younger the woman or the more women he should have. Let us heal this Mind Lie now.

Success does not mean spreading your seed; in thinking so, you would be spreading your seed from the space of needing to be successful: "I do not feel successful now, so I will create children who will not feel successful." You may think your sperm does not reflect the space you are in when you ejaculate, but it does.

Having sex with a younger woman in order to feel younger does not make you younger, truth does. When you reach this level of truth, you will make decisions based on what will make your life better, richer, and more sustainable instead of what gives you a quick adrenalin hit. Think not in terms of people solving your Mind Lies—they cannot, they just amplify them—think rather in terms of others being attracted to your Mind Lies to raise them up for you to see and deal with. Truth will heal them, leaving you to attract in or remain with the person who best complements your level of evolution.

What keeps you young is truth, not hiding from it or supplementing it with nontruth. This is where free will comes into play. There are times when you are far more comfortable with nontruth than truth, and there is absolutely nothing wrong with that, because you will get to see the truth at some time in the future. You may need to suffer in the meantime in order to bring it up nicely and clearly.

Notice what you are attracted to, because this is what you desperately want in yourself. It could be youth, physical fitness and a toned body, money, or a carefree attitude.

Be aware of what draws you in. What you are drawn in by is also what you are running from, yet it is already available to you from yourself.

"I Need To Be Distracted; I Need Options"

This Mind Lie leads you to have a perpetual fear that if you actually focus on what is right in front of you, on what is important to you, you will die of boredom, or worse, lose your identity. Variety is the spice of life, or so your mind believes. But in actuality, success in all areas of life comes from focusing on what is truly important to you, not on what you think will help you focus on what is important to you.

You want to keep your options open, but being distracted takes you away from what is important and ultimately closes your options. Options exist in abundance when you are focused and looking in the right direction. How can you see options when you get distracted by thinking you need options?

You say, "But I need options; surely I need choices."

Options is another word for *distractions*.

You think options are pathways and opportunities, but the way the mind believes, options are ways away from something, as if you need to run away from something that confronts or scares you. This could be being a dad, being married, or staying in a worthwhile career or business. It is amazing how many options appear when you are confronted by such situations. These options are not a coincidence; they are self-generated. You manifest new pathways to avoid your confrontation and fears. But what you fear is what you seek, and each pathway offers a diversion away from what you seek, despite the pathway that appears to be heading *toward* what you seek.

A diversion is something that promises fulfillment but offers the same predicament you confronted in the first place, be it commitment, self-realization, or even self-love.

You see, what you are avoiding, is the recognition that you are enough with what you have. Always seeking new and alternative paths is not—as you would think—living life to the fullest; it is living life at the emptiest. You are most empty when you believe you are not enough.

So what is the truth? To sit and be with what you are confronted by brings you to the peak of the discomfort, and with that comes the clarity and certainty that the discomfort is not arising out of the new situation but out of an old one. It has always been in you. The discomfort is the thought or feeling that you will never be happy just as you are. You need to be more, have more, have a variety of things, and so on. But the truth is that you actually need very little, especially of distractions, when you believe you are enough. Life becomes very easy when you have modest needs. The truth is not something you have been able to see until now:

You, the real You, is life itself. To think you are not enough makes no sense. You are all there is. You are more than enough.

You may have difficulty taking this in because you believe that there is more to life; in fact, you have needed there to be more to life—adventure, lust, validation, conquering, achievement, awakening—but there is not. Life just is. Life is all-encompassing, so to think you need more is erroneous. You actually need less, in the sense that once you understand you are life itself, you will have fewer needs.

You can need less by realizing, "I am already that which makes me whole. I am the very substance my mind believes I must receive for fulfilment." You are it. You have it already. Be it!

The resistance that comes up is that "I will miss out on the sweets life has to offer." But you already have missed out; distraction took care of that. To ensure this missing out stops, realize that you are already enough. The sweetness of life can be felt in full realization of truth, not in running from truth. Remember:

The secret to being happy is liking yourself,

the secret to a great life is loving yourself, and

the secret to being fulfilled is knowing that you are life.

These realizations are essential ways of keeping your focus, and keeping your focus is essential for such realizations.

When you try to live life, you have forgotten that you already are life. Do not live it; this is not required of you. Just see yourself as life.

"When I Am With A Sexy Person, I Feel Sexy"

The next Mind Lie to deal with is the sense of validation a person receives when sleeping with a sexy woman or man. The Mind Lie is, "If I am with sexy person, that makes me a sexy person." But sexiness is not transmitted through having sex.

Sexiness can also be talked about in terms of the feeling of being attractive, being a stud, feeling sexy, feeling desirable, and so on. The truth is that there is nothing sexy about a man or woman who needs someone else to make him or her feel sexy.

Sexiness is an innate trait that increases the closer you are to your true power and decreases the further you are away from it. This is why celibacy is a conduit to realizing your own sexy nature. To eliminate inauthentic sources of feeling sexy and replace them with finding your inner truth is highly sexy. Have you noticed how attracted women and men are to those who show no interest?

What you are being attracted to is not what you think is attracting you. It is not them as your mind has you believe. It is like light refracting through a lens: The person who is being perceived as sexy is the source of the light. Their light is penetrating your lense, activating your Mind Lies or better said, placating them. What shows up are all the reasons why this person is the solution to your woes, how a sexual dalliance with her or him is the answer you have been searching for your whole life. This feeling happens in a split second, and you believe all your problems will disappear. It is the closest sensation to the afterlife that most humans get without having to endure a horrific trauma.

In this moment, you are catapulted out of your world as you know it and into bliss land, where everything is heavenly. But this comes at a cost. To entrap yourself into this space, to be seduced by this process, locks you into oblivion, denial, and resistance to moving forward. You have been seduced, and to your spouse, you are as good as roadkill while you believe the other person is the answer.

What does this sexy person represent? Nirvana—the end of your problems. But in reality, this person represents the beginning of even more problems on top of the ones you think just disappeared.

Talk about a highly addictive drug high. You crave that rush pumping through your veins, that excitement, the thrill of the chase, only to realize later that your problems did not go away, they multiplied, and you hate yourself even more than you did before. It seems like a no-win situation. Or is it?

Mind Lies do not make you sexy. The truth is, you are sexy, but only to those who see beyond your Mind Lies. Sexy in its truest sense comes from an absence of Mind Lies. But sexiness in today's low standards as depicted in movies, magazines, and TV shows comes from people who need the rest of the world to find them sexy. They ooze out their sexual energy to give you the impression that they are sexy, trapping you like a fly in a spider's web. But if you could see what their energy really looks and feels like underneath the sexy smokescreen, you would run the other way.

"Someone Else Can Validate Me"

It is absolutely a Mind Lie that someone else could validate you. This Mind Lie is behind the need to be with someone sexy, the need to be impressive, and countless other Mind Lies. So many of them slip through the cracks, blending in with what you consider to be fact. So much is done, so much is attempted, and so much energy is wasted in needing the approval of others. The illusion is that approval from others will validate you. It will not.

You know by now that what you truly seek is approval from yourself. Seeking it from others is meant to give you the permission to get it from yourself. If others think you are great, then maybe you can think you are great. That is the thought process, but it is flawed. What you receive is someone else's endorsement, not your own. You see yourself through their eyes, not your own. What you really crave is not to see yourself through any eyes, but to see yourself without any context or reference point.

Let me explain. Your mind is fixated on reference points and comparisons, but without time and space there are no reference points and no need for them. Move away from any fixed point of reference, because the mind is this fixed reference point.

Seek to transcend needing any reference point, and the truth will open up to you.

You do not need validating, because there is no you. All validation does is keep in place the Mind-Lie you. You do not need a reference, because the real You spans the depth and breadth of the Universe. You do not need to understand this yet, because needing it is coming from "I am not it." Relate to yourself as the truth itself, not as the body that holds it. A shift in perception changes everything.

"I Need To Be Thought Of As Sexy, Or I Will Not Get The Attention Or Love I Deserve"

Why do you need to be sexy? Is it because Hollywood says so, or is there more to it than that? Unfortunately, this Mind Lie is underpinned by many others, so you have to do some digging to get to the root of it.

The identity clings to the unattainable and keeps you chasing and running toward something that is always changing, always distracting you from your most glorious truth. If you could see what you really look like, you would see that the true You is radiant light that knows no limits.

As radiant and beautiful as you are, there is still the desire to look physically beautiful and to be considered sexy. Understand that the mind is attracted to what it believes it should be but is not. In other words, you are attracted to what you believe you do not have but should have. You are drawn to others that seem to have what you are missing, and this is what makes them sexy. As you see it, your lack of attraction is what makes others seem highly attractive.

As you crave in another what you crave for yourself, you still feel it is of utmost importance to be sexy. Your need to be sexy stems from needing to be loved, wanted, desired, held, accompanied, and respected. You want to be sexy because you want to be desired, to feel OK in your own skin, because right now you do not. You believe that to be sexy means to be lovable, because you are not sure that you are lovable. For some, being sexy has come to mean being respected (by those who do not believe they aren't sexy!).

You want to be sexy, and you see sexiness in others, so you seek to be like them. But they do not think they are sexy (or rather, they do not see themselves as worthwhile human beings), so they seek to be sexy like someone else who seems sexy, who also thinks that they are not anything special, either. Sound crazy? It is. It is like a new pair of shoes that everyone wants because they think it will make them cool, when all along it was never the shoes that made them cool, but believing in themselves. When you believe in yourself, you do not need shoes to be cool, because you just are cool. The same goes with being sexy.

Being sexy is another, perhaps more fashionable, way of feeling OK about yourself. The more you are desired, the more the void of feeling undesirable is filled, yes? No. No matter who you attract in, when you come from the Mind Lie of "I am undesirable," you will be left feeling undesirable. Undesirable in, undesirable out.

You may think that if someone else thinks you are desirable, then they must be right and you are desirable. Here enters another fantastic Mind Lie: "What others think of me makes me that."

"What Others Think Of Me Makes Me That"

If someone thinks you are sexy, then you must be sexy. Maybe in their eyes, but that is not really what you desire, is it? What people think of you is not an indication of who or what you really are. Yes, there are those who can see your light and see into you, see the real You. But they see themselves first, which allows them a brief glimpse into your soul. The same can be said about someone seeing you as sexy: they see their own sexiness when they see you. Remember, you are a mirror to the world.

Allow me to take you deeper. This need to be seen as sexy and the need to have sex with a sexy person can be seen as not only validating yourself but also as needing to be one with your True Self. This is why you crave sex with beauty.

You are trying to return to how you once saw and loved yourself.

Sex has become twisted into a way to bring in what you most desire: desire itself. Not desire for others, or even being desired, but more importantly, desiring yourself. Why do you find yourself so undesirable? You may think, "I don't find myself undesirable; I think I'm pretty sexy." If this were true, you would not need other people's thoughts and opinions to give you your own.

Metaphorically to have sex with yourself is what you desire most. What does this really mean?

In truth, sex as it can and should be is the union with body and spirit, body and Universe becoming one again and returning to love.

Is this not what you desire for yourself in every moment of the day, this level of connection? Of course it is, whether you are aware of it or not. You experience disconnection fueled by your Mind Lies, yet it is reconnection that you are chasing. Not more money, not being more successful, and not being more sexy. It is just reconnection.

"Everyone Else Knows More Than I Do"

Imagine an image of the human brain, and you will note that each section of the brain plays a unique and important role. You will also note that to maximize the brain's full potential, it needs to draw on all aspects of itself: the interaction of parts that, when combined, produce a total effect that is greater than the sum of it individual parts. Now picture planet Earth as representing the human head and all living creatures representing parts of the brain. It is only when all parts interact purposefully and in combination that you get the results you desire.

Each human being represents a piece of the larger puzzle, or the Universal brain. You come gifted with the capacity to channel your talents and abilities toward the greater good and your total satisfaction. You come with a unique purpose that, when combined with complementary people, produces a total result greater than the sum of its parts.

The truth is that everyone else knows different than you, not more than you.

The deeper you look at it, the more you can see that everyone is You, and by that reckoning, everyone has the same access to the same knowing; it is just being channeled via you for specific purposes.

The Mind Lie is once again comparison—how much others know versus how much you know. Do not confuse meaningless knowledge for inspiration. There are a plethora of people who have accumulated libraries' worth of general, scientific, academic, and other knowledge. This is not a relevant point of reference. Does this information add to the quality of their life, or does it just add to the stability of their identity? Will this knowledge shift the identity, moving you and others forward?

It is not what you know, who you know, or how much, but how agile you are to change.

Knowledge can either help you to change or hinder you from change. Your mind's identity relishes what you know, so much so that it sees itself as an intrinsic part of your self-worth. To question what you know may lead you to becoming more, which is exactly what the mind does not want for you. What if you move beyond who you think you are? What if you sway into no longer seeing yourself as the big fish anymore? What if you see that what you thought you knew is not actually the whole truth, or even part of it? These fears can be scary, and looking at them is terrifying for anyone basing their whole identity on how smart or knowledgeable they are.

Obviously, these fears are all Mind Lies. It is your ability to make changes that allows you to stand out from the rest, to thrive and be happy. Knowing what you know to be correct reduces your need to look further, but when you realize that the greatest obstacle to discovering the truth is believing you already know it, then you keep an open mind. Open minds grow much more quickly than closed minds. In fact, it is an evolutionary advantage to be open-minded yet not gullible; there is a difference. Those who seek to feel truth resonate on a cellular level are most likely to prosper on Earth.

Ask yourself, "How quick am I to change and evolve?" because that is far more important than what you know. In truth, knowing how to change is the most useful knowledge there is.

"I Do Not Know Enough"

As you get out of your own way to evolve, your knowing surpasses what your life has taught you; it goes deeper than your intellectual brain knows. Beneath the mind that you have come inaccurately to think of as your source of knowledge is an infinite well of knowledge, far beyond any resource or brain on Earth. In truth, You are this knowledge.

Believing you are the mind reduces you to knowing only what the mind knows. Believing, or better—knowing, you are the infinite knowledge of the Universe grants you access to it. You have what you are.

Normally, and for most of your life, the mind has been trying to accumulate something it believes exists outside of itself: more knowledge. And it is right. Truth and universal knowing are not part of the frequency of the mind; rather, the frequency of the mind is part of it.

To seek knowledge and truth outside of yourself makes little sense, if any, when you are the bubble that houses both knowledge and truth. You are the body that contains it all. How can anyone know more than you? It is simply impossible.

This leads to the two ways of gaining knowledge. You can learn it from outside of yourself, or you can remember it from the inside.

When you realize that you are knowledge, it quickly becomes available to you, like a frequency being drawn into your hands.

Everything is a frequency—hatred, love, all the answers you seek. As they exist as frequencies in the Universe, and as You are all frequencies, all knowledge is yours; all knowledge is You.

"Other People Are More Talented Than I Am"

You believe that others (*which* others is not clear) have more going for them than you do: more skills, more talent, the ability to learn more easily and understand more—they are just more capable than you. But who are you to judge what your ultimate skills and talents are? Have you discovered them all? Have you begun to master any of them? The act of comparison is your greatest saboteur. It stops you from ever allowing your true talents to shine. Comparison does more to stifle achievement than to spur it on.

Those who appear to exhibit a greater skill level than you, whatever it may be, have less to do with core talents and abilities and everything to do with how they have been raised to see themselves. Self-belief is the key to limitless talent and ability. How much of that were you raised with?

The people who excel at something better than you do have just reached a point where they happen to have fewer Mind Lies than you in that area, so they are able to tap into their core abilities more easily than you can. This is the case with professional tennis players, mathematicians, business people, and anyone else in any field at all.

You are gifted beyond what you can allow in right now. If this does not seem the case, it is because there is a labyrinth of Mind Lies blocking you from recognizing it. Not seeing it means not being able to access your hidden talents and abilities. You can draw on only what you believe you have. This is why shifting beliefs is critical to advancing your growth. It is not that you are not smart, gifted, strong, and so on; it is just that you do not believe you are any of these things.

"Self-belief is the key to unlock infinity." [From *The ALL KNOWING Diary*]

This is a good time to remind you of how pointless it is to compare yourself with others. It is futile, in fact. It creates a holding pattern in which all you can see is someone else, when all you need to see is yourself—You.

You are the real You!

The real you has no limits, because You are all frequencies, consciousness itself. Musical notes, engineering principles, love-making magnificence, success principles, peace, harmony, and infinitely more exist within you, within your consciousness.

The best artists, composers, tennis players, and the like all have a basis in your reality. All the best of the best principles live within you. This is not to say that they are all readily available; some may prove to be more of a distraction from your purpose than a worthwhile pursuit, while others are just not for now. But many are.

Consciousness is You. You are it, and as You are it, you are endowed with its inherent characteristics—in this case, *all knowing*. It is currently squeezed into the tiny body you call you, despite such appearances being deceiving, but, so too are the Mind Lies that say otherwise. The mind says that you are really small on Earth, but the truth is much bigger, as are You.

You never need to look outside of yourself to wish for what another has, never need to be envious or jealous or resentful. You already have what you need to be fulfilled; you just need to tap into it.

Many spend their entire lives following in the footsteps of others, believing that if they do not have the same skills as other people, then they can not be counted or make a difference. How can they ever succeed if they are not exactly like those they aspire to be?

The truth is that those who are truly successful are this way because they believe in themselves. This frequency of belief has catapulted their thought waves into new heights, showing them the exact pathway to manifesting their own success their way, not someone else's.

"I Need What Other People Have To Be Happy And Successful"

This Mind Lie can easily be replaced with truth. A simple subtraction and rewording should suffice. Let' firstly subtract the nontruth—'other people'.

What's left after removing other people and a slight shuffling is "I have what I need to be happy and successful." That is the truth. You already have what you need, but you will not recognize it by looking at other people.

There you go, that should do it!

"I Should Be Great At Everything"

This Mind Lie shows how your beliefs can go from one extreme to the next. This is characteristic of the mind—to go from not believing you are great at anything to needing to be great at everything.

This is not about whether you should be great at everything; it is about being great at what you love. Follow the love, because what you love is what you are inherently great at. To need to be great at everything is to be fooled by the mind into needing approval and validation. Do not get pulled in. Following what you love is the opposite of the mind.

You are not here to do everything, nor to be great at everything. The need to be great at *anything* is a Mind Lie. The truth is that "great" evolves as fast as you evolve. What is great in one moment changes in the next. You think that there is a singular definition of great, but there cannot be, as it would defy the laws of evolution itself. "Great" is an ever-existing and ever-changing notion. If you need something to hang on to—which you do not—I will give you this: doing what you love is great!

When you do what you love, you excel faster than when you do anything else.

The mind wants you to be great at everything so that you and others can think of you as great. But when you do what you love and your heart sings with so much joy emanating widely, everyone will be inspired to do the same.

People who exhibit great talent also exhibit great love for what they do and who they are. The world needs more people doing what makes their hearts sing. It does not need more people seeking recognition by trying to be impressive to others, making them jealous and sending them back into needing to please their Mind Lies. Be inspirational. It keeps you and others out of the mind instead of being in the Mind Lies.

Love yourself enough to do only what you love, and you will get to see just how amazingly talented you are.

"I Am A Nobody If I Am Not Really Smart"

The world has seen many smart people do all kinds of stupid things, with the result that they became nobodies in the truest sense of the word. Where do you think the atom bomb came from? It came from people who thought they were being smart. The same goes for the inventors of plastic bags, the combustion engine, insane taxation, monetary systems, and so on. To be smart is one thing, but to be wise is beyond smart; being wise takes you far beyond being a somebody. Without wisdom, all being smart creates are failures, disappointments, and disasters rather than successes. Wisdom is the guiding force of intellect. It governs how best to harness it and where to apply it for the betterment of humanity, your family, and yourself. Unfortunately, the sole focus for most of school systems is intellect, leaving wisdom to be learned in later life. Should it not be the exact opposite?

Unfortunately, you are living in a society that values intellect over wisdom, which is anything but wise. Until now, it was believed that wisdom followed intellect, that it came from the learning experiences that the intellect provided. But, of course, this is not true.

Allow wisdom to provide the learning, not the other way around.

Wisdom is innate to you. It comes standard in you, and what it does, which very few realize, is open the vault to more knowledge than the sum total of every book on Earth.

Without wisdom, you will destroy yourself. Without wisdom, the mind runs rampant, creating solutions to problems that create more problems. There are countless examples of this all over the world.

Smart is not what you should be aiming for. To do so is just not smart!

Are you a nobody unless you are really smart? The truth is that, without wisdom, you may very well be a nobody. But before you start believing that you are without wisdom, know that you are not. Wisdom is who you are; it is your very nature. It is just the mind that values itself above and beyond what lies hidden underneath.

Wisdom is the ability to know what is smart and what is not. Smart knows that wisdom is smarter. Could it be that limiting yourself to just being smart made you a nobody? The world needs wise people far more than it needs smart people. Smart people cannot see where their smarts are taking them and the world, whereas wise people can. You desire to be smart because you believe that it makes you a somebody, but it is being wise about your smarts that makes you a somebody, and *to be wise over being smart is both smart and wise.*

Let us go deeper; with wisdom you will see beyond needing to be a "somebody" and into realizing there is nobody, and there was never a somebody, only a need.

"I Am Not Loved, Nor Am I Lovable As I Am"

Many people believe the Mind Lie that they are not loved and not lovable. What is not lovable about you? What makes you this way? Can you put your finger on it? Even if you could, you know by now that whatever your reasons are, they are not the truth.

You might not have the body shape you want or the youthful glow you once had. You may have been accused of having a temper or much worse. But you are the only one who believes that these things make you unlovable. This is the critical point your mind is distracting you from. The judgment that you are unlovable is not "out there in the world." Only in your mind are you not lovable; it is your own definition. Your mind has you believe that there is some invisible committee out there deciding on what lovable looks like. The good news is that there is not. It is within you, which makes it fixable.

When you look closely, you can see that this is a vicious cycle. The made-up you, your mind, says that you, your mind, is unlovable. It says that you and it do not meet the criteria of what is lovable. Your mind is the judge and the accused. So what is the truth?

To be lovable is to see yourself warts and all and be OK. The thought that you could have been anything else is completely erroneous. The thought that you should be something else is equally erroneous. The you that thinks you should be more to be lovable is the very reason you cannot see just how lovable you already are.

Love is what transforms the unlovable into the lovable. It is simple: You believe that you are unlovable. If you take away the love, you are left with being unable. But if you bring back the love, you are lovable—able to love. Taking love away makes you unable—unable to love, unable to be happy, unable to be healthy, unable to reconnect with your true nature.

Loving all facets of yourself is the quickest way to heal what you hate about yourself. But you and many others were not taught that as a child. You were not taught to love all parts of yourself, to have unconditional love for yourself. By being scorned for your misbehaviors, you were taught to hate parts of yourself. Mom and Dad yelled at you for your "disgusting" behaviors or for failing at school. They withdrew their love from you when you displeased them, and so the pattern continued. They thought they were doing you a favor by correcting your behavior with a few firm or even harsh words, but what they did was teach you to scorn yourself. Now you withhold love from yourself if you display anything you deem displeasing. Your parents only did this, because they were taught to do this to themselves by their parents.

Scorning yourself has become the way you deal with the parts of yourself you do not like, so you are in a self-hating loop, finding it difficult to love anything about yourself.

Your very definition of what is unlovable came from your upbringing, what you experienced and what you witnessed others experience. So you hate anything about yourself that you do not believe is desirable. You scorn yourself for these aspects, keeping you in hate and out of love for yourself, as if hating parts of yourself will get rid of them. Hate plus hate equals more hate. It comes back to your equation. You are desperately trying to return to being lovable, but you replace the love with hate and end up with hateable.

Love exists in you already. Only when you believed you had a reason to hate yourself did you stop feeling the love.

It gets worse, because now you are being told to love yourself but you cannot; you hate yourself. Then you scorn yourself for hating yourself: double whammy! In truth, the problem exists because you resent that you cannot love yourself. When you love the fact that you have hatred for or discontentment about yourself, then love can begin to flow. Making the hate wrong just adds more hate into the equation.

Love the hate, laugh at it, make how many things your mind finds wrong with you humorous. This is important, because even though you have been told just how important self-love is, you will never achieve it by hating yourself for not having achieved it yet.

Keep this in mind, however: the you that hates all these parts of you is both the giver and the receiver of the hatred. It is like a mess that is both the mess and the creator of more mess. Do not fall for your mind's trap of believing any of this is real in the first place; the hatred you experience is fiction to begin with. It is the mind that hates itself. A made-up mind, made up hate about its made-up self.

All self-hatred is underpinned by Mind Lies. There are many Mind Lies that perpetuate it. Let us examine some of them.

"There Is Something Physically Unattractive Or Downright Ugly About A Part Of My Body"

This Mind Lie is understood by a simple truth: what you are repulsed about in your body is simply what repulses you about your mind. Whether you are too fat, too thin, have warts, scars, hair, or no hair, it is not your body that you hate but what is in your mind. Go easy on your body for reflecting the self-hatred in your mind, as hating it will not make it go away; loving it will.

You may be wondering what there is to love about too much fat, a bald head, toenails that keep falling off, and worse. It is difficult for the mind to let in, but there is much to love about all this. The first thing to love is that these symptoms are your body's way of bringing something to your awareness that you otherwise refuse to acknowledge. Do not get cross at your body; it is cross at you!

The second thing to love is that self-hatred did not originate with you; it came from years and years of societal conditioning. You do

246

not need to hate yourself for the self-hatred that didn't originate from you in the first place. You may not love this, but there is no need to keep hating it, either.

The third thing to love is that each part of your body is a teacher. As you heighten your awareness, your body begins to whisper to you, communicating as clearly as if you were sitting across from a long-lost friend. The information that comes from each body part rivals any medical encyclopedia. In fact, if it were heard, it would prove most medical books obsolete. Your body is here to teach you about your evolution, just as the Earth is. Your body and Earth are one, connected in every way. You might see having to sit and listen to your body to heal it as a burden or inconvenience, but the bigger burden would be to allow your body to deteriorate even more.

It is a gift that your body can show you in this way. It prevents worse things from happening in your life. You only hate what you believe is not OK, and you think that it is OK to do so because you believe others will think the same. But they will only think you are not OK because you remind them of how much they are not OK with themselves. That is what the body is reflecting back to you. Be OK with this.

"I Have A Temper, I React Too Strongly, And I Can Be Mean And Rude; There Is Something Wrong With My Personality"

This Mind Lie can be very powerful and difficult to overcome. Realize that your personality is absolutely priceless and as unique as a fingerprint. What makes it less appealing or less useful to you are the Mind Lies trapped within you. Your overreactions and lashing out, even your violent tendencies, are not you or your intrinsic personality. They are Mind Lies, once again coming up in your awareness to be dealt with and healed. You are not irrational, highly reactive, or anything similar, but Mind Lies are. They drive this type of behavior in seconds—faster than seconds.

Behind every reaction, every yelling match, and every time you allow others to walk all over you are Mind Lies. That is not your intrinsic self; it is just a shadow version. You can hate this about yourself, see it as dysfunctional, and aggravate your Mind Lies further, or you can love and embrace this side of yourself as simply a work in progress. Love that this is the experience to overcome. This is the fastest way to keep all these reactions at bay. Nothing makes a reaction go to an extreme than self-hatred; you feed it every time it happens. Love that it is not the real You and never was.

"There Is Something Wrong With My Health; I Have An Illness Or A Disability"

There is no question that it can be immensely difficult not to hate having health problems. However, they are opportunities for self-love through compassion. Be compassionate to yourself for having thoughts of hatred about certain conditions you are going through. It is not unreasonable to hate these experiences, so be loving about how natural it is to despise serious impediments to living.

Understand that the biggest reason for self-hatred is once again the belief that it should not be this way, that others do not suffer this way, that you never dreamed of life going this way—why you are the only one, and so on. Who said it should not be this way? Just because the majority of people are not dealing with whatever you are dealing with does not make it any less purposeful. The thought that your life should not be this way is one of the biggest causes of self-hatred. Have you ever heard a more blatant nontruth? The mind is playing a trick on you with this one; thinking that your life should not be this way is how the mind keeps holding you back. It is difficult to imagine, and equally difficult to accept, that all things are the way they should be. This is opposed to the way they could be, but there is an infinite number of those.

What you are experiencing is necessary in order for humanity in general not to experience it any longer. You are living a by-product of what humanity has on some level created for you. To believe it should be any other way is naive, inaccurate, and against the nature of flow and cause and effect. It is like watching the rain outside and saying, "That is not right. The leaves on the trees should not be wet." Or worse, it is like burning your hand on the oven and saying, "I should not be burned right now." Why should you not be burned? The oven was hot, you put your hand onto the hot surface, and the laws of physics dictate cause and effect, so now you are burned.

I am not saying that you put yourself in a wheelchair because you were a clumsy idiot and gave yourself an illness. What I am saying is that cause and effect are the bottom line. Nothing happens by itself. What has happened to you and what is happening to you is happening for a reason: it should happen. Remembering this will take away a lot of the self-hatred that bases itself on this Mind Lie—because yes, it should happen, and yes, it is meant to.

What does "meant to happen" mean? It means nothing. It just is; simple cause and effect— physics. There is no hidden meaning other than the truth. Truth and physics are one and the same.

Things are as they are meant to be, for they cannot be any other way until the reason for why things are the way they are change.

There are plenty of other reasons why you think you hate yourself or believe you cannot get past self-hatred, so let me sum up the truth like this: what you hate, the you whom you are hating, all the excuses you believe you have to hate—all the justifications are there to do just one thing: to hide how much you really do love yourself.

People who hate themselves fit in perfectly in this human world. People who love themselves do not. It has become the norm to despise something about yourself, so you believe hating yourself causes others to love you so that you feel included in society. But this inclusion comes at the greatest cost of all: loving yourself. To be included in another's love means that you do not get to be included in your own.

To hate yourself about something is viewed as protection from those that will hate that something about you. "If I get in first, I won't feel the hate and the pain," you believe. Insanity! Hating anything about you does not protect you. Rather, it guarantees even worse pain and suffering than what you imagined you needed to protect yourself from. In fact, it gives you more to hate later on, not less. Love heals, hate destroys. Self-love is the best form of self-protection and defense available.

Defy the convention, defy fitting in, defy the norm, because these are the access out of self-hatred and back into self-love.

"The More Things I Have, The More Status I Accumulate And The More Worthwhile A Person I Become"

Fortunately, a new understanding has recently made its way into popularity; that is the paradigm of Be-Do-Have, a stark contrast to the Mind Lie of Do-Have-Be. You see, Mind Lies such as "I need to do more or have more in order to be happier" sentence you to needing things outside of yourself in order to achieve inner states of greatness or happiness. But as the Be-Do-Have paradigm suggests, the truth is quite the opposite. It says, "When I am being more, I will need to do less to have more."

In other words, the more you are and the more you see yourself, the more you have and are able to experience. Everything begins with the space; it is the very reason behind this book. Once you master the space or state of being, the doing and the having are natural extensions. Creating from a Mind Lie space, such as lack, insecurity, frustration, and other forms of fear, takes from rather than adds to your life. To create or make decisions from truthful spaces, such as love, abundance, self-belief, and knowing, will add to the quality of your life and that of and others.

The need for status comes from a nontruthful space, such as not feeling OK as you are, not feeling loved enough by others, and so on. Creating anything from this space will not be your most direct path to happiness. The need for status creates high amounts of pressure on you and fuels the need for accumulating things, as if things and pressure are what you were searching for in the first place, whereas what you are truly seeking is just love.

At the end of the day, if you choose to live a pressured life, you are not guaranteed more fulfillment than if you have learned to relax more. In fact, if you are living under extreme pressure to acquire more, you will end up less fulfilled, because it will be hard for you to find yourself under the burdensome weight of things.

Do not sacrifice your health and happiness for the attainment of things; rather, sacrifice the attainment of things to put your health and happiness first.

Remember, things do not equal happiness, but happiness can easily create more things. The most wonderful things to accumulate are wisdom and love in your heart. It is not about looking good, being impressive, or needing to compensate for not feeling enough. Rather, it is purely an act of self-love.

Success is not measured in terms of possessions but in terms of letting go of possessiveness, for this is the end of the ego, your false identity. If you truly want to be impressive, if you truly want to feel that you are enough, aim for this; it is the shortcut to happiness.

Realize that you cannot be added to. Nothing can make you more, no matter how much you try. "No thing" will make you more. Only letting go of things you have already added to yourself—like this Mind Lie and others—will truly make you more, be more, and have more!

Everything begins from the space in which it is created.

"I Have To Compete With Others As A Way Of Constant Improvement"

There is a perpetual belief throughout humanity that you are in some way akin to the animal kingdom, that its laws of survival of the fittest somehow apply equally to humans. In truth, survival of the fittest actually refers to your ability to evolve, not to compete. This simple misunderstanding often gets in the way of seeing the truth about human nature and drives you away from, not toward, becoming more.

You believe that without these drivers you will never become an equal to others—or worse, you will never get to be more than they are—and that this constitutes failure. Once again, this is a Mind Lie, and the truth is quite the opposite. You have a natural, inbuilt drive to be more, to keep growing, and not just as individuals, but collectively. This drive is called evolution, and it is constantly pushing for you to see yourself as more, not through using mind-based comparisons or ambitious pacesetters, but through revealing new and deeper truths to take you to the next level. You do not need others to race against to go faster; you do not need to go faster and deeper. This competitive mindset is causing havoc in your life!

> ***Daniel speaking:*** *This reminds me of a movie I recently watched about master chess players from the United States and Russia. I found it funny how both countries were so invested in their respective chess player winning. It was as if whoever won at chess represented the superior country. How ridiculous! Nothing changed after that; the people of the winning country did not immediately become saints or enlightened masters on the basis of that chess game. The fact that both countries were consumed by the Mind Lie of having to compete and win in order to look good showed neither to be the superior one. They both struggle with fundamental and*

basic belief systems, just like a teenager competing at school to win the approval of their parents.

The truth is that it was just a game of chess between two people who were either in the zone—in truth—or not, and for how long. It had nothing to do with who the superior country was. What it amounted to was who could be in a space of truth longer than the other for that moment for each game. If each country were focused on that unique skill, the world would be a very different place.

Truth equals checkmate, and truth will make you far superior—not against another but against yourself. It is not about others, it is about You, the former you, and the constantly evolving and growing you. In sport, you do not play against your opponent, you play against yourself—your mind; or rather, you play to stay out of your mind.

Those who stay out of their minds the longest win, and not just in sports but in life. You win true happiness, enlightenment, health, and fulfilment, none of which you get from winning against another person; you only get it by winning against your former self, the mind filled with Mind Lies.

Constant improvement comes by way of perceiving a nontruth, be that a reaction in the mind, a symptom in the body, a blockage, a disconnection from a loved one, or an apathy to life itself, and then doing the most competitive thing of all— discovering the truth.

This is called life, and life is the continuous unfolding of truth. It happens naturally and will keep happening until you have become everything you truly are, which of course is superior to anything you could become by competing against others. This process is happening right now; but the more you compete with others, the less you see the real opportunities for breakthroughs, starting with the realization that there is no "you," nor anyone else, with whom to compete. It is just minds competing against minds.

"I Am Not Liked As Other People Are"

This Mind Lie is a subtle twist on "I need to be liked" and one definitely worth exploring.

Wherever you look, there will be those with more friends, more party invitations, and more opportunities at hand than you believe you have.

But ponder this: what will it take for what others receive not to matter to you? What will it take for you to see what you yourself have? I could go on about how meaningless many of the achievements of others are and how it is who you are as a person that creates your opportunities, but that is not the truth you need to focus on.

You seek validation as a human being, and being liked as much or more than others is a substantial validation. But do you really need to be liked by others to be validated? Needing to be liked as much as others is like needing any other kind of outside validation; it is just a poor substitute for receiving inner validation. It is a surface-level thrill, a Mind Lie, that needs constant feeding because it has an insatiable appetite for more.

Feeding yourself from yourself is a quick and permanent fix.

What do you need to know to help yourself like yourself? Needing to be liked is a distraction from your higher purpose on Earth. Nobody is here to be liked by as many people as possible. Being liked can lead to reaching others with an important message or touching lives all over the world, but center your focus on what is important.

When you hold a certain frequency, no matter what it is, a certain number of people will be attracted to you. A business expert attracts those who want to grow their businesses and are serious about listening. The Mind Lie that "I am not liked as other people are" works the same way: if you focus on needing to be liked, you attract others who need to be liked but are not necessarily open to what you have to share or give. If you focus on being your truth, you attract others who are also focused on being their truth.

What is more important, living your truth or needing to be liked? In the end, if you live your truth, you attract both.

By turning your mindset away from Mind Lies, you become a magnet that attracts opportunities, and interest around you intensifies.

You become a light that can be seen far and wide. This light makes a bigger difference to people's lives than if you are focused on quantity over quality. There are those who have a huge following of people, lots of friends and so on; and they deliver profound truths affecting people in incredible ways. This is because they do not care about numbers; they just care about being their truth. The more unattached you are to numbers and quantity, the more quantity multiplies.

What will it take for what others receive not to matter to you, and what will it take for what you already have to matter? If all someone has is the need to be liked, then he or she has nothing. Now you have everything, because you no longer need to be liked.

Interestingly, needing to like yourself is also a Mind Lie. But it is a good place to start, one that will spur you on to even greater realizations; for underneath such a need, is the ever-present well of self-love.

"I Am Strange, And Strange Is Unwanted, Unattractive, And Undesirable"

255

You now know that being different is what is needed. It is, after all, what makes life so interesting. But being strange has accumulated all kinds of unwanted connotations. At the end of the day, strange is just another useless label given to those who are not understood by the norm. It is just another Mind Lie.

Because of these connotations, it is wise to reframe the word *strange* and use more appropriate words, such as *unique*. Unique applies to anyone who exhibits character traits, skills, or abilities that stray from societal norms. This, in truth, is actually highly desirable. Societal norms have you where you are today—still wondering what went wrong in your life and where on Earth you can find fulfilment.

There are so many prevalent societal norms that you cannot see how dysfunctional they are. Some that come to mind are some of the obvious ones I have covered so far: the need to dislike yourself, the need to keep striving to be more, and the need to make money in order to find true happiness. Or this one: It is normal to experience pain during childbirth. This societal norm has become a fact of childbirth, but pain is not a symptom of birthing itself, so in the true sense it is not normal, just common. Birthing was designed to be a natural, safe, and wonderful experience. Just ask Daniel's wife, Sonja, who had all-natural and completely pain-free births for both their children. This is a perfect example of a norm that has gone unchecked.

Another societal norm that is so common yet dysfunctional is society's views on marriage. This, too, has become so contaminated by innuendo and connotations that, for most people, marriage is doomed from the start. Your beliefs have polluted the higher purpose of marriage, which is to celebrate the greatness that you are individually by collaborating as a couple to build upon each other's strengths. Together, you will go much farther than apart. Marriage is perfectly designed to heighten awareness, but most people use marriage to keep each other small and belittled. It has become a power play, a competition, with each of you moving on opposite paths and heading in different directions. It is a game of spite with no synergy, no collaboration or partnership in healing and growth. Divorce is certainly preferred to this outcome.

The point is that to lean toward societal norms shrinks you back into ways of being that are highly dysfunctional.

Comparison to the norm happens throughout your life, by your parents comparing you to your siblings, at school in terms of your grades and fitness, at graduation and into university, and all the way through life. Society needs more tests that measure and celebrate true uniqueness!

What you truly need right now is a departure away from norms, away from being like others. Being like others is what stifles society as a whole and condemns you to repeat your past, over and over again, with just slight improvements.

You must celebrate who you are as being unique instead of how similar you are or how much you do conform. Look at your fingerprints. They tell you that uniqueness is perfect, intended, meant to be, so honor it. You may not fit in now, you may not understand why you have this uniqueness, you may not know where it will ever fit in, but know this: like every molecule in your body, your uniqueness plays a vital role in achieving your success. The sooner you align to it and the faster you embrace it, the happier you will be.

You are strange, different, and unique—and thank goodness, because what you really are, what you have to bring to this world, is the best way for you to change lives, starting with your own.

Your uniqueness is a message. This message may come in the form of something you need to say or write, or it might be conveyed through others being in your presence—an invention, a mindset, a perspective, a flavor—but it is unlike anything anyone has seen or heard before.

"Strange" is what those who reject themselves call those who embrace themselves. It is a societal norm for people to reject their uniqueness. Play a role in changing that norm to one of embracing uniqueness. Make it a wonderful accomplishment for every human being to look forward to.

Congratulations to you on recognizing that you are unique!

"Everything Is Always My Fault; I Keep Getting Everything Wrong"

You believe nothing you do for others is ever right, but it is hard to see the truth when so many Mind Lies have been your truth for so long. To see this, you need to go to the other end of the spectrum, which is the realization, "I make an awesome contribution to this Earth and its inhabitants." Now that is a great truth! But can you believe it? What will it take for you to let it in? This truth depicts someone who loves what the Earth provides, honors the Earth, and will do what is necessary to protect it. Does that sound like you? If so, then you can start to allow in that you make an awesome contribution to this Earth and its inhabitants.

The problem, however, stems from your belief that your mistakes are failures. The truth is that a mistake does not equal failure. A misjudgment does not equal a flop, and attempts at pleasing others who remain displeased do not make you unsuccessful.

There are many run-ups in life before you get enough speed, enough momentum, and enough self-love to jump all the hurdles successfully. A run-up is not classified as a failure, so you must not classify any of your attempts at success or attempts at making life better for yourself and those you love as failures.

Remember, there is no you, so nothing can be wrong and be all your fault. This Mind Lie has you believe that the mind-made decisions that did not work out as hoped—that were based on what the mind knew at the time and believed about itself—were somehow wrong and your fault. But how on Earth could anything be more right? This is like saying that $1 + 2 = 3$ but should not, and that it is all your fault that it does!

You are not willing to let the truth in so easily on this one because you want the concept of failure still to exist in your life. You still want to think that you keep getting it wrong for others. This is because believing in failure keeps you trying and trying. It has you feel like a good, unselfish person who wants the best for others. But trying is a Mind Lie stemming from "I am not good enough in the first place," so you must make up for this wherever and whenever you can. Who you are does not provide enough, so you will do more, and doing more makes you a good person who is really trying and making an effort.

However, life is not about trying or making an effort to get it right for another. This is a huge mistake, because trying to better yourself in the eyes of others does not fix anything within yourself, it just glosses over the problem. Rather, you need to see yourself for what you are: a worthwhile contribution.

Recognize that by wanting the best for the Earth, helping to protect it, and being in gratitude for all that is does infinitely more than you realize. This is what is needed now. This beingness has sadly been lacking among those in power for centuries, by captains of industry and so-called leaders in politics. You, holding the space of gratitude, will turn these tables.

This is the simplest thing to let in, but the simplest thing is often the hardest. Just you being this way makes a powerful contribution to the Earth and those who inhabit it.

Perhaps you think I am avoiding the real concern here: "What about making a worthwhile contribution to those in my own life?" They are of the Earth, and being closest to you, they benefit the most. Being a compassionate human being makes you all-around compassionate. People in your life need this and benefit greatly from it. Your wisdom illuminates them. Your love warms their hearts, giving them drive to move forward. And your glances, the way you look at them, makes them feel loved through and through.

You are enough, just as you are.

Stop trying. You are only trying to get it right for them so that you can take credit and say, "Well, at least I tried." But trying is not worth taking credit for. It makes you resentful and unpleasant to be around, and it has others feel they can never get it right for you. Knowing you are enough frees you up to love yourself and spread that love all around. This is what moves you out of getting it wrong and accidently into getting it so very right.

"I Need For People To Listen To And Agree With Me"

The belief that you need people to listen to and agree with you is a Mind Lie. In truth, you do not need for anyone to listen, and you do not need for anyone to agree with you.

You may wonder how you can make a point, do your job, make money, get others on board, and make a real difference to people, but that is not actually what you are wondering. What you are really wondering is, "How do I get to feel right if nobody listens? How do I get to feel good about what I say?"

The need to have people agree with and listen to you is not about creating a necessary result at work or home, or even in the political arena. You think the issue is about agreement or comprehension, but it is actually about your neediness; the need itself is the issue. This stems from subconsciously seeing others as an extension of you; if you cannot validate yourself, perhaps they will.

The truth is that you are heard by the Universe all the time. The Universe understands you better than you understand yourself. How many times have you looked at yourself when you were speaking and said, "This person is amazing! I know exactly why he is saying what he is saying; I get him fully!" How many times do you say that to yourself?

The Universe says that about you every single time you have a thought, every single time you utter a word under your breath or shout something from the rafters.

You see, right now the difference between you and the Universe is that the Universe believes you; it believes in you no matter how crazy what you are saying is. It fully understands why you say what you say, or think, for that matter. "I get you," it says. "Your reality is valid. Not entirely truthful, but valid." The Universe sees through your eyes and understands why you see life the way you see it: so you can feel completely and wholeheartedly validated. Everything you say makes perfect sense in the context of who you believe yourself to be. As this is the epitome of what constitutes being valid, you are valid!

Now there is the next layer to tend to: that validation does not equate to truth. Either something is true or it is not. It is time to stop seeking validation and agreement from others and to aim higher and seek to be truthful. History is full of people agreeing with people who were talking absolute nonsense. The agreement never makes what is said any more truthful. If it is not truthful, the agreement makes what is said much more dangerous. Seek to speak truth, because others hear what you say. Nobody needs for people to agree with anything more coming from Mind Lies.

The Mind Lie that "I need for people to listen to and agree with me" is about feeling good and the feeling that comes when others agree. You want to feel good, so I will offer you an even better feeling: the feeling that comes with speaking truth. It feels amazing whether or not others agree with the truth. This is a guaranteed feel-good strategy, vastly superior to anything being agreed with can ever offer.

"I Need To Prepare For Failure"

You believe that failure is imminent, so you prepare yourself for its eventuality and carry failure around with you wherever you go. You believe that preparing for it, anticipating it, will in some way cushion you from its wrath. If you are already falling, then somehow falling from failure will not hurt as bad. Unfortunately, this Mind Lie singlehandedly creates more experiences of failure than does failure itself.

This belief sets you up for failure, so much so that it blinds you from any and all successes, when all along you were heading into success. When you believe failure is a certainty, you take steps toward greater success, and anticipating failure is lumped in as one of these steps. Believing in failure and believing you need to insure yourself against it by bracing yourself, being on guard, and looking out for it, just brings it closer and makes it imminent. Not only that, it ruins any chance of realizing success or simply experiencing it. This is why so few successful people are able to see their successes. By the time outward success coalesces, it is invisible to them because they are still entrenched in the strategy of failure avoidance.

The truth is that nothing will cushion you from failure better than having a successful outcome, so prepare for that instead. Smiling takes far less effort and energy than frowning, and like smiling, preparing for success takes far less effort and energy than preparing to fail. So how do you prepare for success?

It is simple: know that there is no such thing as failure. Failure is mind made, the same as is this Mind Lie. It is all made up. You wonder, "Then what do you call the loss of money, bankruptcy, products that do not sell, business not doing well, going backward instead of forward, and too much stress in the body? Surely these are the hallmarks of failure." They are not. They are hallmarks of acting from your Mind Lies, not from the center of your inspiration. The trouble that you will encounter while making the transition from Mind Lies to inspiration is the leftovers—the seeds planted from the Mind Lies.

What is created from Mind Lies grows more Mind Lies. Do not confuse leftovers for failures, for they are not. Instead, see them as the end of creating from nontruth. You have spent your life creating from Mind Lies rather than truth, so all you know are the experiences they bring. You label this as failure, but the truth is that it is just nontruth created from a mind made of nontruth. Know this: anticipating failure is not wisdom, it is fear.

In wisdom, you can see that there is no failure until you label it a failure. If you refrain from using this label, you stop having anything to fear and no longer need to anticipate failure. Said another way, you are not nearly as afraid of failure as you are of yourself calling something a failure. Failure does not exist until it has been named or labeled as such. This is what the fear is really about. If you never labeled anything as failure, you would have nothing to keep you in fear. Get this word out of your vocabulary, and half the battle is won.

The second task is to realize that there are either Mind-Lie outcomes or truthful outcomes—there are no failures. If you experience an unwanted result, you can either label it as a failure or realize that it came from Mind Lies. This, in and of itself, is success. Success is seeing truth. Remember, success occurs in the moment of seeing truth, not as an outcome. It is like playing billiards: you know the second you hit the white ball whether you have been successful or not, long before a colored ball is sunk or not. Successful outcomes occur from successful—truthful—states of being.

In short, all outcomes lead to success when you refrain from labeling them as failures. Do not label failures, and you will find success is inevitable.

"I Do Not Know Who I Am; Everyone Else Knows Who They Are"

This Mind Lie is revealed with a little rephrasing so that you can see how ludicrous the belief really is. It goes something like this: "Everyone thinks they are their mind, but they are not."

You now know that there is no "I," so not knowing who you are and thinking everyone knows who they are is all quite funny. Who others think they are is not really who they are, and not knowing who you are is actually a major step forward from thinking that you *do* know who you are. It is a big advantage.

Being sure of who you are and having it not be the truth makes it harder for you to open up to who or what you *really* are. If you do not yet know who you are, congratulations! This is a great place to enquire from.

While many people seem confident about themselves, and self-belief, if it is authentic, is very powerful, it does not follow that such people are living at the pinnacle of what is possible. Confidence can certainly lead to taking charge of your life and creating success, but coming from confidence and nontruth does not lead to happiness, nor health, for that matter.

You take many cues from others as to where you should or could be. But to aspire to be like people who seem to know who they are will only limit what is possible for you. The space to come from is to release the need to know who you are, because this need is misleading in itself. Humans are chasing this answer their whole lives, running around in circles. Instead, be open to simply being, which will bring you back to your true nature, unlike the searching will. Defining or looking for ways to define yourself is a mistake; rather, remain open to just being; this is a blessing. You have just had it backward.

By now, you have come to see that you are not fixed in any way. Since the time you were born, everything about you has been changing. To look for who you are is to try to take a photo of a Formula 1 racecar around the track: all you will see is a blur.

The need to know who you are is based on the need for confidence in yourself, but these needs are both just more Mind Lies. Certainly, confidence can come from knowing that you are strong, attractive, wealthy, admired—a judge, a doctor. But real confidence, or absolute knowing, will come from an absence of Mind Lies. Confidence is not predicated on appearance, skills, or abilities but on the quantity and intensity of Mind Lies. You can be a model and lack confidence in every area of life except modeling. You can be a famous sports star and lack confidence in being a great parent—you get the picture.

Confidence, true confidence, is an absence of Mind Lies. The less you search for who you are and the more you dissolve who you are not, the sooner your confidence will bubble to the surface.

Knowing is the next level of confidence for humanity. It comes from existing beyond the mind, from no longer needing the mind. By comparison, confidence loses its shine very quickly. The trouble is that the mind thinks very differently when it compares itself to others. It looks for similarities and where it can fit in rather than for where it can truly stand out.

People do not know who they really are, but as soon as you discover what you are, you will notice others wanting to grow and realize the new level of contentment that they see in you.

Lead the revolution from feeling confident to knowing.

"I Do Not Deserve To Spend Money On Myself; If I Spend Money On Myself, I Will Never See It Again"

There is a widespread misconception that to give to yourself—be that in the form of nurture, such as a massage, facial, expensive food, or a night in a luxury hotel—is indulgent. For some, even getting help from an expert or undertaking training is seen as extravagant, unless you are wealthy. That is when it all becomes OK.

To do the opposite, to withhold such experiences from yourself, has been termed frugal and responsible. This says that to deny or deprive yourself will in some way lead you toward more fulfillment and enlightenment. People are constantly depriving themselves of what has been put on their path for the betterment of their lives. This is where you get to see how clever the mind is.

To deny yourself of indulgences that stem from the ego is wise, but to deny yourself soulful, nourishing, and uplifting experiences that come from self-love is irresponsible.

To deny yourself what creates or solidifies a True Self-connection is not enlightenment but self-defeat. You might ask how a facial, massage, or nice hotel room brings you closer to enlightenment. The answer is simple: it is not what you do, but the space or state from which you do it, that is important. Self-love is the most powerful connecting energy there is. Self-hatred, the energy behind denying yourself many of these experiences, disconnects you from your True Self. Anything that comes from Mind Lies recreates connection back to the mind. That which comes from truth realigns and solidifies you back to truth.

Frugality means spending what you have in the wisest way. *Irresponsibility* means spending what you have to try to appease your Mind Lies. There is nothing wrong with that, and to beat yourself up for it is unwise. Spending money from a space of self-love is often as powerful for your connection as is ten hours of meditation. There are many paths up the enlightenment mountain, and many experiences lead back to truth as long as they come from truth. Do not rule out spending money on furthering your connection back to You.

Self-denial is not truth; it comes from the Mind Lie "I am not worthy of self-love." The truth is that money is an extension and expression of self-love itself; it came from love, and more is made from self-love. If you stop loving yourself by not spending on yourself, you stop generating more self-love energy and stop the flow of more money coming to you. This is an important lesson to learn.

Bear in mind that money is made in three simple steps:

1. Self-love: knowing you are worthy of it

2. Self-purpose: living your purpose to make it

3. Self-awareness: knowing You are it

"I Need To Be A Somebody; Without An 'I,' I Am A Nobody"

Being a somebody is one of the most addictive needs a human being can have. People travel the world in search of themselves and spend their whole lives trying to figure out who they are. "I need an identity," you say. "I need to be this way, like him, like her, like I have always imagined," and "It is the way I need to be, or I will just die." In truth, it is the "I" that is slowly killing you. Let me explain.

There is no "I" on Earth that carries the same vibrational frequency as your True Self, your identity-free self—You. As such, all "I"s in some way reduce your life span, because anything less than your True Self carries a frequency of nontruth. After all, your body is made from 100 percent truth; it is 100 percent truth, so any thoughts or identities less than truth puts it in jeopardy.

"What is so addictive about this?" you ask. The need to be an "I" comes from needing direction. The belief is that you need to find yourself in order to know where you are going. The need for an "I" and the belief "I need direction" are Mind Lieds that create a vicious cycle. The need to know where you are going comes from the need to know who you are. The need to know who you are comes from the need to know where you are going. The truth is that it is not where you are going that matters, not even in the slightest. It is not who you are that really matters, either. The simple reason is that both cloud the truth. Focusing on where you are going causes you to miss where you are now, and it is the now that defines where you end up. Needing to know who you are clouds who you can be, which also dictates where you will end up. What is the missing truth, the key ingredient to releasing the attachment to these misidentified needs?

Life is not about finding your identity. It is about losing your identity.

Life is not about where you are going; everyone is going to their death. "But where am I going before that?" you ask. This is not the correct question because, in asking it, you are always avoiding the now.

Having goals, ambitions, and direction that comes from needing to define yourself is departing from your True Self. The more you look for outside indicators, the more you miss the point—the inner point. You are addicted to these two things because they give you the temporary reassurance that you are OK, but it is at the expense of your entire life. The inner point, the inner wisdom, recognizes that life is in the here and now and that "I" does not exist. Why spend your whole life searching for it? Why spend your whole life validating the path you have chosen? Thinking that you are lost as you are in the here and now is what drives all this searching. But the more you search, the more you come from feeling lost, and the more lost you become.

Realize that there is no finding yourself, because you do not exist. You cannot find what does not exist. And the more you look, the more you distracted you become from what *does* exist: the now. You will not find yourself out in the world; you will not find yourself in a job or in someone else. Leave the identity by realizing that it does not exist unless you search for it. Just stop searching. If you search for something outside of yourself, it will remain hidden inside, but if you search for it inside of yourself, it will remain hidden outside. Just stop searching.

If you let go of the search, you will realize that everything is the Self.

The world you see,

Is what is inside of me.

I am the world.

I am the water, I am the air I breathe,

I am the mountains and the trees.

I am the blue sky above,

I am the blue seas that I love.

I am the whales and dolphins, too,

I am the snow and what leopards do.

I am all I see and everything else,

I am all things, this is my True Self.

"Clearly I Am Just A Body, Nothing More"

People often believe only what they can see, and when it comes to the body, there is little exception. Nearly everyone on Earth can see their bodies, and so it has become the given identity of what it means to be a human being. But looks can be deceiving, especially in this Universe.

The resistance to seeing past this belief is the fear of "I see my body, I know it is real, but if you tell me there is more to me than that, a huge can of worms opens up. There will be too many questions, most of which I am unwilling to look at, as they will rock the very foundations from which I base my life."

But why the avoidance why the presence of fear? Fear has been ingrained in you over eons of life on Earth, the fear of allowing in the deep, hard-hitting truth because others out there in the world—specifically some of today's largest institutions—will be rocked to the core. It is these institutions that have perpetuated a climate of fear, keeping You hidden in the dark.

Consider people in the health industry as an example. They worry about their credibility if all of society realizes that the body is impacted by the mind and years of beliefs, generations of beliefs. They worry about losing their perceived authority if people learn that illness and disease is created first in thought from the mind, that thought is the cause and what occurs in the body is the symptom. The mind is the illness. The fear is about both reputation and loss of profits. The truth is that those in the medical industry would not suffer; rather, they would become more empowered and more profitable by embracing this truth rather than by practicing without it. Truth grows profits and reputations; it does not diminish them.

Far too many people and businesses have a vested interest in the perpetuation of nontruth throughout the planet and throughout time. Their profits depend on you being distracted from You.

You can take comfort in the fact that You are not just your body, nor even your mind, but rather something infinitely deeper that does not depend on these industries for its healing, salvation, and enlightenment. The industries that service your body and mind depend on your ignorance for their well-being, but your well-being depends on you realizing the truth—which is in You, not in them.

The Mind Lie that "I am just my physical body" keeps many in business and empties the pockets of millions every day. If everyone knew who and what they truly are, many of these professions would not get away with malpractice. The truth is, when you view your entirety as just your physical body, several things happen. The first is that you hand over your power to those who "know more" about you than you could ever know; and the second is that you inevitably give up being empowered, because you are led to believe that there is just too much to know about your body to bother trying. In turn, you give up on truth.

You are here to evolve from realization, and there are those who profit from you not evolving. These institutions and their beliefs exist within your mind; they are Mind Lies created. In fact, they are not the problem. The problem arises when you believe the Mind Lies that "I am just my physical body" and "I can believe it only if I can see it." You believe your mind, yet you cannot see it. You believe that you are your thoughts and your memories, but you cannot see them. You believe what others have wanted you to believe, and many of those people have made some pretty convincing arguments.

Know this: the body and its secrets exist in your blood, in your every cell, but you can never get to these secrets believing that you are just your body. You get to them by believing that you are these secrets and they are readily available. Your body already knows how to cure illness, avoid aging, and have a pain-free birth, but the Mind Lies block them out like clouds eclipsing the sun and getting in the way of truth, blocking the light from reaching your awareness.

You are the Intelligence behind all bodies, behind life itself.

The more you believe you are this, the sooner you will see things you never believed, such as how this Universe really works, and most importantly of all, the fact that You are the Universe. You made yourself; you just forgot.

"If I Do Not Make The Most Of My Time Now, My Future Will Suffer Because Of It"

Many of your activities are about safeguarding yourself against the future. Nest eggs, investment strategies, insurance, body building, and so on often come out of the need to prepare for the worst. You hope to prepare yourself for a better future than that of your parents, but are you going about it the right way? Or are you going about it the exact same way your parents went about it? Let us explore.

You fear being stuck with debt, poverty, poor living conditions, the need to rely on others for help, and the inability to help yourself. So you take many precautionary measures in the present, which seems wise, at least to the mind. But what are you really preparing for? Is it your future, or is it your past?

Wherever fear is present, nontruths are present. In fact, they are one and the same. As you know by now, to create from a fearful state of mind creates something to fear and takes something away from you in the here and now as well as into the future. But safeguarding against the future is a nontruth because it stems from the belief, "My future will, or could be, worse than my past and present, and I cannot allow that to happen." Why is this fear there? Is it because of your parents, the government, or people you have seen grow old and poor?

Or is it because you do not trust your innate ability to live purposefully in the present?

You are so afraid of squandering your time in the present that you honestly believe your future will be a by-product of it. So you take extra steps and exert additional energy to prepare, hoping to avoid this imminent failure. You believe that you will squander the here and now because there are other beliefs at play, one of which is, "Youth is wasted on the young," and any other beliefs centered around being young and foolish, carefree and irresponsible. This has been drummed into humanity to the point that you are on high alert, trying to catch yourself from squandering your precious here and now.

But here is the truth: in being afraid to make such a mistake, you are actually making a whole set of new ones. You are more exhausted than you have ever been, working more hours, stressed more than not, ill more than ever before; and yet you call this state of affairs preparing for your future. In the fight to protect your future, you are destroying your present. In doing so, you may not even have a future.

Foregoing on quality now to ensure a quality future is a doomed strategy; quality now actually creates a quality future. You cannot preserve the future by seeing it in isolation from the present, because the future *is* the present. What you do today, how you feel today, leads into how you will feel in your future, just magnified. To hold off in the present to protect your future creates a future with holes throughout.

A classic example is the parental conundrum of working long hours to prepare for a better future for the children. But they want you now! You prepare for a better future for your kids not by being absent but by being present.

When you fear being too poor in the future, you work tirelessly now to live comfortably in your older age, piling on the stress while you are young and believing you can handle it. This just creates a future in which you are too exhausted and unwell to enjoy it. So stop busting your gut now for the sake of your future unless you want a busted gut in your future.

You have to be now as you want to be in your future. If you want to love your life in the future, start loving your life now.

The present and the future are the same moment, despite what your mind has you believe. The here and now is the future, yesterday's future, last week's future. Tomorrow is here and now, and it is today's future. But the mind has you believe they are different from one another, disconnected by space and time, in the sense of hopping from one island to the next. Where is the separation between this moment and the next?

Plant seeds of love today, and you will have fruits of love tomorrow. One perfect yet harrowing example is the fear of people during the Cold War. Americans were so afraid of a future global communist regime—of losing their identity as a power player—that they began stockpiling nuclear weapons. The more they stockpiled, the more the Russians stockpiled. Now both nations sit on tens of thousands of these potentially Earth-destroying weapons. Both now have to deal with the environmental fallout of managing all the nuclear waste. One wonders whether their prevention took them further away from their fears or brought them closer than ever before? How safe do Americans and Russians, and the rest of the world, feel now? Not very.

Preparing for a worst-case scenario in the future brings worst-case scenarios into the present.

Digging Deeper

If it were up to You, you would be enjoying the present rather than preparing for the future. The mind separates the two as if they were mutually exclusive: "I cannot enjoy the present and simultaneously be safeguarding my future." This is the source of the problem. Such a tiny belief causing so much damage!

In truth, only enjoying the present ensures a future worth enjoying, and not just enjoying, but having the resources fully to do so. Ask Steven Spielberg whether making each movie was about preparing for his future or the best way he could enjoy the moment. Without enjoyment in the present, there is little or no inspiration flowing through you. It is inspiration that directs and guides your actions to the greater good, which is the greater good for the present and for your future.

Who you are today is infinitely more capable and abundant because of the steps you took from the guidance of inspiration years ago, and even last week.

Where there is joy, there is space for inspiration. Delaying joy until sometime in the future delays inspiration, which in turn makes your future suffer.

By preparing for your future, you are squandering the present. Enjoying the present safeguards your future.

"I Cannot Trust My Joy To Be For The Greater Good"

You ask, "How can I trust that joy now is not squandering my time when everyone advises to prepare for my future?" The mind will squander time whether it is preparing for the future or overindulging in the present. This is what you are really fearing. So where is the balance—or is balance even what is needed right now? No, there is something far more important: the truth. There is no

276

such thing as squandering your time when you exist in the space of truth. It is not about balance of work and play, it is about surrendering control. The more control you attempt to exert, the less you protect your future. So far, you have been attempting to control the outcome of your life, of your future; but it is not control that makes all the difference, it is surrender.

The trouble for you and many others is that, growing up, you were scorned so many times for playing too much, being irresponsible, and not working hard enough that you have a warped view of how life is safely and prosperously lived.

When you hurt from the stress and fear about preparing for your future, you choose to utilize your time in a way that continues the hurt and stress. You create more than you need, and you take from yourself more than you have. You can see this happen all over the world.

You need to realize that there is no future. This takes the mind out of the equation, giving you far greater clarity to access inner truths. From a reality where there is no future, how can you squander your time? If you cannot run out of time, how can it be squandered?

From this understanding you can now see a deeper truth. The fear behind not making the most of your time is not that you will live in an unpleasant future as it appears—as the fear says—but that you will be responsible for that unpleasant future. There is something worse than dealing with struggle, and that is dealing with struggle that you have blatantly caused. To condemn yourself for not making the "right" decisions when you had the chance is a fate worse than death.

Healing this sense of responsibility and the fear of squandering time requires several releases. The first is to realize that taking away from the present takes much more away from the future. The next release comes from knowing that punishing yourself in the future for time misspent in the present happens only when you look back over your life and see how you missed the best opportunities in trying to gain something for the future. Instead, you can choose to spend time with your children, pace yourself through work, spend holidays with family, enjoy still times sitting in nature, have investments based on seeing the truth instead of acting from fear, and so on. You will not punish yourself for having more joy, but you will punish yourself for taking joy away from yourself.

Life gives you what you need to experience in each moment. To neglect any one thing in preparation for future moments is to neglect life and its nourishing gifts. It is in neglecting these moment-to moment gifts that you compromise your future.

Imagine that you have a backpack, and everything you put into it now represents what you have in your future. Most people think that the more they leave out of their backpack in the present, the more they will have in the future. But of course, the opposite is the truth. The more wonderful experiences you allow and open yourself to now, the more can go into you backpack and the more you get to bring into all future moments.

It comes back to a lack of trust in yourself to make the right decisions in the present. Because you do not trust yourself, you follow the way of others, defaulting to what society believes, such as the Mind Lie, "Spending the present preparing for the future is not squandering your time, it is producing something you can bank on." But the only true safeguard is to trust yourself.

If you trust yourself in the present, you will have no problems trusting in your future self and the life you create.

The mind is the past and the future. You look to the future or the past for your salvation, because they are the only place in which the mind can exist. You fear the present because you believe that it will be horrifically lonely and unsafe, as very few you grew up with spent any time in the present. It is just not somewhere to visit, so you think it must be unsafe. This could not be further from the truth. The present is where you are most safe.

278

"If I Squander What I Have Today, I Will Have Nothing Tomorrow"

The mind would have you believe that your biggest fear is the fear of squandering what is important to you, such as money or your time. You think, "What will happen to me if I do squander away my savings or choose to use my time ineffectively?" This creates anxiety and leads to poor decisions. In truth, your deepest fear is not in looking back and wishing you had used your savings or time more wisely. Your deepest fear is that you already *have* misused your savings and time.

The mind projects you into the future, when all along the fear and worry is, "What if I actually *have* misused my time poorly? My life could have been infinitely better now." You seek to remedy this undercurrent of anxiety by perpetually rectifying your future, persisting at taking course corrections and maneuvers, so that your future will not repeat your past.

Nothing you do now will replace the decisions of the past except to cover over them so that you can stop torturing yourself, because your belief is, "If I make good decisions from now on to protect my future, then I will erase, or at least make up for, the poor decisions of the past." For the most part, this is accurate. However, what this course of action will not do is remedy your fear of making bad decisions. This fear will haunt you even when you are given new opportunities to make new decisions. It comes back to the fear of "I will squander my precious resources, my time, my money, and my relationships, as I have done many times before."

What is the remedy? It is the realization that it was not you who squandered anything; rather, it was the mind's need for validation.

You cannot repeat the decisions of yesteryear if your mind no longer carries the beliefs of yesteryear.

Your mind never stands still. It is always morphing from one state to the next, from one need to the next. It is just an opinion that it, or you, will morph back into the old you to repeat the past decisions; it is only an opinion, not the truth. As you get older, and more importantly, free of Mind Lies, you will become much wiser; but the wisest of all know that the fears of the past create the struggles in the now, for there is no future. From that knowledge—that the squandering is in the present—it is happening already, even as you do your best to avoid it. You cannot help it because it is your mind, and not You, who is in control. Indulging in fear is the mind once again, but this time it is playing tricks on you. It has you thinking that what messed things up for you was the decisions of the past, so you are taking charge to fix things in the present in preparation for the future. Who is fixing what now? Still the mind.

The mind has you running in circles, pretending that you are somehow avoiding new mistakes and so getting rid of old ones. In fact, you are creating new ones. Running in circles is exhausting and stressful; it creates illness and ages the body. How would you rank this in terms of squandering your precious resources?

The realization to have is that you are in your mind the most when you are in fear. Fear takes away, it does not give.

Love gives and does not take away.

The real question is, "How do you leave fear and return to love?" The answer is simple. You will squander your precious resources in fear, but you will add to and augment your precious resources from love. The answer for which you have been searching to remedy your past is to stop coming from fear and to trust in love.

In love there is no future. The future is mind made. It never actually happens. It is like those signs in bars that say "Free Beer Tomorrow."

When you realize the future never actually comes, you will ask yourself a whole set of different questions. Instead of asking, "How can I best prepare for my future years?" you can ask, "How will I most enjoy today? What will bring fulfilment today?" The beingness of fear asks questions from fear and creates a reality of fear.

A beingness of self-love generates a whole new set of questions that create a reality full of love.

But the mind asks, "What about my retirement? What about the economy collapsing, and what about losing my job?" When you come from love, you allocate your precious resources to those things that you love rather than avoiding what you fear. Squandering comes from a lack of self-love. You squandered in the past because your decisions came from fear, from the mind, from Mind Lies. Love dictates how to spend time and money better than fear ever will.

Now you come from love; love is purpose, and purpose brings expansion into your life.

Now you can let in the deeper truth: "I exist across time and space. My future is my present, and my present is my future."

It is only the mind that squanders. Truth savors, leaving abundance in your midst.

"If I Am Not Attached, Then Where Is the Fun?"

How often have you found yourself excited about something and believed that if you did not stay excited, the thing would never come to fruition? It could have been a job opportunity, a new car, or a new business idea. At some point, you got the need for attachment confused with the need for excitement. You can be excited about something without holding it back through attachment. Attachment is fear disguised as possession. But the opposite is the case; all fear does is push something away from you.

In truth, attachment is the fear of loss and the disappointment resulting from loss. You hope to ensure that something enters into or stays in your life by approaching it with fear of loss and fear of disappointment. Where do these fears come from? Many come from the Mind Lies of "I do not deserve it anyway; I am undeserving" and "Without that thing I will be a nobody, destined for misery and unhappiness." You can see how excitement and attachment are never one and the same thing. What is really going on is that you are excited about something and want to ensure that it comes into or stays in your life, but you begin by feeling undeserving and unworthy. You fear that you will never be a whole person if you lose that something, and you want to be guaranteed that it will be yours forever.

Now you can see how devastating attachment is to creating a reality for yourself; it pushes things away. But how do you stay unattached to things you want or desire? Simply realize the truth behind the attachment: the only thing that could make you undeserving would be if the thing was never meant for you in the first place—such as mail destined for someone else's mailbox. Being undeserving is not a bad thing; it is just a word that has bad connotations.

You resist this concept because you are told that you can have anything you want if you set your intentions on it. This is frankly just not true. You cannot have someone else's child, or someone else's husband, or someone else's driver's license. These may be obvious examples, but there are many less obvious examples of things not being meant for you: a part in a movie, the lyrics of a song, a particular house or car, a career or job opportunity. *Undeserving* simply means "out of alignment with something." The resistance that can come is, "I should be allowed whatever I want"—which is another great Mind Lie.

The real truth is that you are allowed what is rightfully, truthfully yours when it is rightfully and truthfully yours—no sooner and no later.

You will feel residual resistance to this truth because of the rest of the Mind Lie-generated attachment, which is: "I will not be whole unless I have the thing, and therefore I will not be happy, because on some level I need it to see myself as worthwhile." Really?

Let us clean this misconception up. Your identity wants something because it believes it is essential to make the false identity more whole and happy. But how can you fill a hole that does not exist in the first place? The mind is worried that one of its Mind Lies will not get placated by another of its Mind Lies; that is, the mind sees that it is full of holes, so it tries to fill them by believing, "I do not think I am deserving, so, despite feeling undeserving, I want that thing to make me happy rather than healing the feeling of being undeserving and void of happiness."

The truth is clearly that attachment carries an even deeper nontruth: "I will never get it, anyway." You are worried that you will never get the thing because you are undeserving, and this worries you because you believe that there is something missing inside of you that results in your needing this thing.

What is the truth? You will never get something if you keep worrying that you need it to fill an imaginary hole in an imaginary mind. Why? Because the mind is not worried about getting what you think you are attached to; the mind is worried that it cannot get the satisfaction it seeks, and it is right. You cannot get that missing piece that you desperately crave because it is imagined.

Let us look at an example. You are excited to get a new car, so you attach to it, thinking that attaching is the way to bring it into your life. Here you have confused attaching with manifesting, hoping that they are one and the same. But secretly, attaching is just about your being worried that you are undeserving of this new car. It is not about being worried about missing out on getting the car; it is about being worried about not getting the feeling you desire, such as accomplishment. But the mind is right; it is not ever going to get that feeling, because what it seeks does not exist. You cannot feel accomplished by getting something you didn't feel you deserved in the first place.

The point is this: do not seek something because of the reason you are attached to it. See the truth; then you will see all the reasons why you actually deserve it. Seek not to be attached, but to be allowing. From this space, that which is truthfully yours will enter your life much sooner.

"I Am A Mistake"

Many kids are raised in families that did not plan for, or even want, them. They are then swept into the "I am not wanted" string of Mind Lies, including "I am a mistake." Any belief in this set of beliefs is quite challenging, and it takes a lot to get through to the other side if you do not have access to the truth.

The truth accelerates your understanding and, of course, the healing of such an erroneous belief. Without the truth, many turn to drugs and even suicide to put themselves out of the constant emotional suffering.

So what is the truth? It is time that it was shared. It is simple: for your parents not to have had you would have been the mistake. Even more importantly, as your parents twist and turn with regret and resentment for allowing you to enter into their family, they begin to resent themselves for not being adequate parents, since they did favor you coming into this world. This haunts most parents to the point of believing, or remembering, that they themselves feel like a mistake. Could it be that parents who, deep down, feel they are a mistake inadvertently create healing for themselves by having a child under similar circumstances? The answer is yes. The healing occurs when the parents finally realize that their child is no mistake at all, and they can see the reward. When you were born, you brought an opportunity for this healing, in the same way that your children bring an opportunity for yours.

Delving deeper into this healing, and what do you see? Despite the hardship, the inconveniences, and the cost of having a child, what you brought into this world was priceless. You can see this in your own children.

You may now be covered in Mind Lies unrecognizable from the child you once were, but underneath the veil is still that beautiful child. That is the one constant; your glowing radiance never changes, it just gets brighter. It can be very difficult to allow in this truth, because you need another truth, as follows.

What your mind thinks—what it believes and convinces you of how you feel about yourself—is but a mirror of what those around you as a child believed and felt about themselves. Your mind has been a catchment, a net that has held on to all the thought energy that was thrown at you in your formative years and into adulthood. Your mind does not represent your identity; it is a collection of everyone's minds and their false identities. The mind you see is the mind humanity believes is real. But it is not your truth; it is not anyone's truth. It is just a mind dancing around on planet Earth, hoping that you will never fully see how mischievous you have allowed it to become.

A mind is not you, it is just there as a warning for how bad things can get when you neglect self- love and over-supplement your identity. You are, in truth, pure love, so there is nothing out there in the world that can bring love, but you can receive it when you stop believing that you never had it. The judgement was the mistake, that is it. Attaching labels to a human being is a mistake. It was your parents' label, not yours. It came from them. What came from you was love, that is what you are, that is your True Self.

The cost of another child, the stress on the relationship, the inconvenience, and so on, gets in the way of seeing the child for what he or she really is: an unexpected blessing.

You were an unexpected gift. As tough as this blessing may have been, it was still very important that you made your way onto this Earth.

"I Am A Nobody Without My Parents"

You have often felt you needed approval from your parents in order to feel on track and to feel that you made the right decisions, whether you are conscious of it or not. This is one of the most devastating Mind Lies there is, and it leads to rebellion, exhaustion, and addictions to drugs and alcohol.

The need for this love and approval becomes the driving force behind many of your decisions, severing you from moving toward what is in your highest good. From career choices to life partners, money decisions, and your views on business and relationships, everything gets skewed. But the need for your parents' love and approval actually stems from something rather unexpected. You think you need, or at least want, their love, as that is what human beings need. But this love you seek comes from the need to validate the identity you have chosen. Let me explain.

As the seed for your identity is laid and as it gathers momentum, your identity becomes more and more unsure of itself. You would think that the more layers of identity you have, the more secure it becomes in itself, but that is not the case. This is because the identity is not gathering layers of certainty; it is gathering layers of uncertainty.

While they seem convincing, all the identity traits you accumulate end in question marks. For example, "I am not good enough, right? I do not belong, correct?" As these are questions themselves, they can never be fully satisfied because the answers become questions, too. "I am not enough" gets answered by, "I cannot make the cut for now, I think."

Your entire identity is one big question made up of countless little ones. This is why it needs so much constant reinforcement. Even the mind does not believe it is the truth; even as the nontruth, it is not solid enough to be called a nontruth.

What does this have to do with needing Mom and Dad's approval? Usually, your parents are the first humans with whom you come into contact and whom you believe have any authority. As such, their word is key, and what you seek is their word on whether all the question marks you have accumulated about yourself are in fact accurate. You are subconsciously enquiring, "Is who I have come to think of myself as in fact the truth?"

What you need to know is that your parents cannot give you the nod of approval, as they are not actually qualified to do so. This is because the part of them that is being called forth to make this assessment is their own identity, and identities look for similarities. Your mom and dad's identities believe that if you have what they have, then they can safely say you are on track. For example, if you believe the same nonsense they do, and if enough people believe that same nonsense, it is fair and accurate to say that it is worthy of Mom and Dad's stamp of approval—in other words, their validation. So to be validated by your parents is to be validated by hundreds or thousands of years of beliefs being believed in. Talk about two wrongs not making a right! You seek other identities to validate yours because this perpetuates rather than eliminates the identity. But what you need is to see the truth, not get validation. You can never get clear on what you really are by seeking validation from others. It only perpetuates who you believe you are.

Who you have come to think you are is not who you truly are, so why seek validation for being something you are not?

In this moment, you may get a tiny glimpse into just how perfect you really are, as you can see that it is not validation you seek; it is invalidation. You seek to have the identity you have so trusted in to be shown as the farce that it is. This is where joy is found and the release occurs.

The identity seeks Mom and Dad's approval, but the identity is false. Because it is false, it needs others to see it as real. The more approval or agreement you get from others, the more the identity lives on. The less approval you get, the worse you feel, unless you realize a lack of approval means a lack of agreement. This shows that others' identities do not share in what you believe. This is a good sign, because it shows your uniqueness, not your mind's questions. The less others validate you, the less mind you have running the show. Follow this further: seek not validation; seek only invalidation. Be steadfast on the path of least validation.

The release occurs when you realize that you have *believed* you have spent most of your life trying to validate your identity, but what has actually been happening—all the struggles and all the suffering—is because you have, in fact, been achieving invalidation of the identity. If you had known this from the start, then failures and rejections would have be seen as victories, as bringing you further away from the identity and closer to truth.

Now you know that you do not need anyone else's approval, because it takes you back into believing your identity. As the identity is false, you can now know that there is no part of you that needs validation.

"I Do Not Exist Without My Parents"

The belief that you do not exist without your parents is a bit of hidden Mind Lie lying in the shadows of the previous one, "I am nobody without my parents." You now feel that you are inadequate on your own and unable to truly shine without the blessing and support of your parents. But this Mind Lie is even worse than the last one, as it has you believe that there is no freedom from them, no freedom truly to shine in your unique self.

In truth, your identity has nearly everything to do with your parents and their identities, but it is not so linked that there is no salvation. Let us explore.

Human parents gave birth to you; on this we can agree. But recall from earlier Mind Lies that birth is part of the cycle of existence and actually is nothing personal. "Nothing personal?" you say. "They are my parents!" Yes, but the truth is, they are parents to your body, as they were the ones who grew and raised you. But the real You already existed long before they became your parents. What is more, it is the other you, the nontruthful you, who was born as a result of them; this is why you feel helplessly tied to them.

In actuality, your parents are just part of an evolutionary cycle that keeps consciousness in the flow of life on Earth. The real You chose these parents as part of an elaborate experiment to see how far human life can be stretched beyond the filter of the mind that gets created during your upbringing. This experiment is not personal to them; in fact, it is personal to no one. Yes, there is incredible bonding and love shared between a child and his or her parents, siblings, and others, but this does not make it personal. Let me explain.

For something to be personal, people must be involved. It is fair and reasonable to assume that you and your parents are people—but they are not, and you are not. What you are instead is life itself appreciating itself in another form. You are life enjoying itself and smothering itself in more and more love so that the whole can benefit from increased love on Earth. You can make this personal, but if you do, you will miss a crucial part of the whole experiment, which is for you to not see it as personal.

"But," you ask, "why can't I keep the fluffy good feelings of parent and child, brother and sister?" You can, but not in the way you have understood it so far. This new level of understanding does not take away all the love; rather, it heightens it to a whole new level.

When identity is brought into an equation, the love that could be experienced is rapidly filtered to match the degree that the identity is prepared to see and feel. When you no longer make it personal, you remove the identity and see the love that is truly present.

The identity filters love from your experiences, making the experiences impersonal. And here you were thinking that what you already had was so very personal. It is not personal until you see the truth of it, see it for all that it is: love. Simply love. The identity does not stand a chance against pure love. It cannot exist because identity is the absence of love. It will do its best to avoid pure love from ever being experienced.

This brings me back to your not believing that you can exist without your parents. In reality, it is the only way that the true You can exist. If love is ever present and you are love, then being your identity eclipses the true You out of the picture. Conceiving of your parents in the way you see them currently—as intimately connected to your creation—reinforces that aspect of your identity. In other words, part of your identity is contingent upon those who created you being parents. As long as you relate to them in this way, you keep that aspect of your personality alive.

To fully be rid of mind-made reality and of the mind itself, you need to transcend all nontruths, even those that may seem to bring warm and fuzzy emotions. To do this, recognize that those warm fuzzies are easily amplified through truth, through seeing your parents for who and what they really are beyond the identities they portray to you. This takes fortitude, but you have it in you.

Your parents *are* You. They come from the same genetic makeup as you do. You may wonder what genetics have to do with this, but bear with me. Genetics is not just physiology, it is also cosmology. It is the key ingredient of the star and space matter that goes into making life possible. Even as a cellphone depends on software updates, evolution depends on genetics. DNA is always being upgraded along everyone's journey, allowing in more and more new programs, new levels of consciousness.

From the perspective of DNA, your parents are part of a continuum that you, just by being you, are helping to evolve and perpetuate.

"How does this make them me?" you ask. A DNA linage is like a hair attached to its follicle: it leads back to its source. All the hairs on your head lead to follicles, and each hair follicle represents a family linage. All the hair follicles belong to the same head—yours. If you have not had children yet, then you are at a follicle starting a new hair, helping it grow and evolve. Once your kids are born, they will be at the tip of the hair, growing it longer and brighter!

As you are connected to your parents through your lineage, you are part of a magnificent line of beings helping to raise the consciousness of the Universe. Your essence, your True Self, extends back through your family's roots, but just because your body was born through the bodies of your parents does not mean that you are from them. You can exist without your parents; you already do and already have.

Do not be fixed into a certain reality just because you have parents. It is time to unground your identity by seeing the truth about you: that You are in fact the Universe. As such, you transcend all identities, and with this comes a tiny but significant glimpse into a greater truth: You, as the Universe, made your parents. They did not make you.

"I Am Wrong To Abandon My Parents"

Becoming one with your True Self can be seen as abandoning your Earthly self, human needs, and human societal norms. Many attachments get created when living a human life, but some of them happen for the wrong reasons. Take the need to stay small so that others do not feel abandoned by you. This is a perfect example of an attachment that will harm you in the long run.

To abandon is to leave someone in need, never to return, but this is not what is being asked of you. If anyone is being abandoned, it is your former self. By growing and evolving, you are continuing to advance what your parents first started. No one on Earth, least of all your parents, can rightfully encourage stagnation. You are free to grow, no matter how many people find it challenging and confronting. Remember, the more resistance and backlash you get, the more you are clearly on the right track. If this means abandoning the relationships you once had, and the perceptions you once had, in the name of something infinitely greater for you and ultimately for your parents, why wouldn't you do it? The trick is to know that it is for something greater. But how can you be sure?

Know this: to abandon your identity is to live a life free from inaction and fear. To hold on to any part of that identity may seem to bring comfort, but all it will give is a repeat of the past—not just the highs, but also the lows, warts and all. Contrary to what the mind has you believe, you are not here to keep repeating the past. How is your life ever to expand into something greater if you keep doing this?

Abandon the old mind in search of truth, and you will be rewarded with depth of relationships never yet experienced and an ability to see the truth where you never could before. In this space, love— unconditional, unbinding, eternal love—can be felt.

Your parents' identities caused you to abandon yourself—and them, for that matter. Abandoning their identities will allow you to reconnect to your True Self and help them see that they need to do the same; it is therefore healing for you and for them.

"I Have To Record All Negative Experiences In My Memory"

Memory is an important subject to address now, especially as this Mind Lie wreaks havoc with memory.

The beliefs you carry exist in your memory, and the traumas of your past also exist in your memory. What set this in motion, and does it really have to be this way?

There are several key beliefs that support the need to record and remember the negatives of the past. After all, that is what memory is: the need to store and recall. It is a need that you really do not need. It comes from the beliefs that "I will fail again if I do not remember my past failings" and "Who am I if I do not remember all the bad experiences I have endured, especially if I have nothing to show for them?" and "Others need to know where I have failed so they can avoid my mistakes and I can pass this wisdom on to future generations."

The mistakes and the experiences do not need to be retained; only the lessons do, so why do you insist on remembering all of it? A key reason is because you believe that to make the same mistakes over and over again is simply stupid, but what your beliefs have not accounted for is that remembering the past failures and all the bad emotional experiences is stupid. Perhaps you are reacting to this information right now, but a reaction is present because a great deal of your identity actually hinges upon these beliefs. Your identity thrives on remembering the past, so opening yourself to not remembering is abhorrent to the identity. Who would have thought something so simple could be the cause of so much damage?

Another Mind Lie shows up in this respect as well: "I am nothing without my experiences. They define me; they have made me who I am today." This sounds very dramatic, almost poetic, but it is just more nontruth.

What has defined you are the outer limits of your belief systems. What your experiences have attempted to do is either reinforce your existing beliefs or chisel away at them so that the true You can be revealed. Who you are today is a by-product of how you insist on seeing yourself versus the core self underneath.

Why make the delineation? Why exclude experiences in the shaping of who you are? For the very reason that you are clearing this belief: you believe experiences create who you are, and so you end up as a by-product of that belief, not the experience itself. Likewise, you can see the truth and realize that it is your beliefs, not your experiences, which shape you. This realization frees you from needing experiences to shape you or the past to haunt you as a way to avoid the same mistakes in the future. Believing that you must remember negative experiences defines you as far as your identity goes, but there is a deeper truth: the need to be remembered is even more defining.

"Are you saying that this is all about posterity and not learning from past mistakes?" you ask. Yes. The mind has you believe that you are trying to avoid repeating the same mistakes over and over again, but it actually wants posterity. Just look at your life and see how remembering all your failures has not empowered you but instead has crippled you into making new versions of the same mistakes. Past patterns repeat over and over until you see the cause of the original mistake, the nontruth. But do not substitute remembering for learning the truth. They are not the same thing.

Remembering past experiences is a way never to forget the false you. The mind keeps track of all the you-defining moments, which become its anchors in keeping your identity from changing.

The mind thinks that if it does not remember, then you would be lost. These anchors in memory are reference points from which to take identity. What is the truth? It is not past experiences that make you who you are, because You existed long before you witnessed these experiences. You are the witness, not the experiences themselves. How can something that is being witnessed through you be You? The way you experience something is a product of the mind, but who You are is not the mind.

The mind evolves from one experience to the next. That means that only the mind is a product of your experiences, not you.

You do not need to remember the past; it is the past you need to forget. Then you can allow your experiences to be just that—simply experiences. To see an experience as defining or worth remembering is to see yourself as definable and worth remembering.

Are you worth remembering? Absolutely not. Believing this Mind Lie is one reason your identity remains unshakable. To remember this Mind Lie keeps it alive; to forget about it opens up new possibilities never yet imagined. What is it going to take to let go of the need to remember negative past experiences and the old self?

Realize that it is not the experiences that define you, that it is not the lessons you have learned that define you. What defines you is truth.

The Mind Lie that "life is about learning lessons" is what makes this realization virtually impossible. You need to move away from this fundamental human belief, because it is keeping you imprisoned in your past. It is a perpetual cycle of "I need to remember my life experiences so I do not repeat past mistakes. If I learn the lessons I need to learn, I will not repeat past mistakes. If I remember the mistakes and the lessons, I will not repeat my past mistakes. Life is all about lessons, so the more I remember, the better I will do." The mind chants this over and over again—except for one small thing. Life is not about remembering lessons, nor is it about the lessons themselves. Lessons are a means to an end, and what end is that? It is chiseling your mind—your identity—back to your ultimate truth.

When you ask the eternal question, "Who am I?" new experiences and new lessons show up. But just because they show up does not mean that is what life is about.

In fact, what life is about is equally as undefinable as you are. It is not about just one thing; it moves and expands and serves an eternal purpose of catapulting consciousness forward. Right now, for humanity, life is about carrying the wisdom forward from each life experience to enable you to see yourself as part of the whole. The more you see yourself as the collective one organism, the more consciousness grows. The more you realize that you are life itself and see your magnificence in every flower, every tree, every cloud, and every drop in the sea, the sooner life can become about something else. But how are you going to get there if you keep dragging around life experiences from the past?

Once you move beyond this stage of life, humanity can move into something so exciting that it is scaring you into staying small. When you truly see that you are life itself, you will remember that you created your own DNA. From that perspective, even the sky is not the limit.

"I Cannot Grow Faster Than My Partner"

Fear stops many couples from growing. You fear rejection from your partner. You fear attack and judgment, harsh criticism, or worse. If you are a highly considerate person, you fear belittling your partner. You believe that the greater you become, the smaller your partner will see herself or himself. Yet, as real as these fears may appear, what do you really fear? Who is your partner really mirroring back to you? You, of course. Let me explain.

Remember, the greatest fear in this scenario is not rejection or criticism from another but from yourself. You do not fear another's words or harsh looks; instead, you fear your own words and harsh looks. The first layer of fear is in fearing your own judgments, your own criticisms. But in truth, it goes deeper than this. You fear something far worse: the realization that you were right about yourself all along.

If your views and opinions are attacked, condemned, or judged by your partner—or anyone, for that matter—your mind goes through a series of checks and balances, either validating the attack or seeking to invalidate it. Instead of realizing the truth in the moment, your mind defers to past experiences that brought up certain doubts and skepticism about your ability to make smart or right decisions and assessments of yourself. "Am I right, or are they right?" This is a terrifying place to be, because if you cannot depend on yourself to get it right, who is left to depend on? Or worse, if you cannot rely on yourself to see the truth in any situation, then you might not be who you have thought yourself to be your whole life.

When the identity comes into question, panic sets in. You preempt this panic by switching off the guidance of your True Self. It is the safest way to avoid an identity conflict, as far as the mind is concerned. You see, there is a battle, a one-sided tug-of-war between the mind and the True Self, as the higher self sits on its rock overlooking a still pond of infinity while the mind wrestles, wriggles, and squirms in protest to the stillness, insisting that it is all there is, arguing that the still pond is merely a hoax.

The truth is that *you* are the still pond; this is your truth and infinite nature. But the mind cannot accept that truth for one key reason: it is too busy defending who it thinks it is. It is one vicious cycle after the other. When you are born, and sometimes even before, the mind is made up. A thought happens, a thought so rapid that it gathers momentum. The dawning of thought is, "What am I?" The need to know more grows and grows, attracting more ideas of itself, like a magnet attracting more and more paper clips until it is completely covered, unrecognizable even to itself. And that is the point: the magnet—the thought, "What am I?"—cannot see itself for what it is: the eternal question, nothing more, nothing less.

What does this have to do with your spouse and what is holding you back? It is the fear of losing your mind. Your spouse is just another excuse not to look at your truth.

The greater truth is that your fears of rejection and disappointment have nothing to do with your spouse and everything to do with that first thought of "What am I?" What if you realize that you are not who you always thought you were? This fear is so great that you forget, or neglect to realize, that this is what you have been searching for and craving your whole life. You have secretly been desiring not to be who you thought you were this whole time. That is the truth. Of course, the mind flips this desire upside down and has you run and hide from it.

In truth, you no longer want to be fearful, needy, scared, and inadequate and to compensate with ambition, accumulation, goals, and superiority. You do not want to be without any longer, so the very thing you fear is the antidote to the fear itself.

Ultimately the fear of your partner's persecution, rejection, criticism, and undermining is the fear of seeing the true You. It is the fear of realizing that you have been rejecting your magnificence, avoiding it every step of the way, hiding from it by being like every other human being on Earth and undermining yourself every step of the way by playing small. You fear yourself, the you that will cease to exist when you stop fearing its existence.

In realizing this real You, you begin to achieve the elusive use of your full brain. Your fear that you are the small you, which is actually a fear of how great you really are, prevents your greatness from shining through.

What is stopping you from being your magnificent self and using 100 percent of your brain? The need to be you. But who is this "you" whom you believe you need to be? This is the most interesting of all enquiries. You cannot stop yourself from being yourself because there is no you. There is only a need to be you. There was never a you; there was just a need.

I will repeat that crucial point: there is no you; there is just a need to be you.

The mind is the need; it is not the You. So where did this need come from?

It came from the realization that there needs to be a you, an "I." But how can this be if there is nothing to begin with? The need to be a you created the experience of you, and you think about yourself in the same way you always have because you still think there needs to be a you. Is this confusing?

Keep in mind, there was never a you; there was only a question. The question led inexorably to many possible answers, none of which were accurate: "I am my red hair, my eyes, my mouth, my heart rate, my money, my car, the light and not the dark," and so on. Yet you neglected to realize that it was just one Mind Lie upon the other, one possible answer after the next, creating the next series of questions after the next, after the next: "Am I this, or am I that? I think I am this and that."

What if, at some point, you realize that you are not any of those things? Then what happens to you? "I will break apart," the mind thinks, which is why it has you perpetually run in circles, validating it and compensating for its ideas of itself.

You will not break apart or die. You will see that there is no you; there is just a single question. You will realize that the only way forward is to disregard all answers to that question because it is a rhetorical question; it was never intended to be answered by you. It is like a seed that never flowers but remains open and able to flower and blossom into the infinite.

But your question is not, "Who am I?" or "What am I?" Your question is, "Why do I keep holding myself back?" Rephrasing the question to be more direct becomes, "Where is the 'I' holding itself back?" When you ask this question, you will discover that it is the mind holding itself back. It is not you, not the real You; it is just the mind, terrified of returning to "I am not who I thought I was." And it is this that stops you from using your whole brain. It is this that fears rejection, persecution, and alienation, masquerading as the Mind Lie that "I cannot grow faster than others."

When you reach your whole brain, there will be no one left to fear anything.

You used to worry, "What will others think of me if I grow too quickly and become my True Self?" But the actual worry is, "What will I think of myself if I grow too quickly and become my magnificent self?" The truth is that there will be no you to think any such thoughts, because you will have transcended the mind altogether and reached a state of being where there is no fear.

You could say that what you fear the most is being without fear itself. Fear lives in the fragility of the identity. It would be like Clark Kent fearing death from bullets when he turns into Superman.

Currently you have what your mind calls very practical worries, such as finances, spending, relationships, and societal norms. The truth is that these are just the mind's way of saying, "The end of me will be the end of you." In this instance, the mind is both wrong and right. When you see that there is no you, there will be no worries, so worries come from the you that the mind has made up. So the mind is right: it is the end of the small you and the beginning of the real You. The truth is always a far cry from what the mind presents.

What you can do is move toward that which you fear: the end of the mind. Move toward where there is panic, fear of rejection, and fear of criticism, because there is peace on the other side. The mind speaks a secret language, so when it says "do not," you must do. When it says "wait," you must go. When it says "fear," you must trust. When it says "to reject," it really means the open up and the end of suffering awaits.

The mind has you running marathons, inventing things you do not need, climbing mountains and running yourself ragged so that you can finally feel free and alive; yet being free of the mind is what you seek the most, and it will not come from being the mind.

Go back to the eternal question of "What am I?" because that is life itself. But remember, the question is rhetorical and not intended to have a definitive answer. It is just a never-ending exploration. Do not seek to answer it, seek to experience it.

Realize, "I am not what I think because I am not the mind. I am the space that allows the mind, an infinite space that needs nothing, no definitions or boundaries. I am a space seeking to be nothing and everything wherever it can."

"I Must Work To Avoid My Eventual Failure"

The feeling of being a failure can be a tricky one to shift, because there are many perceived benefits in holding on to these belief systems. For one, if you view yourself as already being a failure, you do not have far to fall when it does eventually happen. That is what this Mind Lie is about: your eventual demise. It points to the need to cover up or avoid the feelings of an impending failure through your best attempts at creating success. You work hard, desperately attempting to make a success of yourself. You do this for yourself and to look successful to others despite feeling that your failure is an inevitable eventuality. This is one of the hardest Mind Lies to clear for the simple reason that it is so simple to clear. And as in many instances in life, "simple" is easily overlooked.

Realize that failure is not an eventuality but a state of mind. One person's failure is another person's success. What makes it so tricky is seeing that the need to contribute to success, to compensate for the eventuality of failure, stems from the belief "I have already failed." This is like running up a down-moving escalator, hoping to convince someone—ideally yourself—that you are giving it your very best shot.

But what this does is blind you to the truth that is staring you in the face: you, who are running from falling victim to failure, are the very same you who thinks you are already a failure, which is the same you who thinks that running from something gets rid of it. The simple truth, of course, is that all these versions of you are made up. There was never a failure, and you were never able to run from it. The you who thinks you are improving things is also made up.

Essentially, a fake person is running from a fake problem because a fake person said it would help.

Your notions of inevitable failure and of being a failure come from your deepest fears of becoming like other failed people—a parent, aunt, uncle, or other relative—and their failures because you witnessed them. But the truth is, their failures—becoming destitute, being humiliated, being defrauded, going bankrupt, being left, being criticized, dying alone—are in fact the very basis of your identity.

The realization that "I can fail" is what determines the entire course of your identity. You spend your life compensating for it, never realizing that you are running from your identity. You think that you are running from failure, and in a manner of speaking you are, for the identity is the failure.

Believing that you are someone you are not and then living a life mirroring it is the failure.

The inevitable failure from which you are still running has been and gone; it is happening and has happened. You cannot run from it because the failure is not now, nor is it in the future. It has already happened. The minute you condemned yourself into this box you call your identity, failure became real, because the only part of you that understands failure is this failure-based identity. As failure is the identity, it is perpetually fearful and running from some sort of failure. Look at every single one of these Mind Lies, and you will see a pattern threaded throughout all of them: failure avoidance. Believing that you are the mind is the failure. Now that you know you are not the mind, you can immediately see yourself as a success, because if the identity is failure, then the absence of the identity is inherently success.

You need not run nor rush nor hurtle yourself through your life attempting success, because you are inherently a success and have been the whole time.

"I Will Be Sad Without An Identity"

After everything I have revealed so far, do you not see it is the identity that makes you sad? You can think of this Mind Lie as coming at exactly the right time. When you reach a point of enlightenment where the identity is nearly fully exposed, it is normal to start having objections to moving forward.

But the truth is that you will be ecstatic without an "I," because there will be no you dragging you into the mud at every opportunity. You will recognize that all is one and that there is no need for a separate "I." You will feel cocooned and embraced in love instead of looking for it in all the wrong places.

Other thoughts arise that resist the final step:

1) I can't imagine my head space without that voice hanging around.

2) My identity is what makes me, me.

3) My identity is what makes me human. (And this is the truth.)

4) If my identity leaves, I will die.

5) I need a personality to survive.

But what is the truth in this series of thoughts? Let us go deeper:

1) "I cannot imagine my head without that voice hanging around."

You cannot imagine it because that mind has done nearly all the imagining in your life to date. Trying to imagine life without this imagination is very difficult. The truth is that you cannot imagine with that voice because it laces everything with doubt, fear, and disappointment. This is not imagination at all; it is limited by what it perceives as realistic, achievable, and interesting, which is all based on its collection of Mind Lies. A pure imagination now becomes available, a connection to the Divine, where your mind melds into being with the one Universal Mind, limitless and all-knowing. This is true imagination, a new voice fills your awareness, a voice of truth and unconditional support for everything you represent.

2) "My identity is what makes me, me."

Never have truer words been spoken. This is the mind speaking about itself, so yes, it is what makes it itself. However, it is not what makes you, You. Rather, your mind is what hides You from existing in this world. Your mind has you believe in its significance, which hides what is actually significant. It is not saying that you are significant, as you have been led to believe. It is saying that *the need to be you* is significant. But the real You is infinitely more significant than the need to be you. Who wants to spend their whole life being a need? After all, this is all the identity is. Why settle for being you, when you can be everyone and everything?

3) "My identity is what makes me human."

The need to be human strikes again. Everything is about preserving humanity, or at least preserving the mindset that keeps you living as a human being. But a human being, as it is seen by the mind, is not the definition of the total possibility or capability of this species, it is just a label. Even *species* is a label you need to dissociate from. In truth, you are not human, you are energy that inhabits all forms of life, planets, stars, galaxies, and evolution itself. So why stick with one label? Why confine your true mind to just one thing when it can think as everything?

When you see yourself as just one thing, you can only think as that one thing. But as you expand, how you view yourself as including all things, as the knowing of all things, becomes your knowing. You exist in an all-knowing Universe, where the sum total of the Universe is available to those who see themselves as the Universe. All the answers, all its secrets, become available to you when you let go of needing to be human. You are not a human being, you are 'being' itself.

4) "If my identity leaves, I will die."

If your identity stays, you will die much sooner! Without the mind in the driver's seat, your body is free to rejuvenate itself. The cells are no longer starved of the love they need to heal, and your heart beats infinitely more happily and is therefore healthier. Both aging and disease are products of the mind; they are what the mind looks like in the body, because the mind is everywhere. It takes over the body, blocking life-giving energy from reaching vital organs and shortening your life span. Cancer, arthritis, and every other symptom in the body are by-products of the mind. Heal the mind to heal the body. Now you can see why so few cures have been found: because the source itself, the cause of the illness, does not exist in the body but in the mind, beginning as the little seeds of self-destructive thoughts that began all those years ago—thoughts that can kill.

5) "I need a personality to survive."

Have you not noticed how full of personality you are when you like yourself? Your True Self is full of personality; it need not come from your Mind Lies. For one, a personality generated from a space of love is far nicer and more supportive of your longevity than a personality stemming from fear and other Mind Lies. Personality, quirks, and a sense of humor are innate to your DNA. Do not hold on to the mind to keep your personality; that would be like holding on to a disease to keep feeling that you are still alive. The Universe is full of personality, do not be confined to one, when you can experience and see yourself as them all.

These are powerful truths and incentives to release your attachment to the mind. But what is the truth to all of this? What does it reveal?

The body still wants to be human. It has become attached to being one, and the same is true with your mind. Yet there is another belief hidden: "I am mind, body, and soul." This fluffy and seemingly spiritual concept causes more havoc that you could possibly realize. Let us get to the truth:

You have seen that there can be a life without the interference of the mind, so where to go from here? There is no body without spirit; spirit is what created the body. The body is the spirit. It is infinitely more spirit than mind. The mind comes after the body, and the body comes after spirit—thought before creation. Spirit is another way to describe all thoughts, all consciousness driving the expansion of the Universe. That means You are spirit above all else. Your body is just one body that you get to play in throughout eternity.

You are the spirit in all things and in all matter. Spirit is the space where all things matter.

306

"I Am Despised And A Nuisance"

This Mind Lie has to be one of the harshest beliefs you have carried all these years. It would have taken you off this Earth and ended your life had you not addressed it here and now.

The mind despises itself. It knows that it is just a nuisance, which makes it despise itself even more. But why is there so much hatred in such a thing, and why do you feel it as being about you? The answer is the same for both questions: Your mind loathes what it is not. It thinks it can be or should be everything, but only You are everything. You see, the mind is the opposite of You, and You love everything, for it is You. The mind hates everything that it cannot be.

You are truth; your mind is not. It is that simple. You identify with such hatred of self because you identify with the mind rather than with You. You have been taught here and there to be ashamed of loving yourself, congratulating yourself, and praising yourself. You have been taught that it is wrong to love yourself because the mind cannot thrive when love is present.

In truth, You thrive when love is present.

Who are you, really? Are you someone who is despised and a nuisance or someone who defies being any one thing?

Others in the past may have despised what you represent to them, and, as in catching a cold, you caught it and believed that it was true of you. But the real truth is that you cannot be something you are not.

"I Have Not Done Enough For The World"

The Mind Lie of not having done enough for the world is an exhausting belief to have. Even when you have done truly amazing things for people or the planet, or both, you never quite feel that it is enough. It haunts you day and night beneath your awareness, compelling you to do more, achieve more, and be more. This drive is not instinctual but is programmed, for the instinctual counterpart is to be and behave in a way that is balanced with both giving and receiving.

All ecosystems on Earth are based on such a balance, and the reason why the human ecosystem is so destructive is because it swings out of balance from one extreme to the next, from needing to take and keep taking to overcompensating the need to give and keep giving until you are dead. Neither extremes are healthy.

What is the truth? In the center of balance, an awareness become available, a stillness, where just being is enough. There is no need for doing, creating, or achieving, because in being, a giving and receiving loop is allowed to take place. In this loop the immeasurable knowledge of the Universe becomes available: it gives, you receive, and balance is achieved. The Mind Lie, of course, is that "I" must be the giver and the receiver; after all, that is considered balance, is it not? It would be if the "I" who believed this was actually real rather than fictional. How can that which is made up make a significant contribution, such as restoring balance to humanity when it is not even sure of its own existence or relevance? The "I" that matters is already giving; now it is time for that "I" to receive from itself, also. You play no role in this other than to let in this understanding. For you to think that you must keep giving is a fallacy, because the you that thinks this, has no role on this Earth other than, to be dissolved through truth.

In fact, recognizing and embracing this understanding eliminates the illusion of Mind Lies, for the mind cannot and will not exist in this space. It is a space of truth. To create from this space is to create with no need to do more or be more. To create in this space is to allow the expansion of the Universe as it wants, not as the identity wants.

"What does the Universe want now?" you ask. It wants for all of humanity to nurture this space and allow it to show you truth.

This is not something that requires more of anything, least of all more trying. It is not about active participation. Rather, it is passive, a deep surrender into slowing down, so this space can take over as your real mind. You are connected to it, like a computer drawing upon one massive mainframe computer, only able to benefit when you surrender your human aggressive and often forceful will.

What does it tell you right now? It is an important message to free you from the need to keep doing more and more, giving more and more. The message is this: The giving, the most productive way to give back to the Universe, is not through giving at all but through receiving. Receive insights, reassurance, self-love, knowledge, blessings, and peace, for these are the only antidotes to the imbalance on Earth and the imbalances within.

"I Am Separate And Disconnected From Life"

It is odd to think that you could be separate from the very thing that you are. Life permeates every cell of your body, and yet somehow your mind is convinced that you are removed from it—very odd indeed, but nonetheless convincing.

To see yourself as disconnected robs you of your ultimate power as creator in your very own existence. You see yourself as at the mercy of life rather than as what is true, which is that you are an intrinsic part of life as a whole. What is the truth? As I have said before: You are life. But like the many other truths that came before this one, you are going to need more than that.

Your essence, your True Self, is the life force that powers the human body. It is only the mind that sees itself as separate. Can you let that in? When you are stuck in the mind, you feel separated. The mind is part of life but does not see itself this way; it has too many beliefs that it is a victim of life instead. However, the true You is as much of life as it gets.

Life itself is not just a phenomenon, separate and alienated from the rest of the Universe. Life is instead a direct expression of the Universe. In fact, the Universe *is* life, and you are the personification of it. What is even more is that life is intelligent, thinking light. It is what evolved into you and everything else over billions of years.

The mind cannot relate to any of these concepts because it was conceived by life, and all things conceived by life have the virtues of life, which is intelligent matter with the desire to live on and expand. The mind wants to live on not as life but separate from it, because it knows that life is truth and it is not. It cannot live in a sea of truth, so it fights to exist on its own.

Your truth is that the mind does not sustain life but rather takes it away. The more in your mind you live, the less life you live.

Life is a mind itself, separate from your mind. Your mind is simply pretending that you are separate from life itself, but it is separate from a far superior mind called life.

Life pioneered human anatomy and the ecosystems on Earth. It is vastly superior to the thinking human mind. Only the belief that you are separate from life has you disconnect from its mind. The design of the human brain is to draw on itself for daily tasks and to draw on life's mind, the real You, for all decisions. So think of yourself as having two minds, each for a different purpose. One remembers the basics while one knows your path. The trouble is that you have been using the minor mind for the majority of the time and major mind for the minority of the time, if at all.

Life is not how you have come to understand it. It does more than just beat the heart. Life is heavily involved in human life—it pioneered it, after all, and not just its concept but its ongoing evolution, including everyone's day-to-day decisions.

See your life and all its possibilities through the lens called life, not the filter called the mind. From this space, you can plainly see how anything but plain life is.

Your true identity is not as a human being but rather as light being human. Why would light desire a human experience? It is not a human experience it desires, per se, but a truthful one; and so you are propelled forward on your journey of life in constant realization of deeper truths. The light wants you to know that You are it and it is You.

Why bother having this human experience in the first place if what you are is light? Why go to such great lengths to fool yourself into no longer seeing yourself as light, only to go to even greater lengths to remind yourself that you are and always were light?

How can light grow and expand if it always sees itself only as light? It does this the same way you expand by having different experiences, such as starting a business, getting married, having children, traveling; light, too, wants to know itself in unique ways and have experiences that grow its core.

Unlike for human life—where knowledge and intellect are worshipped as the ultimate indicators of growth—for light, knowing everything is not the issue nor the path to growth and expansion of the Universe. That is what awareness is. Having new awareness is what grows all the parts of your Universe. For the leaf to know itself also as the twig grows the whole tree. For the branch to realize that it is also the trunk, again, grows the whole. For you to know that you are the Earth, you are each other, you are the Universe, grows the entire Universe.

What is stopping you from knowing yourself as life itself, as intelligent light? If you knew yourself as light, many things in your life would have to change. Who is ready for cataclysmic changes in their lives? Not many people. But let us assume for the sake of this book that you are. What stops you is the realization that, as life itself, you are as equally responsible for the violence, genocide, poverty, and all other manner of mayhem as you are for the joys. That is the fear. The truth is far more appealing. As life, you are responsible for eradicating all of that from ever repeating itself through the human species. That is the work everyone is doing in various ways.

"How are we doing this?" you ask. It's simple: when you allow in that you are life itself, you stop succumbing to the fiction in your mind and start becoming the truth that is in your heart. The mind does not want you to realize that you are life by pretending that it will be too painful for you; yet by refusing to see yourself as life, you are doing exactly what creates pain for all.

Life is not you, life is what remains when the Mind Lies are all gone. It is You.

"I Am Separate And Disconnected From Earth And The Universe"

Many of the problems you face in your daily lives and as a society stem from disconnection from the whole. You study the Universe, the stars, and the distant planets as if they are not of you but are neighbors to you. You view the Earth as a stand-alone planet, and nobody knows for sure how you ended up there. You see it as your role to make the best life possible for yourself so as to not suffer, not to feel less than, and that is just what you do. You take what you need from the Earth to do this and believe that it is the only way forward. But stop to imagine, what if things were different? What if you did not just randomly end up on the Earth but were purposefully designed for it, like the pilot fish who were designed to help sharks, stingrays, and turtles?

Imagine for a moment that human beings as a species evolved not from apes or monkeys but instead came here to help elevate the consciousness of the Earth. "What? A planet has a consciousness?" That is a radical notion for you.

In truth, you have a consciousness, and a few moments ago you believed you were of the Earth, so it stands to reason that you got your consciousness from somewhere—a parent, so to speak. If you are of the Earth, then Mother Earth is your ultimate parent. You may have noticed how nature works; many of its qualities and physical attributes are exactly like a child's, who in turn gets them from its parents. There is a continuation of being.

Consider that Mother Earth is the Intelligence behind nature, and in this light you can recognize that there is thinking going on, that Mother Earth is thinking. You talk about life and species evolving, but what does evolution really entail? When a species evolves, it grows in a way that is more suited to the upcoming challenges and dynamics of its environment, so clearly there is intelligence involved.

A species of bird does not shed all its feathers in the event of an ice age; rather, its feathers thicken or evolve to become fur. There is intelligence here.

Mother Nature and Intelligence are synonymous. In fact, the very fuel of evolution is Intelligence; you cannot have evolution without it. Where does this Intelligence come from? It comes from the same place where you came from: a naturally occurring mind, a brain bigger than the size of the Universe. You exist in this brain; you are a thought waiting to realize that it is not separate but is part of the whole. This is difficult to see because you are a product of it, and you have yet to realize that you *are* it.

Your brain and the Earth's brain are one, but believing you are separate disconnects the two, leaving you feeling isolated and needing to fend for yourself.

The Earth's brain is one small part of the larger brain. It, too, is part of a collective ecosystem that fuels the growth of your entire Universe; one for all and all for one. Each galaxy is one of the many lobes of this brain, each galaxy serving a purpose, a function, for the greater whole. The Earth is an idea in one of the lobes, a concept that was thought of, and life on Earth is mandatory for this idea to come to full fruition. And the idea that is planet Earth is the idea of love.

Is this so surprising? Love is the greatest human experience there is. It is what everyone is seeking throughout their entire lives. It is what the entire human race is pursuing with everything they have. If the planet Earth is the concept or idea of love, then the ultimate in self-love is to see and experience yourself as the Earth. If Earth were not the concept of love, why are you so hard-wired to pursue it? Why is nearly every song ever written, every festive holiday, every gift you buy, every gesture you make, toward experiencing greater love?

If Earth is the idea of love, what are the other planets for, and what do the other galaxies do? They all have slightly different purposes. You will feel compelled toward a slightly different experience of life, growth, and expansion, depending on which galaxy you are in. For example, life on Earth thrusts you toward self-love and compassion for others. Life elsewhere is about more ascended principles, such as life creation, planetary ecosystems, interplanetary governance and concepts you cannot yet begin to imagine. It is like a grade in school or martial arts. Once you learn the basics, it is time to advance to the next level. Your next level could be as a multidimensional being affecting different layers of reality simultaneously. It may be that you will be evolved enough that you no longer require a dense, physical body, and the need for physical life as you know it on Earth will not be that important to you. Everything that can happen does happen in the Universe. There is a spectrum of realities, different frequencies of existence, all coalescing to create this brain, to power life through this brain, to give rich learning experiences and profound realizations about yourself and your true nature.

Love is what the planet wants, and you are failing dismally. But do not beat yourself up, as that is not self-loving at all. It is time to recognize what the natural currency on this Earth is, and that is to return to love, to be love.

There is no medicine on Earth more healing than resonating in a constant state of love. Your body is made of love, which is why you feel so good when you are in love.

The mind-made identity has cut you off from this obvious fact. It makes it out that love is a luxury, a nice thing to have once you have all the money, fame, and success you need. It makes it out that you can do without love and still thrive on this planet. But you are not thriving without love; it is not working.

Because you are without love, you treat yourself, others, and the Earth in the exact same way you feel about yourself. Think of when you got your first car. You loved it at first and kept it neat and tidy, washing it regularly. But as time went on, you fell out of love with it. Eventually your "No eating in the car" rule relaxed; smoking in the car was allowed, drinking in the car was encouraged, and you stopped caring how much rubbish was piling up underneath the brake pedal. And who cared whether it looked like it had not been washed in two years?

This perfectly describes what is happening to humanity and the Earth. You fell out of love with yourself and are now treating the Earth in the same way as you treat yourself. One is an extension of the other, there are no two ways about it.

This brings us back to the question, "Where is this Intelligence called Mother Earth coming from?" It comes from You. Not the fictitious Mind Lie version of you, but the real You.

You share this light, this consciousness, in the same way that all other animals and plants on Earth share it. It is called instinct, but it is more than a preprogrammed awareness. What you have is that and infinitely more. Instinct was programmed; it learned and evolved and is where it is today. But what will take you beyond your instinct is reconnection to your Mother Earth's intelligence, seeing yourself not as separate but as an extension of it. You were born on the Earth but are also a part of it.

Your nature is nature. Remember that.

"I Cannot Tell The Difference Between The True Me And The False Me"

In many ways the belief that you cannot tell between the old you and the real You—the you and the You—should be the very first Mind Lie you deal with. But having come so far and learned so much, you are now ready to let this truth in at the deepest level.

The blurred lines that occur between knowing the false self and the True Self are blurry for one reason: you have always wanted them there. They keep you, in your mind anyway, from becoming an outlier in society; they keep you in check. If you cannot ever be truly sure which one you are, why not take the middle ground? After all, that is the safest place truly to fit into society because, as you know, extremes inherently do not fit into society.

But remember, fitting into a society is inherently dysfunctional. This is because you are not actually attempting to fit into society any longer; rather, you are trying to stay within the realms of what is understandable and predictable. Failure and struggle have become so much the norm for you that you believe you will become unsettled if excellence becomes your norm. The mind will not accept it, which is why it will not accept the real You. It is so used to having battles and needing to put out fires in your life that you believe that is life.

Let us get to some truth, and fast. The only reason you reject the new norm is because you feel uncertain inside of it. You have become certain in uncertainty; and now, becoming certain in certainty is the new uncertainty. The truth is that you no longer need certainty. You lost your need for it when you lost your need to be validated as the mind. It was the mind that needed certainty the whole time, not You.

Now you are faced with the blurry lines between what is true and what is false. "What blurry lines?" If you no longer see yourself as the false self, then what blurry lines are we even talking about?

There was only ever one You.

Who Am I? (continued)

Or could it be that I am not my mind,
But, in truth, something sublime?

Truth has taken the veil from my eyes,
Now I see what is true beyond my mind!

I am not my years, I am not out of time,
I am what is true, I am the Divine.

Yes, I can feel myself now,
But I am not a who . . .

I AM the NOW.

Visit:

www.**MINDLIES**.com

for more truths,

support and training.

Also From Daniel:

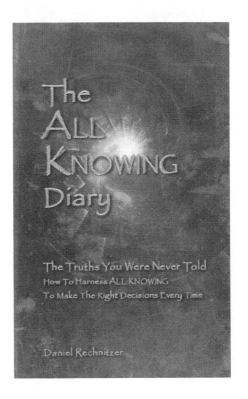

"More Than A Book,
It's A Home Study Course To
Access Limitless Genius!"

Made in the USA
Middletown, DE
23 April 2021